The Author

Joe Martin is a child of the Computer Age and is fascinated by Bitcoin, blockchain, and all things cryptocurrency. As a journalist with over 25 years of professional experience in the world of technology, he is ideally qualified to provide an accessible, understandable and transparent insight into the world of cryptocurrencies.

Through the lens of Bitcoin, he explains exactly how blockchains work and why they will change the world. Bitcoin is the starting point of the fourth industrial revolution, and those who wish to protect their jobs, their property, their families and their futures must understand the basics of the crypto world. The significance of Bitcoin, blockchains, and cryptocurrency in general will be examined and explained in this book in an entertaining and accessible format.

This book will be particularly helpful to those working in professions that are sensitive to the impact that cryptocurrencies and the blockchain will inevitably have on our society and livelihoods.

Bitcoin, Blockchain & Co.

The Truth, and Nothing but the Truth

Information about Bitcoin, Ethereum, Blockchain and other cryptocurrencies for interested parties, for beginners and advanced.

EXTRA: Earning Money With Cryptocurrencies, Trading & ICOs

Copyright

Special thanks to all who help to make this book possible. I am especially grateful to Luccia, Mariana, Susan, David and Matias.
I also would like to thank the organisers of this blockchain conferences where I learned a lot:

https://blockchain-expo.com/ — https://btcmiami.com/
http://tokensummit.com/ — https://digitalchamber.org/
http://finovate.com/ — https://www.crypto-financing.com/

Title elements from:
Blank golden corner ribbon: Author: BSGStudio
Technology-background-in-blue-color: Designed by Freepik

Table of Content

The Bitcoin Exchange Rate

During the writing of this book, the price of Bitcoin skyrocketed against the dollar, euro and all other currencies, going from about $1,000 to over $15,000 per bitcoin. Who knows how Bitcoin will be valued when you read

While this jump in value was great, it has created a few problems in this book. For example, I did some calculations that took the exchange rate into account, such as whether it is worth mining cryptocurrencies, how much you would have been paid for a single pizza at the current price, and how high transaction costs are. Due to the steeply rising price, the results were already outdated by the time I finished the chapter and will continue to change over time. Bitcoin experienced constant increases in value throughout 2017 — though it sometimes felt like every hour! To tackle this problem, I have decided to set a price of $10,000 per bitcoin at the time of printing in January 2018. Thus, it should be noted that all calculations refer to this exchange rate.[1]

Please inform your friends and acquaintances!

Please share the information in this book with others, or simply recommend the book to those who can benefit from it. Your friends, your family and your acquaintances will be grateful if you point out how they can inform themselves about cryptocurrencies. Your friends and family should be able to use the information in these pages to make money. By the time they finish reading, they should be able to buy, trade and invest in Bitcoin, Ethereum, and other cryptocurrencies, while having enough knowledge to arm themselves against the many online scammers who try to take money out of their pockets.

Thank you very much.

---

[1] *Interesting fact: I am at Miami Bitcoin Conference 2018 and the Bitcoin price was two hours ago exactly $10,000*

The Most Important Things on One Page

To be active in the emerging world of cryptocurrency, you must first to understand the systems that underpin it and that will help to shape the future. It is vital that you understand three fundamental pieces of information before you begin any activity related to cryptocurrencies.

Without these **three key considerations**, you cannot fully understand and navigate the intricacies of the crypto world. Without these three foundational rules, you become extremely vulnerable to financial losses if you become active.

The rise of Bitcoin & Co. has created a gold rush of sorts. There are a lot of frivolous offers from opportunists out to make a quick buck from the hype. In a more sinister twist, there are also seasoned fraudsters who actively look for ways to part you from your money and your crypto-credit. These criminals range from the shady opportunist to the seasoned professional. To navigate this world, you must always be on your toes. The best way to beat the fraudsters is to stay one step ahead with some knowledge of your own.

For that reason, you should read these instructions repeatedly. Internalize them and let them sink deep into your subconscious. The following principles must be applied intuitively. Gauge everything—every single thought and decision—by these principles. With these three principles at the core of your every decision, you will be safe from fraud and you will understand how our world is going to work in the near future.

*1. Ensure that **you—and only you—have the "Private Keys"** to your cryptocurrencies (that is, Bitcoin and Co.). Always. No one else!*

*2. You can only unconditionally trust a **genuine public blockchain** with many completely independent nodes.*

*3. The **Computer Source Code** of a trustable blockchain system is always **openly accessible** and can be examined and used by everyone.*

Even if you don't yet understand what "Private Keys" are or know what a genuine Public Blockchain is, never forget these principles. Analyze every offer from this perspective, no matter how attractive it seems. Do not allow yourself to be tempted into breaking these rules. Read this book carefully, understand the importance of these rules, and question every offer with this knowledge. That is the only way to protect your property. Only then is your future on a firm foundation and only then are you capable of taking informed action. With the knowledge contained in this book, you can successfully deal with cryptocurrencies and other Blockchain systems and shape the future so that you and your family are comfortable.

Glossary

Terms Used

Fortunately, there are only a few specialist terms that you need to know to be able to discuss and understand cryptocurrencies and the blockchain. These are initially explained in the following short glossary. Other terms will be introduced successively in the text and explained fully. This book is aimed at the layman and is presented in an accessible and understandable way.

Public Blockchain: The word "public" doesn't accurately reflect the generally accepted meaning of this term. A public blockchain in the sense of a true, genuine blockchain is not a private blockchain nor the blockchain of a consortium or association. The characteristic of a public blockchain is that anyone who has a computer can download the appropriate software and become part of the blockchain system. In general, the data in this blockchain is publicly accessible, although this is not necessarily always the case. The computers creating the blockchain can be located anywhere in the world and work completely independently in creation and management of this blockchain. It is also worth noting that, in this context, "public" does not mean that all data is transparent, just that anyone can participate.
A public blockchain is the only blockchain that is truly tamper-proof. Not all blockchains are created equal, and the differences are crucial.

Ledger: A ledger should be interpreted as a general account record. It is a list or book in which all transactions are stored chronologically from the first to the current transaction. In the case of a blockchain, it is a file. As transactions occur, this ledger continually grows in size. In the summer of 2017, the ledger of the Bitcoin blockchain was already greater than 130 GB.

Crypto: Crypto refers to all systems that use encryption techniques to prevent data from being accessed, or at least read, by an unknown third party or to sign the authenticity of. These systems are summarized under the umbrella term crypto. Mathematical encryption techniques are currently used in these systems, but before the computer age, less secure methods of encryption were used.

Cryptocurrency: If a coin is created by computers with the help of an algorithm, then it is labeled a crypto coin. The algorithms and computing power required for the creation of the coins are very complex and elaborate. This is because mathematical encryption techniques do not just create the coins, they must also calculate or compute other functions. For example, the computers that carry out these calculations also protect the network against misuse and manipulation. This is achieved by applied cryptography. The best-known cryptocurrency in the world is Bitcoin, closely followed by Ethereum.

FIAT Currency/ Money: Fiat money has no intrinsic value — it simply serves as a means of exchange. The opposite of fiat money is commodity money, such as tobacco, rice, gold or silver, all of which have an intrinsic value alongside its exchange value. It's value is not dependent on governmental decree. It holds its value as long as payment can be made with it.
In principle, Euro, dollars, Swiss francs, yen and all other paper currencies are fiat currencies. They have no real intrinsic value. Critics even claim that they are worthless. At any time, fiat currencies can be inflated through additional printing from central banks and governments, thus become actually worthless. For example, this happened to the Reichsmark in 1920s Germany and has been happening to the Venezuelan bolivar since 2014.
Bitcoin is not a comparable currency because, although it also possesses no intrinsic value, it is unique in that it cannot be manipulated or printed by any government. Thus, the Bitcoin is not subject to this kind of inflation. For this reason, it is defined as neither fiat nor commodity money, but as a cryptocurrency.
Bitcoin's intrinsic value can best be quantified in the electrical energy that computers need to secure the network and keep it running. It is reassuring to note that if an organization requires more electrical energy per year for purchasing and provision than Iceland uses to keep this network running, then Bitcoins must represent some value.

1944

George Orwell, in relation to a possible victory by Hitler, wrote that winners have always been able to rewrite the history of humanity at their discretion and to their taste, to shape their own future and remain in power. Truth then becomes a relative concept, which is a great danger.

2014

Julian Assange stated that Bitcoin's most important function is that of an unalterable time stamp which guarantees that news represents the truth and is firmly fixed for all time. Thus, any falsification of history by rulers, a danger correctly identified by Orwell, is excluded once and for all.

Since 2009

Public blockchains have been locking the truth in data blocks and ensuring that no-one, no government, no-one with money or weapons, or lobby groups equipped with whatever, can ever alter this data. For the first time in human history, it is guaranteed that this data — and thus the history of humanity — corresponds to the truth, and nothing but the truth, for all time.

Chapter 1 — What you absolutely need to know

What you will learn in this book and how you should read it

I stumbled across Bitcoin late—not until 2016. Maybe you discovered it even later than me, or years before me. Regardless of when Bitcoin came to your attention, I am sure you have a few questions that no-one has been able to give you a satisfactory answer to. I am also sure—since you've picked up this book—that you are interested in the topic of Bitcoin and cryptocurrency. As an author and journalist, I am fascinated by the subject of crypto. However, no matter how hard I tried to grasp it, to understand it, to get a handle on how it all works, I kept finding myself in a deep dark wood. The more I learned, the more questions I had.

Even after reading dozens of reports, listening to even more podcasts, attending conferences and speaking to lots of crypto experts, I was still in those woods looking for clear answers. But my problem had changed. It wasn't dark in the woods anymore. On the contrary; now the sun seemed to be illuminating my path, but I could no longer see the wood for the trees. Total information overload.

More conversations, more reports, more articles, more podcasts, and none of it really helped. The only reassuring thing was that I was finding more and more people who were experiencing the exact same uncertainty. There was more confusion than expertise in this new, specialist area. Again and again, I participated in conversations until both sides exhausted our logic and still were no closer to clarity. Why was that so, and how could it be solved?

I believe that anyone who has had any dealings with Bitcoin, blockchains and other cryptocurrencies will know instinctually that this new technology will change the world for the better. Many are intuitively of the opinion that we are approaching a new industrial revolution, or perhaps are already within it. But the world of cryptocurrency and blockchain is anything but intuitive.

It runs counter to every framework and system that form the foundation of our modern lives. In large part, it is counter intuitive, strange, unknown, alien. I have often stood with almost literal question marks on my face, my lips forming one astounded "Pardon?" after another. I kept hearing the same stock answer from my friends: "I just don't believe that."

Understanding Bitcoin and blockchain runs counter to everything we know

A change in thinking was not the only thing missing in my understanding of what is happening with cryptocurrencies. I lacked the central theme, the overarching framework, or maybe — as I now think — the deeper meaning of Bitcoin and blockchain.
When I realized something was missing from my conceptual framework, I started to seek it out. I looked for a new paradigm.
Many people who get involved with crypto see it as an opportunity to gamble. They want to take a chance at the possible windfall that comes with investing early in new technologies. With Bitcoin, the rate rocketed from a few hundred to over $10,000 within one year, and investors experienced wild fluctuations, up and down, again and again.
The cryptocurrency Ethereum, whose rate shot from under $10 to nearly $1,000, experienced even wilder fluctuations. Ethereum investors gambled with so-called "Alt-Coins" and via ICOs — but more about that later in the book.
Oh yes, and all that happened within nine to twelve months. Bitcoin shot up 1.333 % in twelve months (December 2016 to December 2017- from $750 to $ 10,000), while Ethereum skyrocketed 5,300% in twelve months (Ethereum from December 2016 until December 2017 - from $8 to $420).
Nearly every crypto-portfolio made the profits of Warren Buffet — the best investor in the world for the last 40 years — look like pocket change. These profits in the thousands of percent were new for everyone, even the high-powered professionals who gamble every day with their financial instruments and move billions back and forth.
But others who come into contact with Blockchain see even more in it. They see better workflows in their company, more peace for

mankind, the solution to all problems, the universal world computer.

The truth is probably — as it so often is — somewhere in between. However, this recognition does help us to further understand what it all means. What are the long-term implications of Blockchain? Are there any? Is it all just hype, a new software? Like Windows 10, 11 or 12?

The aim is to understand without being able to program

I am a child of the computer age, and the rise of crypto reminded me of my lectures from the past. My first home computer was a Commodore VIC-20 — the predecessor model to the revolutionary C 64. I grew up with it and was in the vanguard of the whole development. When Apple released the first iPhone, I stood in line at the Apple store in San Diego, California for hours, but by the time I reached the front of the queue, they were already sold out.

As an entrepreneur, author and journalist, I have done and experienced a lot in the technology sector. However, I have never been a programmer or mathematician. This is good news for you because this book is written for technical laymen. No computer code and everything explained in a way that can be understood by mere mortals, interested non-specialists.

This book is also for those who are already involved in the wild west that is the current crypto world. It is even written for the software experts who, perhaps, after reading it, will have a better understanding of the problems they are solving in the real world, and why that is so valuable and important.

But at that time, when I was first getting involved in crypto, I didn't have the overarching framework to guide me. I knew that there was something there, but for many long months, I simply couldn't grasp it. The further I ventured down the rabbit hole, the more I discovered that many others didn't know much either. Even those who stood on the stage, and certainly those in the audience, didn't fully understand what it was and where it was going. In the coffee breaks, subjects were skillfully avoided, and a kind of pseudo-knowledge was coolly presented without any real idea of the material. Maybe because this knowledge framework was lacking.

I remember a time in the mid-90s when stood on the stage and spoke about the internet. Wide eyes, furrowed brows, disbelief, and then: "Oh, the internet, it's just a fad. It will pass."

Not that it bothered me. I didn't mind whether people believed me or not, but their response did surprise me. As we all know today, the internet wasn't a fad. It didn't disappear. It might be new territory, as German Chancellor Mrs. Merkel postulated even in 2015, but the internet has changed our lives hugely.

Around the millennium, I found myself standing on stages again. My new subject was the great frontier of e-commerce. Again, I heard nay-sayers and disbelievers with all kinds of excuses and dismissive remarks. A common one was: "No-one will put their payment details on a website, it's far too dangerous." Well, in 2016, Amazon alone achieved 136 billion USD of sales from people who don't put their payment details on the internet. So much for that.

Five years later, I spoke on the topic of "social media." I heard the same voices piping up: "No-one will put personal data about themselves on the internet." Today, Facebook alone has over two billion people doing exactly that. So much for that.

And here we are today with cryptocurrencies and blockchain. But this time it is different. People are more aware of the change. They have seen the patterns of the past and are more curious than anything. That's good. Of course, there are still the skeptics. That is the biggest group—interested yet skeptical, and not really motivated to do anything about it.

Why a blockchain?

The blockchain is exactly why I looked for the framework. For the skeptics and the curious, I looked for the real purpose of a blockchain, the real reason for the existence of a decentralized system. I looked for the reason why cryptocurrencies generate such hype. Why large industrial organizations, banks, insurance companies, and even governments are strategically involved in cryptocurrencies. I looked for the reason why many of these individuals and organizations were working together, when in the real economy, they were often bitter competitors. Why this sudden co-opetition? Why are those in competition co-operating at the same time?

At some point in my investigation, it all became clear to me. I had stepped out of the dark of the wood and was now bathed in sunshine. I could clearly see the trees, the trunks, the leaves, the ferns and all the flora. I had found it: the truth!

Ok, that sounds a bit theatrical and possibly even esoteric, but it isn't. The truth is an integral part of a certain kind of blockchain. To formulate it in a different way:

We can rely 100 percent on the information of a public blockchain

Like the Bitcoin blockchain, which is the first and strongest blockchain to date. It contains an unalterable record of all transactions made since the first Bitcoin was created. No intelligence on this Earth can ever change this. No individual person, group of people, computer group or even an artificial intelligence can alter the transactions of the Bitcoin blockchain.

That was the "Wow" moment for me. You're probably thinking that you already knew that. You already knew that a blockchain is a record of all processes and is immune to changes. You already knew that it is a solid database. That is how blockchains are often characterized, right?

Yes, that is how they are described. But exactly what that all means is rarely correctly understood or communicated.

We know how a blockchain works. We know all the things that you can do with a blockchain. But what we don't really know is why you should do all of that with a blockchain. The truth, which is stored unalterably by the data in a public blockchain, will change our world. Certainly, and inevitably.

That is why I decided to write this book. It is a complete handbook for the new age of truth. One which will lead the reader into the fascinating world of cryptos.

What knowing the truth means

What does it mean for us that we can rely 100 percent on the details anchored in a blockchain? That is a question that is difficult to answer, and a new question for us because trusting completely in data is counterintuitive to us. We are often happy to give away the data of our orders, our bank accounts, and our movements to

Amazon, Facebook, Google, Apple and other digital entities, and for the most part, we don't even think about what happens with our data. But sometimes we are alarmed — and rightly so. Maybe we are alarmed because a hacker has stolen 140 million records from the Equifax company or because someone has stolen our personal identity. While we might be more trusting in giving data, we are becoming more and more skeptical of the data we receive and rely on.

Fundamentally, we trust these large companies, these centralized administrators and marketers with our data. We rely on them. We have the expectation that a company of their size must know how to protect their customers' private data. (Ha, ha, ha).

Nevertheless, that trust only goes so far, and it has to stop somewhere. With the number of security failures and leaks that have occurred in recent years, we are beginning to become distrustful of institutions. Blockchain will change all that.

If you can rely 100 percent on entries in a database, could you then purchase something from a third party without knowing who he or she is?

How do you know that this person can pay? How do you know that this person is the legal owner of the goods for sale? Up until now, you didn't. Up until now, you could only cross your fingers or maintain a level of ignorance and indifference.

If you buy a car from a complete stranger whom you have only spoken to briefly on the telephone, you would want the papers for the vehicle, right? You would like a purchase contract and invoice, and you would want a reliable record of the payment you have made by putting it into the bank. If you were the seller, you would want evidence that the payment had been received and assurance from the bank that it is not counterfeit or fraudulent. This is particularly true when we are dealing with someone from out of state or even from abroad. You would ideally like a copy of their ID so you can find them if something goes wrong. At the end of the day, you've got to be a little bit wary of when completing transactions with total strangers. How can you trust them? Is everything that they are telling you true? Do you know the truth?

What if we're talking about buying something much bigger? If you want to purchase some real estate, surely there are lawyers for that, right? True. But that's another professional group that will be made redundant by blockchain technology. What? Pardon? Lawyers are becoming redundant?

Lots of jobs are being lost, and blockchain is making sure of that

Blockchain technology will change the world and how we interact and transact in it. We will no longer need to trust anyone because the truth is anchored for all time, unalterably, in the blockchain.

Whatever is contained in a public blockchain is true and reliable. You can buy a house without a lawyer and even without a copy of the seller's ID. You can trust that it is the real owner from the data in the public blockchain. If the transaction is then closed, you become the new owner and that new information can be found in the public blockchain. The record of your ownership exists forever, or until you enter the sale to someone else into the public blockchain. It is safe and without risk, and it allows for seamless transactions between strangers anywhere on Earth. It all happens without need for a lawyer and with low or no fees involved.

The public blockchain will automatically enter you as the owner if all the preconditions stored as an smart contract in the public blockchain are met. The public blockchain holds the door open to you because your unique cryptographic key fits and that of the previous owner no longer does. (Please note that I quite deliberately keep writing "public blockchain" and not "blockchain." There will be more about that later in the book.)

That is, of course, a futuristic example, and I know that it appears a little contrived. But what if I told you that we already have the technology for that? What if I told you that the first projects in which real estate is being managed via a blockchain are already up and running? They are in Costa Rica and Sweden.

I have chosen this example deliberately because it is very provocative. There are many examples which are less challenging, such as digital money, marriages via the blockchain, automatic electricity delivery from neighbor to neighbor, or automatic betting on anything at all. What about a €100 million bond from Mercedes-Benz via blockchain? This has been in place since June 2017.

Blockchain technology is here and it is not going away. It will not disappear overnight or over the weekend. It is far too late for that.

Having a basic understanding is helpful and necessary

To understand what this means for us all, it is first necessary to understand the basics of the technology and the concepts it is built on. That is what I will explain in this book.

Compare it to the time you were learning to drive. You learned the highway code, the rules of traffic, and the basics of how the car works. The driving instructor explained how some cars need diesel fuel and others need petrol. Some cars have a manual transmission and others have an automatic. You also learned how to calculate braking distances so you don't drive too fast and can stop safely. A little theory was needed before you could get moving in practice.

You really didn't need to know how engine management software is written or what material the drive shaft is made of to drive a car from A to B. Similarly, you do not need to know exactly how the software works to understand the crypto world. However, you do have to know the signs so that you don't end up in a cul-de-sac or drive the wrong way up a one-way street. In the first instance, you get stuck. In the second, you could end in an accident. Both scenarios are unpleasant, potentially dangerous, and completely avoidable.

It is the same in the crypto world. You can easily get yourself stuck in a dead end or run yourself right into a fraud, which amounts to an accident. In this book, you will learn the signs and how you must act in "crypto-traffic" to ensure you get where you want to go safely.

If you master the basic rules, you will be able to trade faster and more independently with cryptocurrencies. You can use the skills you have learned for your own needs, or you can join a blockchain company or movement. In any case, you will be the one in the driver's seat at all times. You will also learn how to earn money with Bitcoin, how you can save, and how you can perhaps make yourself independent of the pension system, which can no longer be financed anyway.

The first part of this book explains how Bitcoin works, what different types of blockchain there are, how you can trade or set up a savings plan with Bitcoin, what other cryptocurrencies exist, and how you can invest in new business models and make good profits in these currencies. The goal of the first section is to give you a thorough framework of understanding for the fundamentals of cryptocurrency.

In the second part, we dive into the dangers and potential pitfalls of the crypto world. We'll discover how you can lose a lot of money, be taken in by fraudsters, and the incorrect ways to set yourself up that will inevitably lead to losing your Bitcoin or other cryptocurrencies. The goal of the second section is to make sure you're aware of the dangers so you don't fall victim to them.

The two halves of this book are essential and inextricably linked. You should study the first section diligently so that the misfortunes described in the second section do not befall you.

After you have mastered the basic procedures and techniques, you will understand and value what it means to know the truth in relevant areas of our life, because it is anchored always and forever in the public blockchain. You will recognize the potential danger of the massive changes that will occur for you, your company, or your industry as crypto shakes things up. And with your knowledge and understanding of blockchain, you will be able to act accordingly. You will understand and be able to see what is coming. You can prepare, position yourself to capitalize on these shifts and set yourself up for success.

That is why I have written this book—so that you are not caught by surprise when the new wave of automation inevitably hits. Because one thing is sure: the world is about to change in a huge way. The data which we will soon be relying on will make millions of jobs redundant. At the same time, it will enable and encourage completely new business models. Be prepared. Be on board.

How you should read this book

I worked hard on the structure of this book to make it as logical and accessible as possible. As with any book, it is recommended that you read it from start to finish. Each individual section is carefully placed to build on the previous, which will allow you to really understand the whole system in a clear way.

By the time you finish, you will know not only how to drive the car — to persist with the driving metaphor — and what signs mean what, but you will also know how cars will change our society. You will understand the significance of cars being able to move goods and people from A to B faster than horses, and how you can be one of the first to position themselves accordingly and trade profitably.

If you don't read this book in order, you will still gain some important knowledge that will help you. However, you will remain as just one of thousands of people in the traffic who take it for granted that goods are on the supermarket shelves. If you know the whole system and the concepts and models behind it, then you will know why the goods are in the supermarket and how they get there. You will understand the overarching principles and you can achieve considerably more in the crypto world. You can calmly and skillfully shape the future for you and your family.

With this in mind, I hope you enjoy reading the book.

Joe Martin

Miami, January 2018

Chapter 2 — The Truth and Nothing but the Truth:

Why blockchain will change our world and our society, and how we ought to manage it

We all know that once toothpaste has been squeezed out of its tube, it will never go back in. Turning back time breaches so many laws of physics that it is just not possible to do. Who among us would willingly choose to go back to the old practice of recording music from the radio onto cassette tapes, when we know the current quality of digital music from CDs, iTunes or Spotify?

These advancements and inventions that characterize our modern lives will not just disappear from use. Unlike advancements of the past, they will not be lost.

Knowledge, on the other hand, can be lost. It has only been in recent years that we have we discovered — with astonishment — why the ancient Romans were able to produce vastly superior and more durable cement than the builders of today. The materials and techniques we use for our motorway bridges crumble after just 50 years of use, while the Colosseum is — more or less — still standing almost 2000 years later. This superior building knowledge was lost to us through time.

Knowledge can be manipulated. In the era of "fake news," manipulation of information is an easy feat to accomplish. Apparently. Because actually, the word was never really any different. Manipulation of every kind — from faked news to counterfeit banknotes, falsified records to forged signatures — has defined our past and created our society.

Why can't we just blindly trust this data and information?

An analysis shows why knowledge is lost through time, and the result is unequivocal: knowledge and information could only be managed centrally up to now. Central management, central storage, central control. Anything that is centralized can be changed, manipulated and lost through destruction.

Who knows what valuable knowledge was contained in the thousands of scrolls and books at The Great Library of Alexandria — one of the largest and most significant libraries of the ancient world — before it was destroyed by a series of fires over a number of years. The information lost could have been the foundation of many great advancements for humanity, and the loss has probably held back the development of the western world considerably. Just as the knowledge of the Inca was lost, no one knows for sure what contributions from other cultures we have missed out on. What everyone today knows, though, is hard disk drive errors and computer crashes. In some ways, that is also a loss of knowledge. When the excel table or the document you've been working on are gone, you have no choice but to start from scratch. Your carefully formulated thoughts are lost. The skilfully created table is lost. Annoying.

Until now, this system of central management was the best solution to maintaining, organizing and protecting our valuable knowledge. States were and are centralized structures; sometimes that took the form of a monarch ruling a kingdom or a democratic government that leads and manages the state. Ultimately, everything is ordered and managed from a central point of control, even if there is devolved local administration.

Even if you live in a democracy or a federalized state, you should be under no illusions. The most important information — for example, tax numbers, our social security number, and our vehicle registrations — are all centralized at the highest data levels and are stored in some linked database. These databases, which can be manipulated at any time, can also fail, be hacked, and are permanently under threat of viruses.

If centrality is the problem, or if centrality is identified as the predetermined breaking point, is there another solution?

Yes, there is. A solution to the problem of centrality came to the fore in 2008 with the birth of a concept called "Bitcoin."

The Bitcoin white paper, the folding paper of the crypto industry, was published by Satoshi Nakamoto. To this day, no-one knows who is behind this pseudonym. It might be a lone wolf or it could be a group of computer software experts. Nakamoto describes how a group of computers can technologically be made to deliver the truth, and nothing but the truth.

A truth that is firmly written for all time and on which you can rely 100 percent. A truth, on the basis of which one can blindly base one's future, and that works completely without any trusted persons or trust in itself.

And so an exciting idea was born. Today that idea is building an ever-growing following of enthusiasts. It is reaching the masses increasingly quickly and efficiently, and it is massively changing our society and its administration. That is why it is all the more important to know the basics of this technology; otherwise we are each facing a fait accompli, wondering how we can jump onto a train to the future that is already departing.

Data that we can trust blindly?

If we could blindly trust data, it would have enormous consequences and that would completely change our future. Without overstating it, you could argue that it's a fourth industrial revolution — that of the trusting society.

By this, I mean a society in which you can blindly trust any offer or transaction, even if it comes from a completely unknown third party. In this version of society, you can purchase real estate by mobile phone without a lawyer. You can have your medical files with you and any doctor, wherever you are, can rely 100% on the information contained in those files, meaning they treat you more quickly, effectively, and safely than ever before. That is the kind of life-changing impact trustable data can have.

In the following section, I will show you exactly how that works and what technical developments would need to be in place to ensure that data is always reliable and reflects the truth — without exception. I will illustrate how this system is constructed and why it is uniquely positioned to deliver the truth. Along the way, you will also discover the circumstances under which it is vulnerable to attack or could be manipulated. All of this is presented in a straightforward way, so that anyone can understand it without needing to be a software programmer.

In this book, I have drawn examples from private and professional areas in which confidential applications, dominated by the truth, deliver benefits, and how these new applications will influence the future. By the end of the book, you will fully understand why this will happen and why the development is inevitable and unstoppable. The toothpaste is just not going back in the tube!

What is the secret of such a trustworthy application, in which the truth and nothing but the truth is recorded?

If the problem is that of truth, the integrity of data, or centrality, it logically follows that the solution can only lie in a decentralized application. I'm sure this was also the exact logical progression that Nakamoto's thoughts took when he began creating a solution. Nakamoto built a truly decentralized application with Bitcoin — one in which data are kept simultaneously on several decentralized computers. This network of individual computers, also called nodes, always optimizes itself so that failures of individual nodes are automatically balanced. As a result, most nodes always have access to the truth. In this way, such a network is designed to safeguard against failure.

In addition, the data must always have a certain structure and be stored in a certain way so that subsequent alterations and manipulations are impossible. Through skillful linking of the individual data sets into a series of data blocks that are linked to each other, an unalterable record is produced, one which always corresponds to the unaltered truth.

The data must be stored unalterably forever, impervious to manipulation or censoring, and must be stored on many computers (nodes), completely independent of each other simultaneously. They must also, though, be linked with each other so that subsequent alteration by an unauthorized individual is denied and ignored by the majority of the computers.

House owners can relate: if the land registry has been tampered with, someone else will then suddenly own their property. That is an entirely plausible scenario that could occur through the malicious collaboration of a lawyer with an employee of the land registry or the escrow company, for example. However, this kind of manipulation would no longer be possible if the transfer of title had been registered and certified simultaneously in the first instance by many hundreds of independent places. That would mean that hundreds of lawyers and land registry officers would have to have collaborated on the deception. That is practically impossible.

Transactions without Witnesses

The real estate metaphor serves only as an example that it is— theoretically, at least—possible to manipulate information when only a small number of participants and witnesses are involved.
A simpler version of this same manipulation, is if you give someone 100 dollars in cash and he later claims to have never received the money. You have entered into a transaction within a centralized system without a third party to witnesses and corroborate the truth of the transaction. Even if you asked a friend to be present when you paid the other party, you still can't be 100% sure that said friend is reliable enough to confirm that you gave the other party the 100 dollars. He could forget, or pretend that he had forgotten because he had been bribed by the other party. Humans error and susceptibility to manipulation is a large part of what makes the centralized system vulnerable and ineffective.
There is a huge amount of literature on this subject and many academics worldwide have tackled these connections. Game theory is a science that attempts to understand systems as a way to predict the behavior of people who interact when exposed to a variety incentives. What the game theoreticians want to understand is how much a recipient who owes 100 dollars must pay a friend for him to "forget" and thus no longer be a witness. In theory, there is always a sum that makes it lucrative to manipulate. Maybe not for 100 dollars; but with sums in the millions, it would not be exceptional or rare to discover that someone's loyalty can be bought for a price.
If the handover of the 100 dollars is observed by 1,000 friends and all 1,000 are potential witnesses, then any judge will believe that the 100 dollars was paid—even if one, 10 or even 200 of the witnesses lose their memory. Thus, the greater the number of witnesses, the lower the risk of interference.

Transactions with witnesses and a dictator

Real estate owners can relax, then. Even if real estate transfers are not recorded simultaneously by all registry office officials, it is unlikely that ownership issues are manipulated by the lawyer and the office concerned.

What about the state, though? The state is ultimately the highest central point. A registry office is only a state instrument — an office. If a lawyer is bound by the laws, are owners threatened by adversity?

As in all centralized systems, there is a danger of manipulation within a state in a functioning democracy through politicians who decide the laws. That is, more or less, simple or manipulative, depending on the state. In Germany, people have been arguing for years about paying fees to the license fee agency for public radio broadcasters. The state, as a centralized point, introduced a system that forces everyone to pay for something that not everyone uses. There are enough examples of centralization and, thus, manipulation by the state — according to budget situation and interests. And there are plenty, especially if you *think* that you are living in a free, democratic state: residence costs for new roads, refuse collection fees, church tax, etc.

In a dictatorship, homeowners cannot feel comfortable. If the son-in-law or nephew of the dictator desires a nice property that already belongs to someone else, then the ownership issues will soon change. That has happened more than once in history. The central element — the dictator — simply changes the rules.

Dictatorships don't often last long. They either die out or are overthrown. Then the big clean-up starts, and the questions arise as to which buildings belonged to whom and when. Mr. Smith claims it was his; Mr. Jones says the same because he paid Mr. Smith for it. There are few witnesses, if any, and each one remembers something different. The simple problem of the 100 dollars described previously has suddenly become the problem of a house owner dispossessed by the state. Since there are no reliable records and no reliable witnesses, what can be done?

The good news is this: All of the problems described so far can be elegantly and reliably solved by decentralized systems.

In a genuinely decentralized system, there are always enough witnesses. Additionally, all records from the past in a public blockchain are unalterable for all time. That is why you can blindly trust these data.

Satoshi Nakamoto invented such a system in the form of Bitcoin, which was the first decentralized system in which one can transfer money from A to B with 100% security against counterfeiting. That is only possible within a decentralized system.

Unfortunately, decentralization only sometimes seems to prevail.

This is the point at which the first misconceptions often occur. The difference between a centralized and a decentralized system is absolutely crucial. A centralized system is easy to define. It is the one point in a network where everything is stored and where all decisions are made. In a computer network, this is the central computer, also called a server.

Of course, a central server can become unserviceable for a variety of reasons, just like any device. In such an instance, you no longer have any access to the information and decisions cannot be made. For that reason, these servers are usually designed so that the important parts are duplicated. The backup system takes over if the original fails.

This is called a redundant system. Redundant systems are standard, for example, in aviation. It is imperative that, should a signal system to the engine fail, the aircraft stays safely in the air; the instruction to climb or descend has to be received via a parallel system.

Loss of data can have catastrophic results.

While it is inconvenient when decisions temporarily cannot be made, it is often catastrophic if the hard drive of a server is damaged and the data lost. For this reason, backups are imperative. However, these are only a partial solution. They have to be played back and the entire server rebuilt. It's certainly better than nothing, but not a satisfactory solution on the whole.

So, engineers quickly came up with the idea of a mirror drive. In this, data are written not to a single hard drive, but to many, simultaneously. The combination of these hard drives ensures seamless and efficient access to data. However, even this does not guarantee the existence of the central unit, as the whole site could go down. The cause of this could be something as disastrous an earthquake or a flood, or something as trivial as a power outage lasting longer than any supply of emergency batteries. Similarly, burglary with material damage and theft of computers is another potential hazard that must be accounted for. For this reason, data is stored on distributed systems; that is, so-to-speak, local separation of the mirrors. This could be entire computer centers acting as mirrors, potentially thousands of miles from each other and, today, might even be located in different countries to be able to withstand "political earthquakes" unscathed.

If one computer center becomes unserviceable, another takes over. This usually happens smoothly, although in some cases, the synchronization may take some time, but, as we know from experience, the internet never actually fails. These distributed data systems can thus be classed as completely secure.

But! These are not decentralized systems; they are just distributed systems, and this is the small but crucial difference that must be kept in mind.

Distributed, safe systems may be safe from failure, but they are not immune to human error and manipulation. Decentralized systems are both safe from failure and immune to manipulation. Those two things are often confused.

Manipulation by the operator

Centralized or even distributed systems are operated by somebody. Somebody — typically a company — programs these systems and thus controls how data is stored in the system. More importantly, it controls what data is being stored. If a malicious perpetrator changes data while saving it, then these data can be accessed securely but are no longer reliable. The truth can never be guaranteed in a centralized or distributed system. It will always be necessary to check the veracity of the data in a multitude of ways.

Herein lies the greatest amount of work generated in our modern world. Millions of people do nothing else but check the veracity of data. If you think that sounds a bit abstract, try cashing in a savings book that is worn and hard to read, or try to register a vehicle without documents.

Historically, we have always had the problem of relying on other peoples' statements or records. Those with malicious intent have thrived on figuring out new ways to circumvent or manipulate this reliance for their own gain. How many wars, skirmishes or local disagreements have happened because news that formed the *casus belli* was based on falsehoods?

False information has repeatedly been used to foment wars, win wars, and gain some kind of advantage over others. It was like that then, and it still is like that today. Forged references, forged doctor titles, forged decrees — all of these have happened and still happen on a daily basis.

The question that constantly arises is that of the verifiability of information. If a seal was broken, the information within could not be trusted. If the seal was unharmed, then it could. Or could it? What if the seal been forged? Therein lies the problem.

Methods have been developed over hundreds of years to uncover and combat forgeries. For example, there are around 50 security features included in the latest euro banknotes to ensure that the note is genuine. Safety features, such as a seal and holograms, are only effective until they can either be forged or — the more common reason for which they are eventually dispensed with again — they become too expensive.

Computers couldn't solve the problem before

This problem was not solved by the rise of electronic data processing. In fact, the same problem was simply transferred to a different medium. Malware, viruses, and hacker attacks threaten our information in new ways on a daily basis. Computerized seals can be broken very easily by insiders with advanced technical knowledge. An example of this is rounding errors. Someone with knowledge and access could transfer the number in the third decimal place to themselves in the bank's software. Tiny, incremental adjustments often go unnoticed and fraudsters can siphon off millions of dollars undetected.

To make matters worse, it does not have to be fraudsters in the conventional sense. It could be the management itself or the state. Information can be systematically altered to gain advantages. Election fraud, for example, is just the prominent tip of the iceberg in this regard.

In contrast, there is the data that is changed by simple, human error with no harmful intent. Transposed numbers are probably the most common cause: illegible figures from a fax, typing into a table, or missing receipts for sums were paid out so that everything balances in the end. Many millions of workers are busy, day in, day out, doing nothing other than shifting data from one medium to another: typing from paper into electronic data processing or from one software program into another. There are millions of writing errors, typos and wrongly understood data in our databases. One classic is, "Dear Mrs. John Smith".

With so many opportunities for error, we really can't trust data! Up until now, we have just had to somehow work around that. In the West, that approach is tolerable, and reasonable efforts are made to reduce risks and safeguard against fraud. The picture is not the same in some less democratic systems. We have witnessed this, for example, in the obvious election interference in Venezuela or in some African states, and before that, in the divided Germany. In these situations, millions of votes were manipulated. This is the problem with any centralized system; an individual or a group of people can suppress others through manipulated information, fake news, and censorship.

It is a worldwide problem that must be solved. We must set the truth as our foundation and build upon it a peaceful social order that is 100% interference-proof and backed by trustworthy databases.

Nakamoto's concept has solved that on the level of a 100% manipulation-proof currency with 100% trustworthy transactions — even if they come from complete strangers. At the heart of his solution — known as Bitcoin — there is, along with efficient encryption technology, a blockchain.

It is now time to examine this ingenious concept.

Chapter 3 — How the Bitcoin Blockchain Works

The invention of the banking system

A solution to the problems existing in the international finance markets appeared in the Middle Ages, with the emergence of the banking system. During these early days, the banker was viewed as the harbinger of truth, and it was the Knights Templar who organized the transfer of money via a large network. Before this, an asset owner would have to carry his physical valuables on his person. As you can imagine, this was a very dangerous undertaking. It was not just Robin Hood waiting to pounce, there also were some really bad guys, too. Regardless of the malevolence of the highwaymen — or even the authorities themselves who imposed many forms of taxation — the valuables were generally lost. The Knights Templar revolutionized that with their network of branches, making it safer and more efficient than ever before to make transactions.

A nobleman who invested a pound of gold could pick up the equivalent somewhere else with an appropriate paper. The Templars also maintained a network of messengers who would report on the transfers. This was not a really trustworthy system because a seal could be forged here and there, messengers could give the wrong news, and all sorts of tricks and manipulations could lead to false information. The system relied on trust and worked because there was no better alternative, and because people had faith in the Templars as trustworthy third parties. They were usually heavily armed and did "God's work" — a factor that, for those times, held incredible weight and should not be underestimated.

The trustworthy third party

This system implemented by the Knights Templar is the first in which a trusted third party played a role in a larger system. The idea of a trusted third party has survived the centuries and is well established in our modern society. We could keep our money under the mattress, but we place it in trusted third parties, like banks or building societies. Or, in terms of the social contract, we feel more comfortable lending our lawnmower to a relative stranger when he is a friend of a friend. In this scenario, our mutual friend is the trusted third party who ensures both sides are fairly treated.

The state has institutionalized the trustworthy third party in the form of the notarial system. Anyone wishing to found a company or purchase a property needs the help of the trusted third party — the lawyer. Another large, worldwide sector of trusted third parties are the auditors. These independent experts check companies' accounts and confirm that all records are correct and verifiable. For example, they check if the company really does possess their declared cash and assets, which the stock value is partially derived from. Does the trustworthy third party really represent the truth, though?

Who has never been annoyed that they lent their lawnmower to that friend of a friend, who returned it broken or never returned it at all?

Who has never been annoyed when their bank suddenly charges some ridiculous fee for a minor infraction of the T&Cs — all because your never read the small print?

Who has never stood shaking their head at the lawyer's office when buying or selling a property? Unclear issues of ownership are not unusual.

And then there are the auditors. Enron — and many other scandals in which investors lost billions — come to mind. When we consider the patterns of history, can we really say that the third-party system represents the truth?

Data in centralized systems can easily be changed

Information and data in distributed and centralized systems can be altered or manipulated by the operators of these systems, so the truth is not guaranteed. We just have to accept that's how it is. Don't we?

Actually, we don't have to accept this anymore. In fact, we have the mysterious Satoshi Nakamoto to thank for not having to accept a flawed system anymore. His concept has demonstrated how we can guarantee the truth through the integrity of the data within a genuinely decentralized system. His concept, which is only now gaining mass awareness, is ideal for changing our systems. This revolutionary system of data and information processing can change the very foundations of our system, but also, leading on from that, our entire social structure.

In essence, Nakamoto combined a number of existing approaches in such a way that the combination creates a guarantee of truth. A core component is computer encryption. But that alone is not enough; a further building block is required: the linking of older data with new, so that a chain of data blocks is formed. Within this chain, the current data always relates to the previous and that in turn of its predecessor. That is the principle of what has come to be well-known as blockchain — a chain of data blocks that are linked to each other.

A chain consisting of data blocks results in the legendary blockchain

This chain itself is, however, only one single (but important) component of the whole system. And it is worth nothing in and of itself because it can be changed and it can be destroyed. It can just be deleted from the server and replaced by another chain containing different data. Both must be prevented if you want to — or must — be able to blindly trust the data presented.

For this reason, Nakamoto additionally distributed these data chains — which will be referred to as "blockchain" from now on — over many different, completely independent computers.

But even that alone is still not enough to create the level of certainty and security that we require. Under certain circumstances, the blockchain can be replaced at some point, and this can be transferred at the speed of light to the other computers, thereby interfering with data. Manipulated does not necessarily mean a huge event in which millions of dollars suddenly disappear. As already described, it is enough to manipulate the third decimal place to become very rich over time. To withstand this danger, Nakamoto cleverly integrated a brake into the system to prevent the quick dissemination of manipulated data.

In the following section, these individual component parts will be presented in turn. You quickly will see how effective the combination is. You must not be deceived by the term "blockchain" alone and that is why other places are indicated where dangers might lurk. You can't automatically trust the trendy term "blockchain" alone.

The truth is not in every tin that says "blockchain" on it

Nakamoto first split the system up into individual transactions and then collated them in data blocks. In this process, some additional cryptographic formulae are used to encrypt the data blocks. Thus, we enter the field of cryptography.

In the following section, we will use the conventional nomenclature of the cryptography sector. We will call the participants "Alice" and "Bob" and use the virtual currency Bitcoin, or its abbreviation, BTC. Alice and Bob are synonyms for sender and recipient of a transaction or message. "Carol" and "Dave" are further protagonists in a cryptographic system. They also represent senders or receivers. They represent people who are exchanging assets, so one is selling to another and gets paid. That is a transaction in the sense of Bitcoin.

So, if Alice wants to send 5 BTC to Bob, that is a simple transaction. Alice owns more than 5 BTC and sends 5 BTC to Bob. He now sends 3 BTC to Carol and 1 BTC to Dave. This is two further transactions. The Bitcoin system now collects these transactions and packs them in a data block.

This block has a specified maximum size and is packed and bundled by specialized computers. The system is designed so that a block is produced about every 10 minutes. It is this that acts as the brake mentioned previously and that brings other benefits with it (more about that later).

This data block is now not just bundled up like, say a .zip file, but cryptographic procedures are used that enable this block to be provided mathematically with an unequivocal label. This label, which is called a "hash," is the result of a calculation from the data of the info-block.

This hash is a very interesting piece of mathematical work that is based on so-called "trapdoor" functions. Exactly how it works is a source of fascination for mathematicians.

Trapdoor functions for the layperson

It is enough for the non-mathematician to understand that the formulae concerned can only be calculated in one direction. If you can normally calculate x if, say, 2+x=5, then that is not a trapdoor function, because it works in both directions. A hash algorithm, on the other hand, works in only one direction: forward.

Even if you know the result of the calculation and the associated calculation path, you cannot return to the starting value.

That sounds fantastical, but it really is possible and it is fascinating. As already stated, as a mathematical layman, it enough for us to simply know and recognize the existence of this phenomenon to understand the whole system. Those who wish to delve into it further will be able to research the mathematics of it easily on the internet.

The transactions are then collated in a data block and assigned a hash value through a cryptographic algorithm. This hash value cannot be changed, nor can the initial values be deduced from it. If you were to change only one single, tiny part of the transaction data that makes up the data block—say, adding a comma at one point—then that would result in a completely different hash value. Here is a real, calculated example that illustrates how an individual change delivers a completely different hash value.

If, for example, you generate the SHA 256 hash from the following sentence:

I am Satoshi Nakamoto

becomes:
c8bb907d49983cfd5b1db28be3fe3c2c5ade3a2b2995bd56f8b4203f74345caa

If you change only one single character by adding a full stop at the end, then the 256 hash changes drastically:

I am Satoshi Nakamoto.

becomes:
80cd76ffd0af98e2fbe066cda10847e7edbaa4caabb4fbf14d317b9cbbc4c963

The two hashes are in no way related. The period at the end of the statement was the only thing changed.
This hash, and the fact that it changes so radically through a minor change, is one of the foundations of data integrity — also known as "the Truth" — of blockchain technology and the Bitcoin cryptocurrency.

The data blocks are interlocked with each other

In the Bitcoin system, Nakamoto decreed that the data block will not just hold the current transactions, but that each would also hold the hash of the preceding block. The next block can only be linked to its predecessor if the hash values can be linked — that is, if the new block can be calculated together with the hash value of the previous block. Thus, a conclusive blockchain is made from data in which the information is unalterable and protected from manipulation. There is an important safety function in this compared to conventional systems, which is what makes blockchain so uniquely future-orientated and forward-looking.
As this is a crucial and very significant function, it is summarized again below.
A hash value is a mathematically derived value that is massively altered even by a minimal change to the data. Even if the result

value and the calculation route are known, it is impossible to reverse the formula calculation to extract the input data.

Every data block is calculated from the transaction data and the hash value of the previous block. In this way, one block can only be attached to its predecessor if the calculation is correct. The trick with this mathematics is principally that, although the calculation of this value can be very complicated, it is very easy for a third party to recognize that the calculation was correctly executed. You can, therefore, recognize that the result is correct without running the calculation again. As I said, fascinating.

Blocks are made under this premise: one after the other and attached to each other; thus, forming a blockchain.

Imagine, for example, that five blocks, exist, each with 1,000 transactions. Block 2 would be generated from the transactions of this block, plus the hash value of Block 1. Block 3 was generated from the transactions in Block 3 and the hash value of Block 2 which, in turn, depends on the hash value of Block 1. You can see where this is going.

If a transaction in Block 1 is now changed, this change results in a completely different hash value for the first block. Seriously different.

Block 2 is then incorrectly computed as the second block used the hash of the first in its formula. But as this is now different, the result cannot now be correct. As a result, a new value must also be calculated for Block 2. The same applies to the whole onward chain.

So, all blocks receive a new hash value because one variable — the hash of the previous block — is changed in the complex hash formula of the next block. This must change all the following hash values. A very ingenious thought, which is one of the keys to the success of blockchain. But is it enough?

A minimal change at the start forces a complete recalculation of the whole blockchain.

For a while, this was pure mathematics, which was of no real use because data can be changed, which just leads to the hash values of the blocks being changed. They change to something noticeably different, and the data do not now represent the truth. But no-one can see that.

Transactions and records from the past have been falsified. The original data are not stored on our computers in a manipulated blockchain. History has been rewritten and the property now belongs to someone else. So, we are not there yet.

Of course, Nakamoto also solved this problem by additionally providing for a peer-to-peer network. A peer is a person, an individual or — in the technical world — a machine in a network. The meaning of "peer" is "having equal rank or status."

In our technical case, it is just another computer called a node. This node is connected to the other nodes and receives the data blocks from its neighbor. It quickly checks the hash value of the new block. Due to the hash procedure used, this is a comparatively easy calculation that can be executed very quickly by any computer. Checking is much easier than the original calculation of the hash value for each block, especially because the nodes will receive a input variable form the hash calculating computers, which are specialized in building the data blocks. If this value is correct, and if it corresponds to the last block, which the node already has, then the node just attaches the new data block to the blockchain that it already has. If the incoming data block cannot be calculated based on the last known block, then the node discards it and waits for the next.

The whole procedure is being carried out constantly on many thousands of nodes. So, local blockchains stored on the nodes are built up block by block. In the Bitcoin blockchain, many thousands of nodes have joined Blocks 1 to 5 in the above example and stored them locally.

The P2P network prevents manipulation

Now, it is extremely hard to carry out any manipulation. If someone on a node (computer) changes one single transaction in the first block, then the hash values of all five subsequent blocks in the example are changed.

This is a direct result of the methodology where the hash of a block is always computed from the transaction data plus the hash value of the previous block. The sixth block is, of course, built on the hash value of the fifth block and fits perfectly on the manipulated computer. However, if this sixth block is now sent to the other nodes, the block does not fit the fifth block that they all have stored locally. As a result, the block is refused and the nodes wait for a different block — Block 6. There now may be one computer that can conclusively show false data, but it is only one among thousands. However, the truth can be found in these thousands because the system has many thousands of witnesses.

To prevent every node from making changes of its own and constantly flooding the whole network with falsified data, Nakamoto provided a further module. This module has another function and rewards certain components in the network with it.

Computers that calculate and assemble the data blocks receive a special position in the network. Nodes store the existing blockchain themselves and hang each new block on it. This is a process that requires comparatively little computing power, but quite a lot of storage space, because each individual node saves the ever-longer chain for all time on its hard drive from the outset. That appears expensive and profligate, but it is the price you must pay for the truth.

Cheaper storage space is the reason for the spread of the technology in recent years.

One of the reasons why blockchain has only really gained prominence over the last few years — and why more and more organizations than ever are using the technology — is the fact that storage space has become increasingly affordable over the years. The crucial reason why Bitcoin and blockchain are only now breaking out from the realms of the experimental by technical specialists and coming to the wider population may be that hard drives, like all other mass-produced technical products, have become more affordable in recent years.

The Bitcoin blockchain has, in the meantime, grown to over 140 GB — which is now no problem because affordable 500 GB or even 1 TB or 2 TB hard drives can cost under 100 dollars today. When Nakamoto presented the Bitcoin concept in 2008, these hard drives did not exist, or only did so at astronomical prices.

Along with the nodes, which each put the blockchain together for themselves as described, there are further special computers in the network, called "miners." They have the task of generating the individual data blocks.

These miners take the transactions which are in a pool, out of this pool, piece by piece, and pack them together in sequence in a data block. All blocks are provided with an upper limit by the underlying technical protocol.

So, if the right amount of transactions are stacked on top of each other while ensuring that the maximum size is not exceeded, or if all the transactions from a pool are in one stack, the miner begins to calculate the hash value described earlier for this data block.

Miners calculate the hash value of the blocks and secure the network

The miners have the task of calculating together the transaction data and the hash value of the last known block in the formula, and one further value that they must guess, so that it falls below a value specified by the basic algorithm of the whole Bitcoin system. At first that sounds like a monstrous task, but if you consider each individual step in turn, it isn't that complicated.

All transactions are then calculated together in the formula with the hash value of the previous block. Creating this new hash value of the block is done very quickly. However, that alone would not solve the problem of new and potentially manipulated blocks being continually sent to the nodes. This could cripple the system because the nodes would easily become overwhelmed. That is why Nakamoto built in the brake, as previously described.

This brake works via a further algorithm in the basic system of the network — the "core" — which produces a numerical value every 10 minutes that must not be reached. In other words, the hash of the new block must show a defined number of leading zeros. Again, this sounds complicated, but is really simple and effective in practice.

If the figure were 6 leading zeros, then the hash value of the new block must be smaller than 0.0000001. This would mean 0.000000999999 and all smaller values would be permissible.

The miners look for these smaller values by using another random number, called a "nonce," in the formula together with the transactions and the hash of the last block. So, for example: 0,745 (sum of transactions) x 0.872571 (hash value of the previous block) x 1.7656 (nonce) = 0.0002338. This means that the nonce with a value of 1.7656 is not correct, because it shows less than 6 leading zeros. The miner must calculate again and try it with another nonce.

The secret behind mining

In principle, it is nothing more than a guessing game. Put numbers into a formula and then see if the result is smaller than the number previously specified by the system. The formula is obviously a lot more complicated than the example given above.

It is crucial that the result of a hash formula is massively different with only a very small adjustment to the starting values, as we have seen in the example.

It is important to note that it is not a case of linear trial and error on the principle that 1.7656 (nonce variable) is too big, so let's try 1.4441, and if that is still too big, we'll try 1.2982. It is just not that simple. In fact, since the result is not linear, it might be that a greater value for the nonce in the formula leads to a smaller final value. As previously stated, the eyes of mathematicians light up with these formulae; laymen just look at it in astonishment. In case you are asked what kind of calculation is required to calculate a hash value, you can just refer to the "elliptical curve formula." But only if that doesn't lead to more questions! Normally, however, that is enough to end the inquiry.

So, for the miner, there is nothing to do but to guess, calculate, compare and, if the result is not small enough, start all over again with a new nonce. To put things in perspective, we are not just talking about 100 or 1,000 attempts. This process can be carried out in millions or billions of calculation operations per second. Each attempt continually creates the whole Bitcoin network, and the units in which this calculation power is measured are the called "mega-hashes", "giga-hashes" or even "peta-hashes."

So, there are billions or even trillions of hash calculations per second. Let me just point out that such calculations are way beyond the capabilities of the average consumer's computer because the computing power required is simply not yet available in commercial machines.

Today, these calculations are carried out through a sharing of work between nodes and miners. The nodes manage the decentralized stored data and the miners calculate the new blocks.

In the beginning — back when Bitcoin system was started in 2009 — it was still possible to calculate the hash values of the blocks with a completely normal CPU (the central chip in our computers; Pentium, for example). At some point, however, it became too complicated and difficult and the software experts shifted the calculations onto GPUs (Graphic Processing Units). These are special chips in the graphics cards. Graphics cards must also be able to process a large quantity of data very quickly so that they can, for example, calculate the background picture in a game and display it on the screen while the player runs through the gameplay environment with weapons and items. Because of these unique characteristics, GPUs are much better suited to carry out the complicated calculations required to create blocks.

Those who are fastest earn more money

A large number of miners are installed throughout the entire system. All are working simultaneously on every new block and try to guess the nonce. As previously described, they take transactions from the pool and pack them together with the hash of the last block into the new block. They then search for a value for the nonce, calculate, and compare the result with the demands of the system. If the value is smaller than that specified by the system, the block is finished and sent to the nodes connected to the miner so that these can hang the new block on their local chain. The miner then sends it on to other nodes, so that these, in turn, hang the new block on their respective chains — thus the blockchain is extended further and further.

What has that got to do with earning money, though? Well, on the one hand, the Bitcoins need to be created. On the other hand, the computers involved may not need pizzas and coffee to do their work but they do need electricity. And electricity costs the operator money. Why should the operator pay for something if he gets no benefit from it and can't even buy himself pizza or coffee, or even a nice steak dinner every now and then? There has to be some incentive to keep the operator interested and active.

Again, another of Satoshi Nakamoto's ingenious ideas comes into play here: The miner gets a success commission for the work they do!

So how does this incentive system work?

Calculation of the new blocks is always undertaken by all the miners in a network in parallel. However, there will always be one miner who is the first to hash a new block; that is, to guess the right hash value for this block. This miner is now rewarded. The reward consists of Bitcoins, which are simply newly created for this purpose.

While the standard bank has to print new banknotes, in the Bitcoin network, the miner is simply awarded new Bitcoins in the block it has just created. For example, 50 Bitcoins as a reward for each new, correctly hashed block. When the block is attached to the existing blockchain by the nodes, these 50 Bitcoins are legitimized, and they belong to the miner who first found the new block. Thus, everyone has an incentive to calculate as fast as possible and hash new blocks.

This is how Bitcoin was born. Technically, the miners just pack a transaction into each block, in which they pay out this reward to themselves. If the block is validated by the network, the Bitcoins exist from this point onwards, because they are in an unalterable blockchain.

Faster and more powerful computers

With this incentive system in place, it logically follows that those who can calculate fastest will earn more money. This created competition and the motivated those involved to use faster chips that could calculate the correct hash value for the block before anyone else. So, after a few years, not only were normal computers too slow, but graphics cards were, too. Special circuits were developed to do nothing else but hash; that is, calculate the hash values of individual blocks. These special chips are also called ASICs (application-specific integrated circuits).

Special machines, consisted largely of ventilation units because they got very hot, large power supplies because they need a lot of electrical power, and small ASIC chips that do nothing but calculate, calculate, calculate. Hash, hash and more hashing. Hashing mega-, giga-, peta- and tera-hashes. Sometime in the near future, the words "hash" and "to hash" are bound to find their way into the Oxford English Dictionary — but that's by the by.

In effect, we have a system in which all the miners around the world are in international competition. They are taking part in what is essentially a lottery, which has a draw every 10 minutes. In each ten-minute period, one will find the right number, the right nonce, and will win. That is the simple principle of mining in Bitcoin.

The purpose of this complicated process in the implementation of a simple principle is to secure the network itself so that no-one can overwrite and thus change and falsify data. As described previously, this mining process acts as a kind of brake and also serves the creation of new Bitcoins. The term "mining" was chosen because — as with gold and precious stones — new riches are found by digging, through work.

The more hash power, the greater the chances

It naturally follows that, just as in the conventional lottery, the person with the most tickets has the greatest chance of winning. Every single ticket has the same chance but, statistically speaking, the chance is higher if you have more tickets. In this case, the chances are higher for those with the greatest hash power in the network, meaning you can carry out more calculations to guess the correct value before anyone else. That is why there is a worldwide competition for the fastest miner, the most miners, and the best locations — ones where electricity is cheaper and mining significantly less costly. China has its nose in front, but other countries like Russia. Sweden, Japan, Iceland, and the USA are constantly struggling for greater power, more computing power, and sites with cheap electricity offers. Mining farms can be found situated directly adjacent to hydroelectric plants in both China and the USA. The first attempts at using renewable energy like solar or wind power are in the offing in Europe. Russia appears to be strategically interested in mining, and it is possible that the competition for reward will get even broader. In fact, that is the best thing that could happen to the Bitcoin network because the more witnesses there are to a transaction, the more secure it is. All of this is factored into a simple profit calculation. For example, let's assume that a miner — in our case, a specialized computer — has a power rating of 1,200 watts. It will be running and hashing 24 hours a day every day of the year. That is 1.2 kilowatt-hours x 24 hours x 30 days a month on average. Altogether, that makes 864 kilowatt-hours a month.

A kilowatt-hour cost around 13 cents in the US. So, the operation of a miner costs around $110 a month in electricity alone. Then there is the procurement, and the site because the machines have to be located somewhere.

The crucial component in calculating profitability is, of course, the hash power that a miner has. This is primarily how much hash power it has in relation to the entire Bitcoin miner network. If the miner has, for example, 13,000.0 GH/s (S9 Antminer), and it is one of two identical miners in the entire world, then it can be assumed that every second block that the nodes accept and attach to the blockchain will be calculated on average.

That means that at one block every 10 minutes, you will find three blocks every hour and the other miner will also find calculate three blocks per hour. You receive a payment of 12.5 Bitcoins per block (until 2020; later, it will be more). In one month, that adds up to three blocks per hour x 24 hours a day x 30 days = 2,160 payments of 12.5 Bitcoins = 27.000 BTC.

Yay, you are rich! Very rich! Stinking rich! Because one BTC is being traded over $12,500 (January 2018). If you are operating one of a total of two miners and, thus, 50% of the entire hash power of the Bitcoin network, then for $110 worth of electricity, you are making around $330 million in payments. Wow — that is some business! But where is the catch?

Get rich with Bitcoin

The catch is easy to find and is not in the mathematics itself. That is correct — as always in the Bitcoin network, that it all comes back to simple yet very complicated formulae.

The assumption that you can have 50% of the computing power — the entire hash power — with just one miner is, of course, utopia. In fact, the total hash power in the Bitcoin network is 17,087,552 TH/s (correct as of January 2018).

So, in fact, you only have 1/1,320,000 of the hash power. To keep things simple, you can just divide the total monthly profit of $330 million by 1,320,000 to calculate approximately what a miner can receive in payments: $250! Of course, if you are paying 13 cents per kilowatt-hour for electricity, that doesn't add up to a whole lot. For that reason, the mining companies are always looking for cheaper electricity. That calculation looks completely different if you only have to pay 5 cents per kilowatt-hour or even less. For example, industrial electricity in the USA in the state of

Washington on the west coast costs 2.8 cents per kilowatt-hour. It is no surprise that a lot of mining farms are established there.

Additionally, mining has other components that need to be considered, each of which—along with the cost of electricity—can drastically affect profits and influence performance. Room temperature plays a role, the connection cables, the tolerances of the chips, and much more. Added to that is the fact that the miners are only computers and, just as with a normal computer, parts inevitably fail. The hotter the things become, the more frequently failures happen. The warmer a room is, the sooner the miners overheat. All in all, mining is something for the experts; mining at home is seldom lucrative, even if there are tempting offers from so-called experts who will lead you to believe that mining at home is an easy way to get rich (more on this later).

The race for a block is over as soon as a miner has calculated the block and sent it to the network. Within seconds, all the other miners are notified and immediately stop their calculations. They immediately start to build and calculate the next block. If Block 6 then arrives as solved, they take new transactions from the pool, take the hash value from the newly found Block 6, and immediately start to calculate Block 7. The miners are in a perpetual race to find the block first and win the payment. It is a constant rushing, mathematical lottery.

Inflation in the Bitcoin blockchain

This race is constantly restarted. This happens, on average, every 10 minutes. A never-ending cycle, hour by hour, day by day, month by month, and year by year.

This means that, every 10 minutes, 50 new Bitcoins are created. For describing the process of creating Bitcoins, the terminology of the financial world has been adopted. As already noted, gold and precious gemstones are extracted from mines or dug out. This process of mining increases the quantity of valuable assets available in the world, and the same is true of cryptocurrency.

Through these special computers in the Bitcoin network, called miners, new Bitcoins are, essentially, dug out. That is where the name miner originates, and those involved in the crypto world commonly talk of "mining." However, there is an important difference between this and money: While we can never get an accurate estimation of know much gold exists in all the mines of the world, we know exactly how many Bitcoins can ever be mined. In the core algorithm, which no-one but the ominous Satoshi Nakamoto can change, it is specified that 21 million is the maximum number of Bitcoins that can ever be dug or mined by the system. That specific number is locked into the core algorithm and, without the key, which Nakamoto presumably has, it cannot be changed. There are rumors that Nakamoto destroyed the key for security reasons, making the system impregnable. So – 21 million Bitcoins, and no more.

There is, then, only a precisely defined quantity of Bitcoin, which restricts the availability. Just like any other asset or good, limited availability often directly increases the value. We are familiar with this concept when it comes to things like gold, silver and other precious metals, or diamonds, gemstones, and rare earth metals. The same principle applies to art, paintings, and even rare stamp misprints like the famous "Blue Mauritius." Limited availability enhances the value of an item – provided, of course, that there is a corresponding demand for it. There is more about this in the chapter about the true value of work.

The issue of Bitcoin is precisely predictable

The core algorithm does not just define the upper limit; it also defines how many Bitcoins are issued. This began in 2009 with 50 Bitcoins per block. Approximately every four years, there is now a so-called "halving" of the payments. What that actually means is that, since the summer of 2012, only 25 Bitcoins were paid out per correctly calculated block. In summer 2016, it halved again to only 12.5 Bitcoins and, in summer 2020, it will reduce further to 6.25 Bitcoins per correctly calculated block.

A natural consequence of this halving is that the remainder of the total of 21 million Bitcoins can be paid out or mined much more slowly. It is precisely the limited quantity and the gradual availability of the Bitcoins that makes them so valuable. Just as with gold, where it is becoming ever more difficult to uncover large deposits, the found deposits are ever-harder work to obtain. That is why gold holds its value, and precisely why the supply of Bitcoins must be managed. Our current currencies like the US dollar, euro, pound sterling, and the yen are a stark contrast to this. There is no shortage of these, nor are they rare. Quite the contrary, in fact; they are often deliberately inflated by governments and so lose their value. Inflation is brought about centrally by politics, which makes everyone poorer. Inflation is also an effect of a centralized system. We will discuss this further in the chapter on money.

Bitcoin is the answer to inflation. The more intensively it is used as a payment method, the greater the potential it has to become even more stable than gold. As mentioned previously, nobody knows how much gold can still be extracted from the earth. A huge vein might be discovered tomorrow and lead to the bottom falling out of the gold price. Space exploration also poses a potential threat to the stability of gold, should it be found in abundant supply somewhere in space or being produced in the permanent vacuum. Alternatively, if the dream of the ancient alchemists of being able to turn base metals into gold should come true, gold would be worth nothing overnight. The same is true of anything that is assigned a value based on its limited availability. However, that cannot happen to Bitcoin because the system is, as described, secured so that there is no possibility of generating, creating, or forging more.

How you can lose Bitcoin

In fact, Bitcoin has more of a deflationary effect, which is blamed trivially on the loss of access data for individual users. In the beginning, when Bitcoin was worth nothing, or a few cents at most, most software experts didn't pay too much attention to what they had. They simply minted these out of pure enthusiasm for the technology, and the Bitcoins were just stored somewhere on their hard drive. More precisely, the currency was not stored there; rather, it was the access code allocated in the blockchain as proof of ownership, the so-called "private key" that was stored. The next chapter goes into further detail on these private keys and why they are so important. However, for many people, the hard drive was exchanged, the computer scrapped, or the hard drive relocated or scrapped, and the private keys stored on them were misplaced or destroyed. In this way, hundreds of thousands — even millions of Bitcoins — were lost. Not lost in the sense of forever —

because the blockchain, which can never forget anything, still knows these Bitcoins — but lost in the sense that there is no-one has access to them anymore. No-one in the world, not even the largest supercomputers all working together, can succeed in recreating a lost access code, this private key.

This is both really good and really bad news. Good, because the Bitcoins are always securely annulled and cannot be stolen or forged. Bad, because you can never get your Bitcoins back if this access code, the private key, is lost. As stated, there is more in a later chapter on what that actually means, how it works, and why we seemingly hear about Bitcoins being stolen.

Some Bitcoins were lost — or the access to them lost — by the Bitcoins plainly and simply being sent to the wrong address during the payment process. These addresses either belong to no-one, as the system has just accepted the transfer because the formula was correct, or the Bitcoins were sent to an address for which the private key has been lost. Some are sitting for an undefined time in inactive accounts, and it is unclear whether they will ever be reactivated again, or can be reactivated. There are plenty of crazy stories surrounding these lost Bitcoins — or, more correctly, private keys. Remember, it is only ever the private keys that are lost — the Bitcoins themselves still exist, as they always have, as part of the blockchain. One tale, for example, of the person seen with a spade, digging through a landfill for his old computer or discarded hard drive.

Fantastic stories have surfaced, beyond even what Hollywood could come up with. But, when you consider that someone might have once owned a few thousand Bitcoins, then you can perhaps understand their willingness to dig through trash to get them back. Maybe not if the Bitcoin rate is about 30 cents. Then, for example, 5,000 BTC would "only" be worth 1,500 US dollars. But what about a valuation of $1, or $10? Who wouldn't pick up a spade for $50,000? The Bitcoin rate is subject to huge fluctuations, but it certainly traded at over ten thousand dollars per Bitcoin at times. At what point would you pick up the spade or dig through a landfill with an army of excavators? $2,500 per Bitcoin? At a value of $12.5 million? Don't worry. With the knowledge in this book, you'll never have put on gloves and pick up a spade. There will be more later about how to safely store your Bitcoins so that you do not have to make an embarrassing trip to the hardware store.

The successful miner receives more than just the new Bitcoin

It is clear that miners are a crucial component in ensuring the security of the energy-intensive work of the Bitcoin network. The operators run special computers that use a crazy amount of electricity and do nothing else but calculate a certain mathematical formula over and over. They repeat this process until they have found a result corresponding to the specifications of the system. They then report this result and send a data block to all the nodes. The nodes accept it if the miner has calculated correctly. As of summer 2016, the miner receives 12.5 new Bitcoins as reward for the work. But that is not all that the miner receives. That alone is too little incentive because the miner hardware and the specialized computers cost a lot of money, and electricity consumption is also expensive. The miners basically pack into the blocks the transactions that were permitted by the participants in the network. These transactions, in the simplest case, 2 BTC from Alice to Bob, are not completely cost-free, even in the Bitcoin network. A so-called network fee is always due, which the participants can choose freely. So, Alice contacts the miner, "Hi miner, please register that I have transferred 2 BTC to Bob and for that I will pay you a fee of 0.000001 BTC."

Of course, in the network, it is only computer codes that communicate this to the machines, but the miners receive a small fee for every transaction that they carry out in a block. It is important to know this.

Since every miner can freely select the transactions from the transaction pool, the miners maximize their earnings by using an algorithm that selects the transactions with the highest fees first. For example, if Alice offers a fee of 0.000001 BTC for her transaction but Carol offers 0.000002 BTC for hers, the miners will first pack Carl's transaction in the block first, and only then will they pack Alice's — and only if there is still space in the block.

Everything in the Bitcoin network is maximally, capitalistically designed. If Bitcoin and Co. are suitable for changing existing business forms sustainably and for the better, this does not in any way mean that they are "socialistic." Quite the opposite, in fact.

They are pure capitalism, with all the advantages and drawbacks of such a system.

For this reason, the miners obtain, along with the basic income per block that they solve, an additional variable income from the sum of all the transaction fees for the transactions that they pack into that block. That is a huge commercial incentive because added to the current 12.5-Bitcoin payment there are 1-3 more Bitcoins in transaction fees. In winter 2017, that is a simple 15,000 to 30,000 USD dollars in 10 minutes. This is not a bad hourly rate — of course, only if you are the lucky one who was first to calculate the right block hash.

In fact, it is not only a giant lottery for the miner that slaves away 24 hours a day, there is also a residual risk that it must give up its profits again. Once or twice a week in the Bitcoin network, two different miners will find a block at the exact same time, but more on this scenario later.

Ten minutes: the heartbeat of the system

There is one more secret you must know to understand the whole system. How does it happen that one block is created, that is, calculated, every 10 minutes?

Nakamoto set the pulse of the system at 10 minutes — that is, every 10 minutes on average, a new block is found and added to the Bitcoin blockchain. That results in the heartbeat, so to speak, of the system. But how is that achieved?

First, you must understand that the system adjusts itself every two weeks. Each two-week period contains 2016 10-minute intervals. Let's just calculate that quickly. There are 144 10-minute intervals a day, multiplied by 14 is a total of 2016 10-minute intervals in every two weeks.

With that in mind, a further unalterable parameter is built into the basic system that feeds into the formula that the miners have to calculate. This parameter is the so-called "difficulty" of the work. This parameter is adjusted by the system for all 2016 blocks and, in practice, actually works quite simply and effectively. The system measures how long, on average, it takes the combined computing power of all miners to find a block. With this information, it then sets the difficulty of the next 2016 blocks.

If the miners were faster than 10 minutes due to more computing power in the net, the difficulty is increased. When this happens, the miners must guess for correspondingly longer and calculate more cycles before the correct value for a block is calculated. Really simple, in fact.

This system is another one of Nakamoto's ingenious ideas, because it automatically activates additional security factors. The block time of 10 minutes only applies as an average of all blocks since the last correction of the difficulty. Some blocks are calculated much faster than others because it is essentially a lottery. A lucky strike by a miner cannot be excluded and happens more frequently that you might imagine. Therefore, the system calculates the average value of the last 2016 blocks, which corresponds to around two weeks.

More miners, more computing power

More computing power comes into the network if, for example, more miners are connected, or if the computing power on the whole increases. When the first miner used a GPU, that is, a graphics card, to calculate the blocks, it calculated them much faster than every 10 minutes, which was much faster than everyone else competing. It solved nearly every block one after the other and received the payment which, at that time, was still 50 BTC. While the rest were still trying to solve the calculation for Block 5, the GPU miner had done it long ago and was already working on Block 6. The others, which could only calculate considerably more slowly, had to continually break off and start again. By the time they had gotten that far, the GPU miner had already finished Block 6 and so on. It was a constant game of just trying to keep up with the miner with the most powerful computer.

That, of course, is not the sense of the whole thing, because it makes the system very prone to manipulation. This GPU miner would have been able to change data and supply it to the network because it is so fast that the others would not have been able to supply any more blocks to the nodes. They receive a notification in the middle of each calculation process after a short time that a new block has been calculated and that they should start on Block 7. Then, after a few minutes comes the message that Block 7 has been found and they should continue with Block 8. They don't get there either because that gets reported as found, so go to Block 9 and so on. With such a massive computing advantage, the system suddenly became centralized again. That one miner that is calculating with a GPU instead of a normal processor like a Pentium could completely dominate the system and potentially introduce changes to the data at will.

There is no control anymore — pure dictatorship

But Nakamoto had the foresight to solve this potential problem by introducing difficulty as a counter-measure. Two weeks later, the dictatorship was over because, after the 2016 blocks, the difficulty was ramped so high that the GPU miner also needed 10 minutes on average to calculate a block. That means that the system doesn't hyperventilate anymore and the heart rate is stabilized again.

However, in this scenario, it is still only the GPU miner that can find the blocks because it has enough computing power to calculate them. The other miners can't solve any because the difficulty is now too high for their computing power. Now and again, one might strike it lucky because the miners are essentially only guessing. The odds are similar to a lottery player who has only ticked a single box but hits the six correct numbers with the bonus ball. That is the exception, though. The GPU miner will win the most blocks; the only difference is that it takes them a little longer. But it still solves nearly everything, so what has been gained? What was it all about? Here's why:

If the difficulty suddenly goes up very high, a large number of specialists will become aware of this situation. Many clever minds are observing the system, recording data, letting their own application run on the Bitcoin blockchain or supporting miners, which have not accepted anything for days and now suddenly can't keep up at all. A change like this is noticed by lots of participants and, firstly, by the technical experts who can soon work out what has happened.

Bitcoin is no black box that affords access only to a pre-defined group; there is a great number of experts who can react immediately in such cases. They quickly adapt and also use GPU miners. The result is that gradually the total computing power increases massively, but is spread over many so that the system is again decentralized and operated in competition. The pulse is back down to 10 minutes, the hash power is balanced again, and the system is as stable as it ever was.

The advantage of the first one may have been that they won the overwhelming majority of the payments — in the ideal case for 14 days — but didn't the engineer who worked it all out also earn some reward? There can be some lively arguments about the level. If for example, it was 1,800 of 2016 blocks, and at the time it was 50 BTC per block, that would be 90,000 BTC. So, at 1 US dollar per BTC that is $90,000, or $90,000,000 at $1,000 per BTC. Too much?

In truth, these payments are worth it because the system was further developed by it, and it became safer on the whole. Since then, the system has advanced to a point where a huge amount of computing power would be required to bring about changes like this. Thus, the whole system has become more valuable. If you compare it to an invention like the raw plug or the mp3 format, the reward is entirely within normal limits, if somewhat to the upper end.

Nakamoto's system can also balance out exceptions; odd ones out and black swans have no chance

Of course, there are exceptional situations. For example, in the change to the GPU and later to the first ASICs, that is, chips specially manufactured for mining with their special assemblies.

The fluctuations are generally marginal and primarily arise due to an increase or decrease in the number of miners that are connected. For example, if the Bitcoin price climbs in the first half of 2017 from $1,000 per Bitcoin to nearly $3,000 per Bitcoin, then more people will jump on the bandwagon and operate miners. With such a significant jump in the value, it becomes increasingly profitable for them to do so, even at high energy prices.

More miners mean more computing power in the system as a whole, which means more hash-power in the network, which means that the blocks can be found faster. This inevitably leads to a higher difficulty after 2016 blocks — after about two weeks — and, at this point, the system is braked. This occurs so that the higher overall power corrects itself back to the average 10 minutes, just at a higher level.

On the whole, this is good because it becomes much more difficult for a hacker who wants to change data. It also becomes a much more expensive endeavor because much more computer power is required to carry out this change. All of this basically amounts to an economic problem. If manipulation brings in less than it costs to carry out, it is not worth the effort.

For example, if a hacker can net $100,000 but has to spend $150,000, then it makes no sense to try. How much can be gained depends on the price of Bitcoin and — as the system is always gaining more miners — the higher the price is, the higher the hash power and the more expensive an attack becomes. Remember, all of this is done in a system with a limited number of coins, which inevitably drives higher values for Bitcoin. It's an ingenious system, if you think about it.

There is still the problem that there are fewer miners if the price falls. In this scenario, miners may be switched off because the payments achieved are too small and the electricity costs too high. That brings the whole hash power down and because the difficulty is so high, the remaining miners need more than 10 minutes on average to calculate the blocks. This problem can also be addressed within two weeks because the difficulty is then reset lower and the formula can be calculated in fewer attempts. The whole system is reset back to an average of 10 minutes per block again.

In this way, the system regulates itself and grows along with innovations in both hardware and software.

Attacks by switching off miners

The difficulty system represents another security feature, along with the balancing of hash power with more or fewer miners. If you examine this difficulty mechanism more closely, you also find an additional downward brake which ensures that the difficulty can never be dropped by more than 25%. This is defined unalterably in the core algorithm and is designed to prevent manipulation if too many miners under the control of any one owner.

Suppose enough machines belong to one group of miners that they account for 40% of the total hash power in the system. With this power, the could intentionally turn off some machines to reduce the hash power. In simple terms, that means the difficulty is reduced by 40% because the other miners would need a long time to calculate the blocks. Immediately after the difficulty correction, these miners could be quickly switched back on and can now calculate blocks very fast because the difficulty does not correspond to the actual computing power.

In a case like this, this group of miners would have enormous power for two weeks—giving them the ability to potentially destabilize the system and quickly feed in a little new data. This does not need to be in the form of pure transactions; it could also be changes to the algorithms that define the system, which can also be altered to a certain degree. There is more about that later, when we discuss the consensus mechanism.

The maximum reduction in difficulty acts then as a further brake to ensure the security of the system and stabilize the Bitcoin network. All in all, the system as a whole is very well constructed and is designed to protect itself (and its users) from manipulation.

The past cannot be changed

So, what have we learned so far? We know that the Bitcoin blockchain is secured by its miners, which need an average of 10 minutes of difficult calculation processes to fire a series of transactions into a data block. We know that they are rewarded with newly created Bitcoin in a process known as mining. We also know that in the Bitcoin network, many miners are in direct international competition and if a block has been found, they immediately start on the calculation of the next block. So, the next logical question is: how do they find out that a new block has been found?

If a miner has successfully solved a puzzle, it is immediately reported to the nodes connected to it. These computers have the entire blockchain calculated to date stored locally on them. The miner sends them the new block with the request to attach this block to the locally stored chain. The nodes then check whether the calculated hash fits with the blocks already present. If so, they attach the new block locally to their saved chain. They simultaneously propagate the new block to their peers; in other words, the send the new block to the hubs they are connected to after they receive a periodic request from them.

The process of checking whether the hash delivered fits with that already present is a much simpler calculation process than the mining itself, and it can easily be completed by "normal" computers. There is highly efficient mathematics behind it and this process is also an important feature of the system. While the calculation is very difficult and costly, the checking process is very quick and easy.

Every block is then delivered from the miner to one or several nodes, which immediately send the block to their respective neighbors upon their periodic request. In doing so, in quite a short period of time, all nodes and all the miners attached to them know the new block. For the purpose of this example, let's say it is block number 10. The miners "sulk" as they cease their own efforts to calculate Block 10 and immediately start on Block 11.

The nodes attach Block 10 to their chains, which up to this point ended with Block 9. If it fits with Block 9, the chain is extended by one data block, including all the transactions contained within it. Technically, the node does not send the block automatically; it is asked by its neighbors if it has a new block; the node answers accordingly and sends the block. That in itself is not crucial for understanding the system. It is only important to know that the new blocks are propagated quickly to the whole network so that the miners do not continue pointlessly calculating one or several blocks that already exist.

What happens if two miners solve simultaneously?

It does happen, however, that two miners solve a block at pretty much the same instant. While this scenario is statistically rare, it cannot be avoided because all of the nodes and miners are working completely independent of each other. Essentially, each one does what it wants — which is, of course, the whole point of a decentralized system that can't be manipulated. It is a network designed specifically so that no person and no other computer, no matter how cleverly programmed, can control.

Some nodes are attached to every miner, which in turn communicate with other nodes. The connection between nodes depends on which ones they reach the fastest, which in turn depends on how fast the other nodes connect with the internet; all of which is affected by whether they are online at the time and the quality of the connection. It is probable that different miners are linked with different nodes, which are in turn linked to other nodes because the miners are distributed across the world. As a result of this, it can happen that one part of the network knows the Block 10 from miner A, while another part of the network recognizes Block 10 from miner B. Miner B successfully finished its calculations only 17 thousandths of a second after miner A, leading to a situation where there are two correct blocks in existence: Blocks 10A and 10B.

A situation like this would be a catastrophe because the two blocks would have different transaction data, which the miners would have taken from the transaction pool. For example, in Block 10A, Alice sent 2 BTC to Bob, but this transaction is not considered in Block 10B.
Strictly speaking, Alice could now use her 2 BTC again in the part of the network which accepted Block 10B and transfers it to Carol. In the B-part of the network, the transaction would be recognized as valid in the following Block 11. So, Alice would have spent her 2 BTC twice. Great for Alice, but bad luck for either Bob or Carol. Fortunately, this further problem of digital money was predicted by Nakamoto and solved in his scheme.

The so-called "double spending" problem

"Double spending" means just that—spending money twice. The person can spend once from their actual credit and once more because no one notices that the credit has already been spent and the account is empty. Some fraudsters even manage to transfer money twice from an empty account, and really advanced fraudsters can even manage to get away with it three times or more. How does that happen?
In reality, it is quite simple. Imagine for a moment that you only have $1000 in your account. You write two $1000 checks and send them to two different people on opposite sides of the country. The recipient who is the first to receive the check and whose bank cashes it soonest will get the payment. The second person is

already the first loser as the account belonging to the person who wrote the check is now empty. The check bounces and the second person is also charged bank fees. In the age of online banking, it is no longer quite so easy. There is still a number of people in the USA and other parts of the world who frequently pay by check. Traditionally, it was the preferred method of payment and checks bounce like balls in a playpen.

In the digital world, and with electronic payment processes, the "double spending" problem was one of the biggest hurdles to overcome in ensuring the progress of digital payment traffic. How can you ensure that the data from one file—which has been deleted or spent—cannot be sent again? How easy is it to copy a file and send it to Alice, then send another copy to Bob, another to Carol, another to Dave, and so on?

This is exactly what is happening every second online with cat videos and music files. Essentially, social networks like Facebook, Instagram and Twitter do just that, and so bring people together around this content. Of course, many files are illegally copied and shared. Music is pirated, films are pirated, and everyone exchanges electronic copies of everything that has been digitalized. Copyright holders have experienced and are continuing to experience a dark period in which anything that can be digitalized can also be exchanged without credit or compensation.

The problem—and the solution—lies in the system itself. Digital data can be easily copied and sent with just the press of a button or the click of a mouse. Nothing could be simpler, and that is the problem with digital money. That is the "double spending" problem.

Nakamoto solved the "double spending" problem with Bitcoin

Of course, the Bitcoin system has a built-in solution to handle this problem. The system intrinsically specified that this split, known as the "fork" is automatically solved.

The solution falls to Block 11 because this will no longer fit either 10A or 10B. Why not?

In simple terms, the miner—which has calculated Block 11—knows either 10A or 10B. Its node had informed it previously and transferred either 10A or 10B so that it could start to calculate Block 11. So, it begins to calculate Block 11 using one the hashes of Block 10, but it can't have both. Thus, with successful calculation of the right hash value, its block fits for only one part of the blockchain stored by the nodes and not the other.

If it calculates Block 11 based on 10A, then 11A fits for all the nodes that had 10A, but not those that stored 10B. These will decline Block 11A as invalid and wait for a compatible Block 11 with its stored Block 10B. Confused? You need to think this through a few times and it will become logical and easily understandable.

Now the race has started. If a Block 11 arrives, it will be attached to the 10B nodes and refused by the 10A nodes. It is declined for two reasons; firstly, they already have a Block 11 (11A), and secondly, 11B does not fit either 10A or 11A. So, how quickly is a compatible Block 12 going to arrive?

In cases becoming increasingly infrequent, an 11A and an 11B are arriving, followed by a 12A. However, this scenario is becoming rarer because, with every splitting process, more and more nodes potentially change their minds.

A node is also commercially programmed and controlled through software; so, if it receives Block 12 and doesn't yet have Block 11, it becomes "perplexed." It only knows Block 10 and cannot build Block 12 onto Block 10. The node begins searching its neighbors for a valid Block 11 that not only fits Block 10, but is also correct for Block 12. It sounds a little complicated, but it is very simple.

If the node finds a neighbor that has a longer chain than it has itself. It then cancels and deletes its own chain, which it has stored locally, and assumes from the fork the part of its neighbor's chain that is longer than its own and fits Block 12. In the example above, Block 9 would still be identical to both, but Blocks 10 and 11 are different for the neighbor. However, the incompatible Block 12 fits Blocks 10 and 11 of the neighbor. The node quickly decides to delete its own Blocks 10 and 11, takes these from the neighboring node, and attaches them to its own Block 9. Then the new Block 12 fits its local chain again. The system is designed to continuously update and correct itself in the most secure way possible. Ingenious, isn't it?

The transactions present in the discarded Blocks 10 and 11 are dissolved again and placed back into the transaction pool. Of course, the node checks to ensure that the transactions are not also in the blocks it has taken from its neighbor and deletes these from its transaction pool. The difference then remains. If, for example, Alice's transaction is there, then it is removed and can no longer be carried out a second time.

In most cases, a fork like this will only affect one block, which was mined at the same time and whose transactions are then passed back as not completed. In rare cases, it is two consecutive blocks and in very rare cases, it can be more. However, it is so rare and statistically improbable that it could be safely ignored.

There is a lot of money involved

The emphasis here is on the word "could." It could be ignored, if it were anything other than money transfers to be recorded in the Bitcoin blockchain. If we are dealing with a transaction with a market value of $10 million, which then ends up in a fork with three consecutive blocks that are later discarded — well, that would not be good.

For exactly this reason, those transferring large sums of money should wait at least six blocks. This is because six consecutive blocks of all the nodes — from the example described above — are on Block 16, and the mathematical probability that part of the network is still working on a different part of the chain tends to zero. Statistically speaking, six blocks will guarantee safety. While most users of the Bitcoin blockchain wait for two blocks, if you are expecting a transfer of $10 million — or any sum that feels like a lot to you — it is recommended that you wait for at least six blocks. Then you can rest assured that the $10 million is certainly yours.

It is the linking of individual data blocks using cryptographic procedures, combined with distribution over many thousands of independent computers — all of which are independently calculating, checking and managing the data themselves — which leads to the reliability and truth in the system.

Bitcoin is the technical solution which makes blind trust in information from a completely unknown third party possible. It makes the agent — the trustworthy middleman — redundant.

Of course, the system outlined above is far from a complete description. This chapter is only intended to provide a general understanding of a blockchain system. The technical implementation is not exactly trivial; the most intelligent minds of our time are working with and developing this technology.

Chapter 4 — Wallets, Exchanges

How you get and manage Bitcoin

This chapter is especially important because there are a few things that you must absolutely be aware of when you buy, own, or keep cryptocurrencies like Bitcoin. The author of this very book lost Bitcoin because he was not careful enough with his private keys. The instructions in this chapter could save your Bitcoins and should, therefore, be taken very seriously!

So-called "wallets" are used within blockchain systems to manage the crypto-units, coins or tokens pertaining to a certain wallet, which contain addresses. It is these addresses to which the results of transactions have been or are assigned. Once again, it sounds complicated, but this time it really is not!

The concept of wallets has become well-established worldwide. A wallet is a place in which one can see the status or content of a certain address in a blockchain. It is through this wallet that one can both send and receive money. Put simply, it is special software, much like an online banking portal, in which you can call up your account balance and carry out payments.

A transaction in a blockchain is always a transfer of the cryptocurrency from one participant to another. Strictly speaking, it is from one address to another. The participants may be sensors or other computer units which can process the transferred data. If the temperature in the room exceeds 29 degrees, you should close the blinds, for example. You might not need a blockchain for that, but this should show what kind of value transfers could take place in our modern world. It is even clearer if you imagine an electric car stopping at a red light and the battery being automatically charged by an induction loop embedded in the road. For this, the car pays the road concerned for 32 seconds of electricity by supplying, for example, 0.00001 BTC from its crypto-wallet. This is a technology which is already being actively tested, so it is no science-fiction scenario. Of course, the participants may also be people who are transferring or receiving money. Or, in our case, transferring or receiving cryptocurrencies like Bitcoin, Ether and others, or perhaps an important medical certificate or identity documentation, which also count as transfer of values.

Addresses and wallets

Along with the term "wallet," the term "address" is important in the context of blockchains. An address is basically nothing more than a postal address, just like *8 High Street* is an address. Of course, it is a little more than that in a blockchain system because computers first have to resolve and translate *8 High Street* into computer language to be able to work with it. That is no problem at all for a computer; it does that effortlessly with links.

The problem, however, is in the length and uniqueness of the address. As in real life, you can't send anything to 8 High Street if you don't know the postcode or at least the town or city. Just like a physical address consists of more than just the street name, the address in the context of blockchains has to be a little more detailed to ensure the unequivocal identification of the recipient.

Here is an example of an address for the crypto-token SIA:

2077ffcc79143aa8a1ba36ba934873f7e8d65085f212ce220dfacd267c8291e4d6ebc0923f09

And here is a Bitcoin address:

1Po9VrtwJzHQycEDS3i9JojUUT4dkYteMs

It is easy to see the difference between the two addresses — especially the difference between these and *8 High Street, Anytown*. Addresses must have one very important feature that is critical to the success of a blockchain system — they must be unambiguous.

In addition to this, there must absolutely be enough of them. The so-called "Address space" must be big enough to satisfy all possible requirements. In contrast with physical addresses, there are no upper limits because, in theory, everyone can have as many addresses as they wish. This is an important difference to the real world. In most countries, registration of one main residence is legally required, even though some people have a second or even third residence. However, these addresses, whether a summer home or a flat in the city, also generally have to be registered. With the blockchain, there are no such limitations or requirements.

Everyone can have as many Bitcoin addresses as they want

Addresses are handled completely differently in blockchain systems. All participants, be they people or machines, can have as many addresses as they wish. These do not even need to be known to the blockchain to be effective.

That means that no addresses need be registered with authorities and you can have and use as many addresses as you wish. Under certain circumstances, registering one's Bitcoin with the "real" authorities can make sense, especially if you are trading with cryptocurrencies and making profits. This type of setup should be registered with the relevant authorities, especially the tax office. But that is not what this address term is about in the blockchain system, and the legal requirements around cryptocurrencies is still completely unclear in many countries anyway. This is about this specific circumstance of being able to have an address which is not even known to the system itself. It is not known to the miners nor the nodes, and yet that address can still be used as the subject of a transfer within the Bitcoin blockchain. This is a peculiarity and it enables the receipt of money, here in Bitcoin, completely anonymously. More about that later.

If it is possible to create an address like this from outside the whole system, how can you ensure that this address does not already exist? We are back to mathematics, which will only be presented here briefly and simply.

First, it is necessary that there are enough addresses that can be used. Furthermore, it is necessary that these addresses are chosen completely at random. These two factors are very important and are often is beyond our understanding. Anyone who has noted a sequence of numbers thinks that this sequence is random. They would assume that it is impossible that someone else would write the same sequence, but that is a big mistake.

In mathematics, there really can be no talk of coincidence. It is not improbable that someone else would choose the same sequence of numbers. Therefore, this randomness should be calculated by computers—not just by any old program or by every software command. Unfortunately, these do not always produce a truly random number. Only specialized, bespoke programs can do that better than we can.

The sufficiently large address space is a feature which defines the usefulness of a blockchain; but where do these addresses come from, and how are they generated?

Public key cryptography

To understand this better, you have to go back in history a little and familiarize yourself with public key cryptography. Public key cryptography was in use as early as the 1970s and arose out of a necessity to protect private data, including from the state. That was probably one of the main motivations of the software tinkerers who began using it in the early days of the Computer Age, as they began to implement exciting mathematical models into their protocols.

On the other hand, the state itself—particularly the military, which always had to manage sensitive secrets—had to protect itself from attacks by other states and their secret services. Naturally, the secret services themselves were very keen to protect their own secrets. On the other hand, the nascent developments in computing seemed to greatly simplify the dissemination of information and for this reason were quickly identified as potential security risks.

The experts modeled solutions using mathematical formulae, such as the exponents of primary numbers and elliptical curves functions. The fascinating thing about some of these formulae is that they can be calculated in one direction, but not are not calculable in reverse, and how you should tackle unknown variables in a formula is actually taught very early on in school.

For example, x+2=4 could be calculated by any first-grader. You just rearrange it as 4-2=x. Simple—and x is soon solved as 2. It is not so with three-dimensional elliptical curve functions or other cryptographic formulae. These can only be calculated in one direction, and even if you know the result, there is no way back. You cannot simply calculate backward or reverse engineer the formula. That is the trick that makes it so secure; anyone with the result has no way of finding out the input values.

Wikipedia offers another explanation to illustrate this concept:
"An additive cyclic group can be defined on elliptical curves which consist of the multiples of a point of the curve of the generator of the group. Adding to points in the group is easy, but there are curves on which the division of two points is difficult, that is, there is no known efficient process to find for a given point A in a group generated by a point P a natural number, a, such that aP=A. Thus, on these curves, there is an analogy to the Discrete Logarithm Problem (DLP) in multiplicative groups, also called DLP. [2]"

You do not need to understand that — nor even try to! You only need to know that this kind of formula, also known as trapdoor mathematics, can only be calculated in one direction. If you fall through this trapdoor, you can't get back. Don't worry, all this ultimately serves the security of the system and the user.

Private key and public key are a couple

This mathematics is used to generate key pairs, which consist of the a "private key" and a "public key" which are derived from it. The private key must be kept secret at all costs and serves as a signature to transactions, thus legitimizing them. The private key is the most important part of any crypto-system. Therefore, this must be absolutely protected and kept secure at all times.
In turn, the public key is derived from this key pair. This key is public. It could be considered similar, for example, to the account number of a company. There is a mathematical relationship between the two keys. You can reliably sign a notification with a private key. This signature can then be tested by everyone else against the public key, without needing the private key of the sender. The private key is never used to test the legitimacy of a transaction; otherwise, you would have to show it to everyone else, which would undermine the whole concept of a secure private key. This possibly unknown third party could steal or copy the private key, giving them easy access to the corresponding crypto-money. They could also adopt the identity of the original user or owner and sign notifications in that name.

---

[2] *https://de.wikipedia.org/wiki/Elliptic_Curve_Cryptography*

You can consider the private key as the master key of a locking system. You can create sub-keys that will only open up certain floors and not others. To check whether the tenant may enter a certain floor, you only need this sub-key and the tenant can get in. That is the evidence that the sub-key was created using the master key as a template. The master key of the neighboring building cannot produce this sub-key. This comparison is, of course, very flawed and only intended as a metaphor to help you visualize how these digital keys in the blockchain system work. As in real life, copying a main door key or opening a lock without a key is a straightforward task for a professional, and so proves nothing, but the underlying principle is similar in that Bitcoin and blockchain systems that use this mathematics correctly are absolutely cryptographically secure.

The starting point for the calculation of the key pair is always the private key. As already stated, this must comply with certain requirements. The public key can then be calculated from this private key, and the Bitcoin address is calculated from the associated public key. Calculation of the public key and the calculation of the Bitcoin address is completed using the previously described elliptical curve mathematics, amongst other things.

Atoms in the universe

To generate a private key, a random number between 1 and 2^{256} is needed. If you're not familiar with mathematics, let me assure you that 2^{256} is quite a lot. It is generally accepted that there are about 10^{80} atoms in the universe. That is, of course, only an estimate because a number with 80 zeros can't really be counted. Still, 2^{256} is quite a lot. That is about 1.16×10^{77}. Enjoy counting!

The private key is a number taken from a range of a little more than a 10 with 77 zeros, which is marginally fewer than the number of atoms in the universe. You might be scratching your head and wondering what all these numbers mean, but don't worry. All I am trying to demonstrate here is the sheer quantity of numbers to choose from when generating a private key; it is similar to the vast number of atoms in all the universe, so it is safe to say that are plenty to choose from. The only question that remains is how best to generate this random number.

Computers can do that best and — if you don't use the very simple random number generators — they typically carry out this function very well. All the popular wallets on the market do it well enough and you can generally rely on them.

You can try the whole thing out on this website and generate your own private key: www.bitaddress.org/bitaddress.org

But BEWARE: This generated private key is not necessarily secure! The explanation of why not will follow.

Once you have generated the private key, you can now generate the public key from it. The website does that automatically, and also creates your Bitcoin address. You can give this to another person who can then send a few Bitcoins to you using this address.

The Bitcoin belonging to this address can then only be sent on using the private key. For example, the Bitcoin can be sent to an exchange to convert it into dollars, Euro or other fiat currencies. Without this private key, that is impossible. The idea of this Bitcoin address website is that you print off and keep the result page securely, thus creating a paper trail for your digital transactions. The address can be passed on and can receive Bitcoin, and you have created a so-called paper wallet.

This paper wallet was generated without the website accessing the Bitcoin blockchain. This allows it to establish, for example, whether this private key is still available or whether it is already being used by another user. That seems to be a little dangerous, but the number was generated at random and a probability of about 1.16×10^{77}: 1. That is more than sufficient to ensure that this number is not yet in use.

The private key is the basis of the public key, which in turn is the basis of the Bitcoin address

As previously described, the Bitcoin address itself is generated via the public key computation step, which is derived with a formula from the private key. The public key is also hashed, meaning it is calculated with these formulae, also known as hash algorithms. Two formulae are calculated consecutively and you get the so-called "public key hash." This always consists of 160 characters and you cannot use these 160 characters to calculate backward to the underlying private key. As we discussed in previously, this inability to reverse engineer the inputs is what makes the key secure.

20 bytes—each with 8 bits, making it 160 characters long—is a long number. And it is a number you must always have on you if you are active in the Bitcoin world. That is a bit cumbersome, so these 160 bits are coded with another formula—the cool "Base58Check"—and then contains the final Bitcoin address, which is considerably shorter. The final version is a little over 30 characters long and so is much easier to use.

Despite the efforts at simplification, it is still a letter and number monster, so you have to be careful of typos. This is especially applicable when you are giving your Bitcoin address to someone else or when you send a Bitcoin to a Bitcoin address. If an error occurs in typing or even copy and pasting, this Bitcoin address cannot be resolved against the private key. That always leads to total loss! Most wallets are programmed so that gross errors are automatically noticed—the address is then sent back—but permissible addresses will always accept wallets. A permissible address can then contain typos and then the Bitcoin are gone. For good. Therefore, it is to your benefit to always carefully check that the address is correct.

The Bitcoin is not then owned by someone else who could simply transfer the Bitcoin back, as is sometimes possible with an erroneous bank transfer. For example, if you made a typo with the horribly long IBAN or SWIFT number, your bank can then find out and contact the erroneous recipient. If he or she is a nice person, the sum is then transferred back. If it comes to it, a court might have to step in to help, but the problem is clear.

It is a very different situation in a blockchain system. In the blockchain, there may be a Bitcoin address, to which the Bitcoin was sent, but—as we have already established—it is not possible to calculate this Bitcoin address back to a private key. That is 100 percent impossible.

Sending the Bitcoin by mistake to a recipient who notices and is honest enough to send the Bitcoin back, is extremely unlikely at the probability of $1.16 \times 10^{77}: 1$ that was established earlier. Therefore, it is a case of sharp eyes and total concentration when it comes to crypto-transactions. The benefits that a blockchain brings require increased personal responsibility on the other side of the coin.

In the Bitcoin system, there are also even more complex types of Bitcoin addresses, which are probably quite exciting for those interested in technology. However, it is not necessary to know these when establishing a general understanding. This book aims to appeal to the technical layman and those who are confronted by words like "pay-to-script hash (P2SH)," "encrypted private keys" or "hardened child key derivation" in speaking either to a technical specialist or a phony. In both cases, there is no need to worry about the details of other types of addresses.

However, you should always — without exception — worry about private keys!

The most important chapter of the entire book

Consider the private keys as the key to all the valuables that you own. If you own the private key to a valuable that is registered in the blockchain, you own that valuable and can therefore transfer that valuable.

Put another way; if you have the private key to a Bitcoin account in which there are 1,000 Bitcoin, you can send these Bitcoins at any time. This can only be done using the private key. Only and without exception! Anyone in possession of this private key can do the same. The blockchain checks no documents or signatures. The private key is secure and so, any transactions conducted with the private key are registered by the system as valid and secure.

It is different with the public key and the Bitcoin address. The private key cannot, under any circumstances — not even by artificial intelligence — be calculated from these.

It is important to also remember that the Bitcoin or other cryptocurrencies do not lie in the wallets themselves. They are recorded in the blockchain, which accounts for how many Bitcoin belong to which address. These Bitcoins can only be transferred, i.e., a payment can only be made, with the corresponding private key. Only the approval for the transfers in the form of a private key is stored in the wallet. You must keep this in your head. Anyone can see how many Bitcoin are owned by each address but no-one can tell who owns the associated private keys. No-one can move the Bitcoin they can see. That can only and exclusively be done with the private key!

It follows that the private key needs to be considered like cash, gold or diamonds. Those who own it can pay—just like those with cash, gold or diamonds. However, this is not all they have in common. Just as cash, gold and diamonds can be stolen, all kinds of gangsters are after other peoples' private keys. And that is not all. Just as you can lose or mislay cash, gold and diamonds, you can also lose, mislay or just simply misspell your private keys with devastating consequences.

I hope this section has driven home just how important the private key is. You must always, under all circumstances, keep your private key to yourself—and keep it safely or risk everything.

The private key is key to everything

You have to proceed very precisely and carefully here because it is only these private keys that protect your entire assets. If they are lost, so are your assets. Irretrievably! If they are stolen, someone else now owns your assets.

That is why it is critically important that you are always in possession of your own private keys and look after them safely. There are absolutely no exceptions to this rule, at least for the part of the assets that you wish to protect. There are certain reasons why you might wish to keep some less securely, but more on that later. This rule applies absolutely for every coin you wish to protect.

This is what a Bitcoin private key looks like:

L5ZYeDnDgakM5vDfgVGpmhNr8B8UkBdRQGmaZjmNXXkFtdb8xERe

Clearly, this is not an easy number to remember, but it is easy enough to store in a computer by copying and pasting. Unfortunately, that is also very dangerous. Why? Now it gets exciting.

Many data security experts estimate that nearly all computers are infected with sleeping viruses and Trojans. These little villains— mostly sent by e-mail—lurk in the depths of the software and, at some point, activate a maliciously programmed part of the virus. These viruses are designed to take over the PC or misuse it in some other way. Enough cases have become known in which these malicious programs have locked and encrypted the hard drives of companies, or even large institutions like hospitals, and the decode key offered against a ransom payment. Interestingly enough, the payment of a certain amount of Bitcoin is frequently requested. Even fraudsters understand best practices when it comes to safely receiving third-party transactions.

Attacks like these can be annoying; however, in the private sphere, viruses can often be eliminated and reversed through backups. Unfortunately, this is not always the case, as it often depends on how you picked up the virus to begin with. Solving this issue probably involves a bit of trouble and effort, but it is possible if you regularly backup your computer. So, these attacks are not as dangerous for a private PC or a phone as they are for large companies. They are often just very troublesome and incon-venient.

What can be very dangerous for private keys, on the other hand, are the so-called "keyloggers." These are small programs that record every keystroke on the keyboard and send it to a third person—the hacker. These keyloggers operate silently in the background without anyone noticing. Whatever you type is read by someone else. That is not just embarrassing but is also highly dangerous. These keyloggers can also copy and paste commands including data. This means they can easily copy and send your private key to the attacker. If this happens, the key to your assets is now in someone else's hands!

This stranger now has full access at any time to the Bitcoins or other cryptocurrencies, for which he has obtained the private key. He can simply transfer the money at any time; preferably to an account to which he, and only he, has the private key.

Therefore, it is also dangerous to create a paper wallet, which often seems like a good safety measure in itself. If the paper wallet is created with a computer that is, or will be online, it too could be compromised. The details of how you can create a new private key and associated address through the www.bitaddress.org/ bitaddress.org site were explained earlier. It is only safe to create a paper wallet if you get this code from a computer that has never been online, let it run, and then wipe it completely after the generation of the key is completed.

This all sounds very paranoid, but we are dealing with very sophisticated criminals who understand the system ways better than you and me. They actively construct ways to relieve you of your cryptocurrency and other valuables, so it is very important to be ruled by paranoia here.

Passwords, passphrases and mnemonic codes

We have established that the private key is far too complicated for a normal person to be able to memorize, and it should not be copied and pasted into a computer. Indeed, it should not be stored — at least not completely — on the same computer.
To partially get around this problem, so-called "passphrases" were created to generate the key. These passphrases can also be used as a backup, and the private key can be reproduced with them at any time.
Passphrases usually consist of 12 words, or in other cases, 24 words. These words must be entered in the right sequence in the reproduction of a wallet, where some systems change the sequence of the input randomly. For example, some require the third and then the eleventh word of a sequence and so on. Here is a typical 12-word passphrase:

ugly harvest acoustic sand visa gain minimum author hero laundry aim when

These passphrases are built on a so-called "mnemonic code" which is not important at this stage. What is important, however, is to note it correctly, keep it safely, and more than anything else, always have it in your possession. Remember: whoever has the private key has full access to the assets. If the private key is gone, all the assets are lost for good!

Spelling mistakes and the cursed autocorrect

It is safest if you don't keep the passphrase on your computer and/or copy it to a computer because a hacker could have installed a keylogger and be reading everything you type. Therefore, you should actually write down the passphrase by hand and safely store several copies. In the case of private keys, you can actually copy the private key — unlike banknotes — onto paper. There are people who hide the passphrases in letters or engrave them into metal or plastic to make them durable. Everything is permissible, so long as security is ensured.

You can, of course, keep the passphrase on a computer or a mobile phone, but if you do choose this approach, part should be kept on one device and part on another, and, for example, in a different program. So, perhaps you keep part of your passphrase on a Word document on one device with lots of other texts, while the other half is kept on the notebook of your mobile phone, which is not synced to the computer. Screenshots are not safe, nor are digital images because they can be quickly and easily shared, sent or copied.

A really big danger—and the author is writing this from bitter experience—is writing the passphrase on paper and then saving parts of it as text files on the computer. That ought to be okay, as long as you are careful that Microsoft Word, or whatever word processing program you are using, does not automatically correct typing errors. That is a particularly nasty trap!

If you make a copying error in typing and the cursed autocorrect —which often generates funny words when writing WhatsApp news—decides to "correct" a word in the passphrase, then the passphrase is permanently unusable and access to the assets is lost. So, remember, checking it a hundred times is much better than the pain of losing even half a Bitcoin!

Different types of wallet

We've established that it is very dangerous to lose a passphrase, but this does not have to mean immediate loss. After all, a passphrase is only the security, the backup, for reproducing a lost private key. As long as the wallet that you are using is still functioning, it is not disastrous. Even with a lost passphrase, you can still carry on working with the wallet.

It is always advisable to test the passphrase before moving large sums to the wallet concerned. To do that, you should install the wallet, send a few cents or dollars, and then delete it again. You can then try to use the passphrase you've written down to recreate the wallet. If it works with no problems, you can safely send more Bitcoin or other cryptocurrencies to this wallet. As stated, from this point, the passphrase just has to be kept securely and you don't need to worry about your cryptocurrencies anymore. However, if the computer you use to recreate the wallet using the passphrase is already compromised, you have a problem again.

Perhaps all of this sounds like there is no solution and you really shouldn't be touching the whole crypto thing at all? Don't worry, there are solutions—and good solutions at that! We will now look at some of these to set your mind at rest.

Wallets come in various shapes and colors so to speak. Basically, they are split into "hot wallets" and "cold wallets." The difference is easily explained in terms of what we now know. In a hot wallet, the private key is saved in an app or in a computer system and is online via the internet. In contrast, a cold wallet is not connected to the internet and thus the private keys are not endangered.

Typically, you have a few small sums in a hot wallet and keep your main assets in a cold wallet, also called "cold storage." Basically, it is no different to what you would do with cash; you have $60 in your pocket as walking-around money, but you keep your savings securely in the bank.

There are different types of hot and cold wallets. First, the hot wallets: these can be websites, mobile sites, or there are some so-called browser enhancements, extensions for Google Chrome, etc. Otherwise, there are mobile apps which you can get from the Apple App Store or the Google Play Store for Android devices that act as hot wallets.

In essence, you can choose the wallet that offers you the best user convenience. Obviously, it is also important that the wallet provider makes the private key available to the user. That is the most important thing. If a wallet does not do this, nor for the passphrase in the context of a backup, then this wallet is not to be recommended. Seriously. You could even transfer your money immediately to the wallet operator managing it for you.

You must also note that the provider must have published the source code of the wallet as open source. The significance of open source will be explained at another point. The risk of being uncovered by a keylogger exists for all wallet types because they fundamentally consist of a web page or a mobile app, which are online and thus subject to the risk of attack.

Online wallets

What about if an online service offers a wallet or this is available within another application? The classic example of this is online wallets within a crypto-exchange. Here too — as always in the crypto world — there is only one rule and it is this: you must be in possession of your private keys at all times!

That is, of course, something of a balancing act. Let's suppose, for example, that you want to trade with cryptocurrencies. To do this, you have to deposit some of your money in the wallet of the exchange and ideally keep your private keys there too. The exchanges provide secure wallets for that purpose and protect the private keys with all the means at their disposal. But, for one thing, online services are only secure until a hacker strikes and cracks the secure storage, and for another, no exchange operator can really protect you from its own employees who have the appropriate administration rights. That is exactly what could have happened with the Mt. Gox Exchange in 2013, when 600,000 Bitcoins vanished. This case will be described in more detail in a later chapter.

The money — in our case, the Bitcoin — also sit in an online exchange if they are being bought or sold. It is not so dangerous when purchasing because you don't need private keys, just a Bitcoin address. Private keys must be used in selling because otherwise the Bitcoin can't be transferred. At the end of the day, each individual has to decide for themselves how much of their assets they are comfortable keeping in a web service.

Not all online exchanges are created equal. Many offer the possibility that you can export the private key and/or keep the passphrase. This is already halfway there. Exchanges that do not offer one or the other should be avoided — unless you're not bothered with security and trust the operators blindly. Many choose to take this approach, and it cannot be fundamentally assumed that the money will be lost if you follow this path, just that there no absolute security in place.

It is not the same situation as when you transfer your money to an assets manager. These comrades can also run off with your money but are generally caught and you even sometimes get your money back. Most of them are trustworthy in the sense that they don't embezzle your money; at most, they lose it through risky speculations. However, if it is a lot of money to you, it is recommended to leave exchanges that do not supply private keys well alone.

Two worlds collide

Having said all that, in the interest balance, the other side of should be shown. There are a few wallet providers who go in exactly the opposite direction, and they can also logically and understandably justify that choice.

If you have greater assets and have to keep these at home, that can present its own unique challenges and costs. You have to install a safe at home and put your money in that. The bigger the safe is, the more tempting it is for criminals because they assume it probably contains large quantities of money, gold and diamonds. With this increased risk, you are forced to adopt additional security measures. Perhaps you install movement sensors, security lighting or even hire a team of guards to guarantee the safety of your assets.

In this case, it makes sense to give the money to a professional who has already undertaken all these advanced security measures and more. Ideally, this would be a bank because banks house unbreakable underground safes, which are secured by the most current security techniques and technologies. Most burglars would be gnashing their teeth for all time at these. Furthermore, there is the three-person principle for keys and time switches, so that the safe does not remain open for an undefined time to ensure that the bank's own employees can't pilfer anything.

All of that makes sense because if you put your money in the bank, you can't lose it. Wallet providers sometimes advertise using this argument and offer to keep the private keys secure in so-called "deep cold storage" installations. The private keys would be stored in a mountain massif and can only be given out under certain circumstances, under certain conditions, and in certain time windows.

It is a little crazy; a decentralized system is being distorted and violated because, in this process, the keys, which allow access to the safely kept assets, are centrally stored again and you are at the mercy of this central point. Essentially, you can also give your money straight back to your bank — or to the state. The benefit of a decentralized system is gone.

Ultimately, everyone needs to decide that for themselves. The providers take great pains to ensure security and safekeeping of private keys, and we should recognize that. However, they are naturally not immune from state attacks that occur on the country in which the private keys are stored, even if it is deep in the mountain. At the very least, it represents a certain residual risk. Moreover, you might not be able to get at your Bitcoin as quickly and easily as you could possibly need to. In this way, it is just like with a normal bank. If you wish to withdraw a large sum, you need to notify the bank in advance and then pick up the cash a few days later.

Cold storage and exchange wallets

There are exchanges that provide the private keys and/or the passphrases, but there are also some that do not. There are also some that offer to store the Bitcoin in a so-called "cold storage." That means that the private keys are not stored on a system that actively connected to the internet. It is a bit like a concierge service that can give you a spare key, just in case.

That would make it to some extent a "hot wallet," because any employee could take the key at any time, if he finds out, for example, on Facebook, that the owner is on holiday. Technically, an employee with malicious intent could get into the client's house at any time or copy the key at any time and give it to his colleagues who can then strip the house bare. The same is true of hot wallets — they are simply very risky.

Cold storage of an exchange would be achieved in this analogy if the boss of the concierge service would receive the key personally and then keep it off-site in another completely independent safe deposit box; for example, in a bank or in a separate safe.

This is exactly how cold storage works in a crypto-exchange. The private keys are deleted by appropriate staff from the online system and kept on a computer that is not connected to the internet.

Of course, one has to also consider that everyone who has access to the offline computer can potentially use the keys. You can never protect yourself from that possibility if you give your private keys to another person. That also applies to a family member, a friend, or an employee of an organization, such as a reputable exchange. The risk always exists and, therefore, you should give careful thought to how much money you keep in an exchange.

In contrast with the savings bank, exchanges do not generally have deposit guarantees or similar. On the other hand, you have to acknowledge that in some cases where a customer's exchange crypto-asset was stolen, the exchanges have replaced the losses from their own assets.

So, if you don't want to trust anyone, and in addition, you want to protect yourself against hackers and other bad people, what is the alternative? The alternatives, if a little cumbersome, are the real cold wallets. First and foremost, there is a medium that the Chinese were already using 2000 years ago. It was called papyrus.

Everything on paper

The private key is basically just a long number that you can write down on a piece of paper at any time. The same applies to the passphrase. You should definitely do that. The challenge is more in how you generate the private key or passphrase.

As has been described, you should never just create and use this yourself, "randomly." As humans, we are just not capable of removing ourselves far enough from our own psychology to ensure the key is truly random. So, a private key generator is needed.

Such things exist on the internet. Typically, the mouse is moved back and forth over a field until a one-hundred percent random code is created. This takes one to two minutes, during which a private key, address, and the corresponding QR code are generated. You can now send Bitcoins to this address and transfer them with the associated private key. The private key is kept as a paper copy; it can then be photocopied and the paper and its copy kept in separate places. It should ideally be kept in at least two separate locations so that the two papers are not lost together; for example, in a fire. An unfortunate case was reported of someone who lost $50,000 by not observing this rule.

So, paper document or paper wallet? You can use a paper wallet under one definite condition: if the computer that generated this paper wallet is not online and will not be connected online for as long as this paper wallet is in use. Why? Because the website or the computer that generated this paper wallet can be hacked and interfered with. You would not even notice if this happened. Even if a secure connection is shown, software could be running in the background that sends the private keys generated to a third party. This third party then collects these and one sunny day uses them all at once and quickly empties all accounts. Most people would not even notice this because the assets in a paper wallet are usually stored for a long period — you only find out that the paper wallet has been emptied when you try to transfer some Bitcoin.

In such a horror scenario, even a hot wallet would be more suitable because the exchange will notify you when the money is gone. This is not a joke. It has happened.

Bitcoin and blockchain places people, for the first time in history, in the position of being their own bank. They have their own assets available so that they cannot be controlled or manipulated by others. When you have Bitcoin, you are your own bank. This provides a level of freedom that has never been known before, but with this freedom comes increased responsibility. This responsibility is not easy, and you will have to go to some effort. Freedom always has its price. But enough scaremongering — we will now follow this up with a description of a safe alternative.

Hardware wallets

Along with paper wallets, there are also the so-called "hardware-wallets." These look like conventional USB sticks. When using a USB stick like this, you would write the private keys on the stick, remove it, and place it in a safe. So far, so safe — at least, if the computer was not connected to the internet and never will be again. Otherwise, it could be that a malware that was silently active in the background quickly sends the data to a hacker. The same situation would arise as with a paper wallet. So only use these hardware wallets with great care.

For this reason, two (at present) firms have made significant advancements when it comes to sticks like this. They have developed a stick of their own which computes the keys in this crypto-chip and stores them encrypted. The stick — or in this case the hardware wallet — is connected to the USB input of a computer. The transactions are then created with an application or a program running on the computer. If a transaction is created, say, one Bitcoin is transferred from Alice to Bob, this software accesses the hardware wallet and the hardware wallet signs the transaction. The private key is not given out to the software. It stays securely encrypted and hidden in the hardware wallet. This is probably — together with a paper wallet generated on a one-hundred percent offline PC — the safest method.

Hardware wallets naturally require you to write a passphrase — along with the password that you use to open the wallet itself. This is in case the private key itself is needed. The 24-word chain is generally used in hardware wallets and the passphrase is typed in via small buttons attached to the stick. If you use a system like this, no data are fed in via the PC and so cannot be discovered and passed on by a virus or Trojan. Of course, the passphrase must be written by hand and kept securely, preferably several copies in separate, secure locations.

Like all wallets, the hardware wallet has a Bitcoin address and can be left in the safe when someone sends Bitcoin to this address. They will arrive safely and increase the balance to which you have access with the private key, which is encrypted in the safe. Remember, the Bitcoins are not kept in the wallet, just the right to transfer the number of Bitcoin noted in the blockchain using this saved private key.

An important safety notice

There is an important safety notice to be made at this point. USB sticks are often distributed as part of a promotion at exhibitions. This is a very popular method for the bad guys to feed viruses into computers. Therefore, never connect a stick to your PC that is not in its original packaging and comes from a trustworthy third party! A trustworthy producer might be, for example, a company like Wells Fargo, Citybank or Mercedes. It is important that even if the stick comes from one of these big companies, it must be in the original packaging. You can never know what it was connected to before!

It can be even worse. We've established that you can trust hardware wallets. That is what it says in this book and in many other reports. But can you trust a hardware wallet that has been given out at an exhibition or as part of a publicity campaign? The answer is clearly: No! Because they have their own chips, hardware wallets are expensive to give away. In the summer of 2017, there were only two producers left who could be trusted. One is the Ledger wallet (from $70) and the other is the Trezor wallet (from $85). It is highly unlikely products like these would simply be given away.

Other hardware wallets are not as well-known, and unknown products should always be treated with suspicion when it comes to the security of your assets. Connecting unknown chips to your PC is criminally stupid because you can never know what these sticks will do or who is behind them. Even if they do not maliciously send the private key, it would be devastating if a malfunction were to destroy the key or if the passphrase was wrongly generated due to poor quality. The two named producers have been on the market for a long time and have a good reputation.

Multi-sig wallets

Some wallets have additional functions beyond their basic functions. The export of private keys and/or the passphrase go without saying. An interesting additional function is the so-called "multi-sig procedure." This is basically a simple function that is commonly used in everyday life. Access or rights to transfer money do not depend on one private key with multi-sig wallets, but on several. That means that the 1,000 BTC are only sent if two out of three private keys are used.

A procedure similar to this is a daily practice in most businesses. Transfers must be signed by two directors or one director and an agent. It also common with some married couples with joint accounts; both signatures are needed to carry out transactions. This is nothing more than multi-sig, which is short for "multi-signatures."

This procedure is intended to protect assets from being transferred by one single person, especially when the assets in question are joint assets. In some cases, this would be a sensible thing.

These multi-sig wallets are considered especially safe because there is no danger of misuse by one individual. That was the assumption until the "Parity-multi-sig wallet" of the cryptocurrency Ethereum was hacked during an ICO—an "initial coin offering." Hackers siphoned off Ether (ETH) to the value of $30 million at the time. In an ICO, donors can invest in an idea; there is more about this in the chapter on ICOs and other cryptocurrencies.

A group of so-called "white-hat hackers" simultaneously withdrew the rest of the deposits, to protect them from access by the black-hat hackers. The secured Ether were given back to the company that had organized the ICO. The white-hat hackers, that is, the good guys, used the same trick as the black hats, the bad guys, by stealing the Ether from the wallets. It is yet another strange story from the crypto world that you couldn't make up, but there are many such tales and the best that you can do is to learn from them.

The problem was quite clearly with the multi-sig wallet, which until then was regarded as secure. The real problem was that the software was in a relatively early stage of development and the error in the code had not yet been discovered. That is why it is so critically important to use only tried and tested systems, where those that have been hacked, then optimized and secured by the developers can be regarded as tried and tested. For this reason, the same security advice applies to "new" hardware wallets. You should first let the experts test them out. If they find this new thing good, it will prevail, and you can use it. Good wallets always come through because the crypto world is very active and the wheat is quickly separated from the chaff.

So, you can see that owning cryptocurrency is not that simple; you have to know what you are doing if you want to be your own bank. Someone who had lost a lot of money once said in an interview: "When I installed the wallet, I loaded it with $100 and it worked fine. Then it kept getting more and more. When I then had a six-figure sum stolen, I realized that my safety precautions were only worth $100." The reporter asked why, and he responded: "Well I had no private keys and no passphrases, but then there was the password that I use on the online exchange, only two characters long. The numbers one and two". What can you say? If you want to secure $100, you need to think about $100, but if you want to secure $100,000, then you have to consider measures that are proportionate to that. You need to be 1,000 times more secure and know what you are doing much more.

Ultimately, no-one is immune from attacks. If you want to keep your assets or part of them on an online system, then you have to act quickly if it becomes known that this service has been compromised. That would be all over the press for big exchanges or wallet providers. But what do you do then?

What to do if the exchange is no longer responding

Failure of an online system — whether that is an exchange or online wallet — can have various causes. It might be that the internet is down, which is very unlikely. The system's servers could fail. It could happen, but shouldn't. The website could be impounded by the authorities. That has happened a few times, including summer 2017, in the case of the BTC-e exchange. Hackers can also break into an exchange and steal the data. That also keeps happening.
In all these cases, the greatest urgency is required. As a rule, this does not happen overnight. Something happens in the run-up, something that is reported in the media. In the case of BTC-e, the news went through the media that one of the supposed owners, a Russian, had been arrested in Greece at the request of the US authorities. That was the point at which everybody should have reacted. So how should you react? It's quite simple:

1. Immediately start a different wallet and import the private key.
2. As soon as the money is available in the new wallet, transfer it immediately to another new wallet with another provider or a hardware wallet or paper wallet.
Done. The money is safe. Transferring to a new wallet is a very important step because the hacker is very probably in possession of the private key for the original wallet. The hacker can still get at the Bitcoin with this because they are still linked to the "old" private key. Just as you yourself can see the Bitcoin sitting in another wallet with the private key, so can the hacker. That is because it does not depend on the wallet itself, but the private key

which belongs to the address, and that is still in the possession of the hacker. It is only if they are transferred that they belong to a new address with a new private key.

It is even easier, of course, if the exchange can still be reached. If that is possible, you can save the first step and send the assets straight away through the exchange to a different, completely new address.

If the money has not yet been transferred from the exchange by the intruder, then you can do so yourself quickly. Speed is of the essence. If, however, you do not have the private keys yourself, then your hands are tied and you can only hope that it was a false alarm. Which it generally isn't.

Checking does not help

If you still have them, you can't even use the private keys to check whether the money is still there. If the keys are stored online in an exchange or a wallet, then the hacker has them and can move the money at any time. Therefore, you should always transfer to another address immediately. Then the hacker may still have the old keys, but there is no money at this address anymore. The money is now assigned to an address to which only you have the correct private keys.

When you use an online system — which is necessary in some cases — then you have to keep your eyes and ears open and be ready to react quickly. You should be prepared and have at least one additional wallet to which you could send your Bitcoin quickly. But that should go without saying, as only the least money necessary should be located in an online system — most of your assets should be kept securely offline.

Furthermore, it is very important to understand that you can access your Bitcoin directly with the passphrase or the private key of a wallet other than that affected, allowing you to then transfer them from the affected private key and to safety. This is an important point because, under some conditions, you can't even log into the online system anymore. When the US authorities impounded the eBTC Bitcoin exchange, the log-in page showed only that the website had been impounded by the US authorities. You couldn't do anything! You couldn't even log-in anymore. However, that is not necessary, as the passphrase and the private key work with every wallet. It does not depend on the wallet or the website, only and exclusively on the private key.

I have explained this before, but it is good to restate it as a reminder in this context. Always keep in mind that the private keys are the only key to the crypto-coins. Neither Bitcoin nor ether nor any of the other genuine cryptocurrencies are in the wallets or in an exchange or anywhere else. There are only chronologically saved transfers in the blockchain, which create a portfolio when they are calculated together. The private key is the only key to the cryptocurrency.

Anybody can calculate this portfolio — at least, for most cryptocurrencies — but you can only move this portfolio if you sign the transaction with the associated private key. Which wallet you sign it from makes no difference at all. As soon as it is signed, the Bitcoins are transferred. It is like going to the Wells Fargo with your private key and accessing your account at the Citybank if the Citybank is closed. You could do the same from any bank and from every terminal of every bank. In today's world, that is possible — up to a certain transaction limit — with the conventional banks and your bank card. In the crypto world, that seamlessly works with $100 million — if you have the private keys.

Why exchanges are needed

What are exchanges and why are they needed? The fundamental reason for a crypto-exchange is just the same as that of a tourist bureau de change. They are online services that exchange cryptocurrencies for fiat currencies. Dollars, Euro or Yen and other fiat currencies are sent to these crypto-exchanges who then exchange them for Bitcoin, Ethereum, or other cryptocurrencies. That is the basic principle.

However, the crypto-exchanges are not backed by the traditional banks with their appropriate assets; it is individuals or small companies that operate this agency service between sellers and purchasers. That is why a crypto-exchange is more like stock exchange than a bureau de change. Anyone can open an account and place Bitcoin or ether in an online wallet, and then offer them on the website at a certain rate. On the other side of the equation are the purchasers, those who back either their credit cards or bank details with fiat money and use it to purchase the Bitcoin offered. The exchange takes a fee for this agency service and looks after the processing. It is a very simple business model, although it is not officially allowed in most countries because you actually need a bank license to do it. That is how most countries see it anyway, even if they have not yet done anything to prevent or shut it down. The first actions against these exchanges are currently taking place in China.

In the beginning, it was like the Wild West. Anyone could open a crypto-exchange and bring purchasers and sellers together. The first crypto-exchange, the notorious Mt. Gox, was established in Japan. At the time, it processed about 90 per cent of all fiat to crypto transactions. Then something shocking happened; 850,000 Bitcoins disappeared. Arrests were made, the market collapsed, and chaos broke out. The whole story is told later on in this book.

Despite this misfortune, Mt. Gox has been ascribed an important role. Mt. Gox was the first system that could be used by anyone to buy Bitcoin. That was a blessing because up until then, you had to find your own purchaser and make a deal directly. Most meetings were arranged via the popular meetup.com website. They were announced on the site and were sorted by subject. So, if a Bitcoin Meetup took place in San Francisco, you went there and purchased some Bitcoin from another participant in the meetup. This was a cumbersome arrangement, which Mt. Gox made easy by automating and professionalizing the process.

Gradually, more and more crypto-exchanges were founded. Today, they can be found operating in many countries around the world.

Exchanges have also become much more professional in recent years. As a rule, many will meet the stipulations of the state concerned. Some things are still being disputed, but this is largely due to there still being no clear laws around cryptocurrencies in most countries. Who would have thought that computer codes and mathematics would one day be a currency? All in all, the large crypto-exchanges work around the relevant authorities and appropriate regulations, and the laws will surely follow suit.

So long, private sphere!

There is one thing, however, where there is total unanimity. The keywords here are "AML" and "KYC." These abbreviations stand for "anti-money laundering," and "know your customer," which refer to the identification of the account holder.

One of the biggest concerns of politicians, authorities and most private individuals is the potential misuse of cryptocurrencies for financing terror and other crimes, including child abuse. It may be that Bitcoin cannot be transferred anonymously, but it could be done using a pseudonym, allowing you to protect yourself to a certain degree. A US attorney who solved a big case involving Bitcoin and weapons and drug trading explains exactly what that means in a later chapter.

Sending Bitcoin while in hiding is possible, but a person must obviously be in possession of the Bitcoin to begin with. This is where the exchanges come into play. If you want to exchange fiat for Bitcoin, you would probably do so via an exchange. In most cases, these exchanges have best practices in place for carrying out the usual AML and KYC processes, just as any bank is required to do.

The exchanges determine the personal data of the account holder and verify them. In Germany, that is done by post-ident but can also be done by video-ident. In any case, the exchange has a copy of the customer's ID document and every individual transaction can be assigned to a real person through the blockchain. This is a dream for law enforcement agencies — and of course for the tax office.

Decentralized Exchanges and Mixers

These identification measures are naturally a thorn in the side for many, and the call for decentralized exchanges is getting louder all the time. Why should exchanges be centrally organized when we are actively creating and using a decentralized system? By now, the reader will realize that it is exactly these centralized systems that cause the annoyance and represent a weak spot. Consequently, the exchanges should also be decentralized.

An ideal exchange is one that is running in all nodes and is safely secured again within itself. The first developments are underway; eventually, the only bottleneck that the user must pass through will be the place where the fiat is to be exchanged for crypto. If you are changing crypto for crypto, however — say, Ether for Bitcoin or Zcash for Monero — the payment flow in decentralized exchanges will remain invisible or opaque.

As it currently stands, you can pay while staying hidden. This is possible using a so-called *mixer* or *tumbler.* In these, the payments from Alice to Bob are mixed up with those from Carol and Dave. Ultimately, no-one can say for sure whether Alice paid Bob or Dave. With four participants, that encryption could still be worked out, but if it is several thousand, then the number of possible combinations involved make the system extremely safe.

These systems are currently also found in the dark net, in which you only move under encryption and for which you need a high level of specialist knowledge. Mixers and tumblers are under continuous development and will surely be integrated into blockchain systems as standard in the near future.

As soon as you interact with the "real" world, anonymity is over

Despite all the technical measures to protect your anonymity, it becomes very difficult as soon as you interact with the real world. Anyone who buys a physical product, a book, a set of wheel rims, a case of wine, or a new comfort blanket and wants to pay with crypto money will have to provide a delivery address. There is no way around this if the purchaser wants to receive their goods. A false address is of no use either; the goods just won't arrive. So, you have to "break cover," so to speak. With that, a real address gets assigned to a Bitcoin address. It has to be this way.

Additionally, the data is then being used by online traders for tracking for advertising and statistical analysis. This was investigated by the researchers Dillon Reisman, Steven Goldfeder, Harry Kalodner and Arvind Narayanan [3] in the summer of 2017. Their research revealed that many online shops sometimes

---

[3] *https://arxiv.org/abs/1708.04748*

disclose very extensive data about Bitcoin users, which most frequently happened via the checkout basket. From there, the contents of the baskets were passed on — mostly in a targeted way — to advertising providers as a way to facilitate personalized offers. In some cases, the destination target wallets were also transferred, which would make a detailed analysis of payment flows possible.

According to the study, of the 130 websites investigated, 107 had passed on various information about transactions. It was revealed that 31 websites had also granted various scripts of other companies access to the addresses of the Bitcoin wallets, 104 had passed on the value of the transactions in actual currency, and 30 had passed on the value of the transaction in Bitcoin. Other personal details, which according to the researchers were passed on included e-mail addresses, name, username, address and telephone number. To avoid being exposed, the authors of the paper recommend using Bitcoin mixers. But these to not give comprehensive protection; in many cases, the identification of individual users was still possible.

The partial solution then is: decentralized exchanges and decentralized shops.

Local Bitcoin

One of the first quasi-decentralized exchanges came into being as early as summer 2012 in Finland. "Local Bitcoin" is an internet site which brings buyers and sellers together.

Each person places their inquiries or offers on the platform, which is openly visible to others. It is up to each individual to contact the other and close the deal. The way in which the payment flow is controlled is reserved for the participants. In theory — as the name suggests — you can find your trade partner online and then meet locally, in person. Of course, that only makes sense of course if both buyer and seller live in the same city. In the early days, before the online exchanges started to operate, these local meetings were a good method for purchasing or selling Bitcoin.

In contrast with an online exchange, the monies were not sent by the purchaser to the exchange, for the exchange to then manage it and pay it to the seller. Instead, the monies flow directly between seller and buyer. Both parties could then agree on any method.

Cash handed over in the bar or transfer to the seller's account. Any payment method at all. This is a real peer-to-peer business. But unfortunately, without miners and encryption, like a blockchain offers, it is still somewhat unsafe.

Any cash handover without witnesses is unsafe; even a transfer is difficult to get back if the seller does not deliver. These peer-to-peer problems in the real world are solved by Local Bitcoin through an escrow service. In principle, this is a trust account or an escrow account, similar to what is used in real estate transfers or the transfer of business shares or other valuable assets. Local Bitcoin takes the Bitcoin temporarily into its care and the seller releases them when he has received the payment via the separately agreed payment method. If the Bitcoins are not released, then they stay with Local Bitcoin for the time being and there is a court case.

Local Bitcoin fulfills an important role in countries where democracy and freedom do not function well or where the banking system is undeveloped and/or corrupt.

Local Bitcoin helps many people across the world by creating more financial freedom. It makes these people a little less dependent on systems that are sometimes corrupt and helps them to live more freely — or at least buy a few groceries. This is the other side of Bitcoin, which is often judged negatively and denounced as a medium for the black market in drugs and weapons and financing of terror. Anyone who looks into the overall effect of the truth through blockchains will soon realize that Bitcoin can be compared to a bread knife — it can be used to cut bread or to stab someone.

Local Bitcoin is available worldwide and, in theory, makes it possible to help anyone in the world from your own desk or kitchen table. However, you can't help anyone in Germany though because the Bafin (Federal Institute for Regulation of Financial Services) has prohibited Local Bitcoin. Local Bitcoin then blocked access in Germany. Why?

Here is the Bafin's justification:

"Just using BTC as a replacement currency for cash or deposit money in legal currencies for participation in the economic cycle in the exchange business is not an activity requiring a license. The supplier can be paid for services in BTC without this constituting a banking or financial service. The same applies to the client. Similarly, the mining of BTC in itself does not represent an activity requiring a license, as the miner itself does not emit or place the BTC. The sale of dug out or purchased BTC, or their purchase basically do not require a license.

If, however, other circumstances arise, the requirement for a license can be triggered. This applies if BTC are not just dug, bought or sold in order to participate in an existing market, but a certain sum is paid to acquire or maintain this market. Due to the additional service provision element, this is now proprietary trading requiring a license under § 1 Section 1a No. 4 of the German Banking Act. This is the case if a person in the market advertises that he/she regularly buys and sells BTC. Another example is mining pools, which commercially offer revenue shares from dug out and published BTC in return for granting computer power from the user."

It goes on like that for a few more sections and ultimately led to Local Bitcoin not being available in Germany or for Germany. Shame.

Perhaps one day the German politicians will come to understand that Bitcoin is not evil and might open their minds to the thought that they should not deny their citizens the right to freedom and independence.

Blockchain systems and cryptocurrencies offer greater freedom. People become more independent from the central points like banks, organizations and even governments. The trustworthy administrator in the middle is becoming redundant. You do not have to trust anyone anymore because you can blindly trust the data that are stored in a public blockchain. A public blockchain records for all time the truth — and nothing but the truth.

Chapter 5 — The Truth

A blockchain always tells the truth, doesn't it?

Well, you might have this impression. But no, a blockchain doesn't always tell the truth. Unfortunately, there are many people who make this claim without actually understanding how the system works. If you read through the previous description of the Bitcoin system a few times and think about it, you can get some idea of how the precise use of a correctly configured blockchain can, and will, change our lives. But because blockchain systems function differently from what we have seen and learned up until now, there are many false conceptions and half-truths which ghost their way through the media, often propagated by those who call themselves experts.

Many of these "experts" have either drawn the wrong conclusions or simply not understood what a blockchain really does and how it has to be constructed so that the data is incorruptible and the records are 100% reliable.

Others have basically garnered attention as the loudmouths in the industry, while others use the popular slogans surrounding Bitcoin and blockchain as "welcome marketing." Naturally, there are many conmen who are attracted to the idea Bitcoin and prey on those less educated about it. All in all, there is a whole spectrum of con artists, ranging from ignorant laymen to rip-off merchants to malicious fraudsters — and amongst them, people who manipulate the terms *blockchain*, *Bitcoin*, and *cryptocurrency* for their own marketing purposes. Historically speaking, these usually include a colorful mix of half-truths, false conceptions, and fraud, all of which arise when a completely new technology leads to massive changes in our world. For example, the steam engine, the car, electricity, and the telephone were all vilified in their early years. Whenever there is real change occurring, especially at the beginning of an industrial revolution, it is always accompanied (and sometimes ruled) by a conflict born of ignorance, fear, expert knowledge, and fraud.

So, it is important to educate yourself so that you do not fall victim to charlatans or take a stand on the wrong side of beneficial progress. In order to move forward, we have to embrace and understand new systems, staving off the fear and insecurity that they can inspire. The cryptocurrency market is booming. Basic knowledge and general understanding are required, not only so that you can take part in the advantages but also so that you can avoid being led astray into careless investments. Some people have made a lot of money from this boom, and others will make even more from it in the future, but as in any other industry, there will also be many who lose money. Unfortunately, a person's failed investment is all too often due to allowing himself to be fooled and swindled. This must be prevented.

Is all this talk of blockchain a bit frivolous, or is it really a new industrial revolution?

Along with conmen and "embellishment" (i.e., marketing) experts, there are also many companies in the industry who have recognized that the technology of their individual business models will change massively due to the blockchain concept. These companies are jumping quickly aboard a bandwagon that is already moving.

When Satoshi Nakamoto published his thesis, known in the technology sector as a "white paper," hardly anyone took any notice of it. He began by exchanging opinions with another software expert, and gradually he started to attract more attention. Their joint development took place on the GitHub platform, and as a result, discussions popped up on *Reddit*, the forum *Bitcointalk*, and elsewhere online.

Then, on May 18th, 2010 it happened: a hungry developer — in the literal sense of the word — with the pseudonym "Laszlo" offered 10,000 Bitcoins for two pizzas on *Bitcointalk*. He specified that they should be large, so that he would have some left over for the next day, of course. He asked for onions and mushrooms as toppings and left the options open to either homemade or store-bought, delivery by a service or in person. He waited for an answer.

That was at half past midnight. At 6:42 p.m. the following evening, there was an inquiry about his address. He revealed that he lived in Jacksonville, Florida. After a few more exchanges, someone asked whether it was possible to hire a delivery service in the U.S. from Europe, but no one actually took him up on the offer. Finally, Laszlo asked at 7:06 p.m. whether he was offering too few Bitcoins because he still hadn't gotten his pizzas. Despite a posted comment that 10,000 Bitcoins were the equivalent of $41 and this was above the market price of pizza, Laszlo still had no pizza at 7.00 p.m.

At exactly 7:17:26, when he must have been getting pretty hungry, he reported that he had just received two pizzas and had exchanged 10,000 Bitcoins for them. He even linked a photo of the pizzas to his post. This was an historical event for the whole crypto-sector, which at the time consisted entirely of Bitcoin enthusiasts. The equivalent of $41 for two large pizzas! After he ate, Laszlo posted that the pizzas were great and that he was going to leave the offer open.

On August 4th, "MoonShadow" wrote to Lazlo to ask whether he happened to be hungry for more pizza. "Knightmb" commented, "$600 is a good price for a pizza, I think," and followed it with a smiley face. In less than three months, the Bitcoin rate had risen by a factor of 15. So, Laszlo withdrew his offer and expressed his thanks for the pizzas he had received back in May. It wouldn't be so easy to mine 10,000 Bitcoin a day anymore.

Two Pizza for $100 million

Who could have ever predicted beforehand that two pizzas would be exchanged for 10,000 Bitcoins, an entirely new currency, on May 2010 10,000 Bitcoins, which seven years later in December 2017 would become worth 10,000 times $10,000, equaling $100,000,000. Imagine two pizzas for $100 million! Definitely a world record for currency growth![4].

Bitcoin really took off in 2013. The exchange rate rose in April 2013 to over $100 per Bitcoin for the first time. It peaked at $230 on April 9th, followed with a low point on June 5th and 6th at about

---

[4] *The whole story is found here: https://bitcointalk.org/index.php?topic=137.0*

$66 per Bitcoin. From then on, it rose in worth rapidly. Soon you had to deposit nearly $1,150 for a Bitcoin.

Not long after this boom, the system collapsed. The crypto-exchange Mt. Gox — which will be reported on comprehensively in a later chapter — went bust, and hundreds of thousands of Bitcoins were lost with it. The bottom fell out of the rate and dark times set in for Bitcoin. After a brief peak in November 2013, it fell to barely $300 by the end of 2014. By summer 2015, it had fallen to approximately $200.

Of course, that was the perfect time to buy Bitcoin — and as many as possible. From that point on, the rate only went up. Growth was slow at the beginning, but by the end of 2015, it was nearing $450. At the end of the next year, you once more had to pay $1,000 to get hold of a single Bitcoin. Since then, the rate has simply exploded. At the time of printing this book, it was between $12,000 and $16.000. Not a bad performance for a virtual product which had only just grown out of its infancy. You can look up the Bitcoin rate for yourself online. One can assume that it will only get higher. There's an easy way to justify this assumption; if the rate were to collapse, as it did in 2014, most people probably won't be reading this book.

Some people recognized the signs back then and got involved, believing in the potential of Bitcoin. Others turned their backs on the system.

Ethereum

Those who stayed on board saw in 2014 how a young Canadian introduced another blockchain: Ethereum. Up until this point, no blockchain had attracted any special attention. Ethereum changed that. It introduced so-called "smart contracts." There's an entire chapter in this book devoted to this topic. Ethereum generated more and more interest over time, including from employees of major companies. The more people involved, the greater the recognition of the opportunity that blockchain technology introduces.

The concept that a blockchain ensures the truth of data is recognized.

The idea that a blockchain, when correctly constructed, can be a vehicle for the truth, shimmers on the horizon. In 2015 and 2016, the possibility of automation through smart contracts was the dream of many. Numerous trial projects were started and the idea took hold.

Banks began to found consortia with the purpose of studying blockchain technology to find out how it could be used in their industry. The insurance sector followed suit. Energy companies were next to jump on the bandwagon; then the automotive, logistical, medical industries; next, social media and the media sector; and finally, politics and the government. This sequence wasn't static across the globe; some governments—for example, that of England—engaged with the concept very early. In Switzerland and Singapore, core cells soon arose for new companies in the crypto-sector. In the meantime, at least one government organization in nearly every country in the world has been getting involved with the subject of blockchains and many states are positioning themselves to take advantage of it in the future. Dubai, for example, has announced that it will convert all state administrative tasks to blockchain systems by the year 2020.

Naturally, the IT sector also reacted. It is only missing from the list above because it is not simply a user of blockchain—it was and is one of the main drivers. One of the most notable companies involved was IBM, but also Microsoft and other large companies. Only Google and Apple are still holding back officially.

At this point, all industries are on board and are starting to understand how the blockchain functions and what can be done with it. Indeed, they have realized how possible it is with this technology to simplify many processes and cut down on their labor costs. That is always of interest to exchange listed companies, of course, since costs in billions can be saved, which in turn means that the company becomes more profitable. Companies that are more profitable are rewarded more on the stock exchange. When rates go up, the shareholders, the business leaders, and the executive board are happy. Everyone is happy— except the workers who have been downsized. Company leaders have come to understand the trade-off they must make; by this time, they've realized that the alternative to moving forward with technology could be that their entire company may become superfluous, which of course would be bad news.

A deadly threat to some business

Some companies boldly declared that blockchain technology was a deadly threat to their business and claimed that countermeasures had to be taken. The head of J.P. Morgan, one of the biggest banks in the world, announced in September 2017 that Bitcoin was a fraud. Ironically, his announcement carried the implication that he believed his own daughter was stupid or at least ill-advised, since she herself owned Bitcoins and believed them to be a great investment. Nevertheless, anybody trading with Bitcoins in his bank, he said, would be let go immediately for participating in a practice that he didn't want to tolerate. It remains to be seen if his own daughter must be cast out of the family as well.

The man was of course showered with scorn and derision by the Bitcoin community. He was challenged to ask himself, which had needed to be bailed out with billions of government dollars during the financial crisis — Bitcoin or J.P. Morgan? Naturally, he was also asked who it was who had paid billions of dollars in fines due to illegal dealings at a cost to customers or the community in general. It was clear that after years of ignorance and arrogance, the bankers were now in a cold sweat. Too late — the blockchain will prevail.

Just as in any new industry, a lot of public statements have circulated in the early years, from many different and opposing viewpoints, which has created very controversial debates. The overall discussion will get only more difficult for the layman to understand if opinions are expressed only by people of apparent reputation and authority who generate large media echoes. Thus, self-education is crucial.

Some common misunderstandings will be explained in the following section. It is best to start with the various blockchain (and similar) systems that have been promulgated by marketing experts. These include the so-called private blockchains, the so-called DLT ("Distributed Ledger Technology"), and the like. It will get a little technical, but always in such a way that any layman should easily understand. Only those who know their way through this jungle will really be able to join in and separate the proverbial wheat from the chaff.

The difference between centralized and decentralized

All centralized systems can be manipulated. That is the implicit premise of this book.

Unfortunately, the reverse, that all decentralized systems are resistant to manipulation, cannot be so easily claimed. As so often is the case, the statement is both right and wrong. Genuine decentralized systems cannot be manipulated, but, and this is a big but, not everything labeled "decentralized" is actually decentralized. That is the crux of the matter.

Not every system that describes itself as a blockchain system is really a decentralized system. Only genuinely decentralized systems are tamper-proof. Genuinely decentralized systems must avoid the influence of individuals, even if the individuals join forces as a group. Nobody, even in collusion with others, can have the opportunity to change a decentralized system or to influence its workings. Then, and only then, can a decentralized system be called decentralized justifiably.

If one person or even a small group of people can change the defined rules of a blockchain, then this system is no longer decentralized and is worth as much or as little as any other technical system. This system, whatever it is called, can no longer be trusted!

So, you have to use blockchain systems which no one can alter, no matter how much computing power they have available or how many others that person is in league with. In reality, to date, there has only been one such system. That is the Bitcoin blockchain. To an extent, Ethereum also qualifies, as well as all the derivatives which are based on these two chains. These offshoots should all be investigated more thoroughly, however, and we need to understand exactly what is different in them compared to the original. It is to be expected that there will be others in the near future, as the Bitcoin idea has proved to be ideal. What does this realizatdion mean for the citizen, i.e., the consumer and the customer?

Let's start with the fact that this is bad news for company management and for all people who like to exercise power. The practice of power is in the setting of directions; but now and again, power can lead a company in a direction that is not in line with the interests of everyone involved. Power can foster the temptation to bend and stretch applicable laws and regulations. In the spring and summer of 2017, the diesel emissions scandal rocked the world of German car manufacturing. This is a typical example of the abuse and manipulation of power. The reason for bringing up this example isn't about apportioning blame or identifying the villains; it's only about demonstrating what is possible in centralized systems, however broad the management and control mechanisms in the system. The use of a truly decentralized system would prevent any growth of individual power because one of the participants — technically — would shout if he noticed any funny business. In a system with centralized power, interference can remain hidden forever. Decentralized systems remove that possibility — and not just in business.

Power only exists in centralized systems

The next step is to realize that it is not just companies, as employers and suppliers, that exercise power in our society. Politicians exercise their own special powers. We might be talking about a dictator, a king, a democratically elected minister, or whatever kind of states person. A person such as this may be able to give or carry out orders which are only in his own interests or to pass only those laws which benefit himself. As stated from the start, democracies are nothing more than centralized systems, which is not to say that they are or have to be bad systems per se. As always, "good" and "bad" are relative concepts and democracies of all stripes are certainly not ideal solutions. But at the moment, they are the best systems we know of. This also does not imply that decentralized systems must be better systems. They are just different. The people who know and use power become really frightened when they are confronted with a decentralized system. Bitcoin is the best example. All it really is, is a blockchain-based digital currency with all the functions and opportunities described above. What is the problem? This technology can bring with it a loss of power.

A 500 billion-dollar market is shaken.

Western Union is a very large company in the financial sector. It has a network of branch offices which are often functionally integrated into other businesses like smoke shops, phone stores, or even post offices all over the world. Cash can be deposited and transferred at these branch offices.

This is a very important function in our global economy. It enables a migrant worker to find a job in a foreign country and to send his wages back to provide for his family. In England alone, people have sent over $25 billion in total to their homes abroad[5].

$22,861,000,000 was transferred to other countries from Germany
$20,191,000,000 was transferred from France.
$15,599,000,000 was transferred from Spain.
$15,359,000,000 was transferred from Italy.
$8,594,000,000 was transferred from Switzerland.

This service is valuable to families and their employers, but it is also expensive. Depending on which country the cash is handed in and which it is to be transferred to, significant fees and deductions can come into the picture. In extreme cases, this can be up to 20%. That is a lot when you consider that the money being transferred has already been taxed and therefore already reduced by some 20% or more. Added to that is the long transit period before the family actually receives the money. Seven to ten days is not out of the ordinary.

So, high fees and long waiting periods. Both are the price to pay for what is undoubtedly a very valuable service which is a great help to many people but one which certainly does not make the investors and managers of the service any poorer.

Western Union and other similar providers hold the power in this so-called remittance market. Along comes a genuinely decentralized system named Bitcoin, which takes minimal fees — less than 1% — and allows the family to receive the money within an hour! What a loss of power! Less power due to strong competition means less turnover, falling share prices, and less money for the shareholders and the management.

---

[5] *in the year 2015*

These changes take some time, of course, because workers are inevitably laid off first. This causes a reduction in costs for a company which allows profits to be maintained. This does not immediately affect wages and share prices, but in the long term, the sector will die, just as John Maynard Keynes predicted long ago in his 1936 work entitled "General Theory of Employment, Interest and Money", which is still regarded today as probably the most influential book on economics.

A genuinely decentralized system replaces trust in an institution

There are indeed reasons for financial service providers to be fearful. Their very existence is under threat. The threat is more than real — and it's not just the remittance market that is affected. Every bank service is threatened because a genuinely decentralized system can carry out all the functions of a bank without any further need for the middleman. Frightening, isn't it? Genuinely decentralized systems will massively shake up and change the established systems. It is shocking how far-reaching these changes will inevitably be.

This section is about power and politics.

While people who have to live in dictatorships or quasi-dictatorships cannot yet really use genuinely decentralized systems, it is possible for people who live in democracies — and in such places, these systems will quickly become established.
People living in dictatorial systems have the opportunity to take up arms today by using Bitcoin to purchase their country's currency at its real value or to trade in the "hard" currency of Bitcoin. They can't otherwise use decentralized systems because dictatorships are even more centralized than democracies. Decentralized systems are the antithesis of dictatorship.
In any case, by doing so a little power is taken away from the dictatorship. Dictatorship can only defend itself by prohibiting such systems — which is a nearly impossible position to take, as we shall see later.

Let's go back to a democracy. Here, power is generally distributed via elections. The parties and their leaderships regularly apply to voters so inclined vote for them and their parties, so that they can govern in peace for the next legislative period.

Some do a good job, others a less so. It makes no difference because once they are elected, they are in power, at least for a period of several years. Unless they make a real mess of it, they will stay in power for these years and may even get re-elected. This is the system which has functioned very well in the West for the last 70 years. The voters elect their representatives, and if they're lucky, they are elected on the basis of their own marketing and their party's.

Election promises

This democratic system is far from perfect though. Who has never heard of an election pledge that isn't kept? What about the decisions of the governing party or its representatives in an unexpected situation, one in which voters can't be consulted? It's not possible to keep continually asking voters, for practical reasons alone. In Switzerland, there is a manageable electorate that can be repeatedly organized, but even there, as everywhere else, representative democracy in all its forms is the best form of government for the current era and has created the greatest prosperity for the population.

But what if a genuinely decentralized system were to change this democracy? What if blockchain allowed elections? If blockchain could ensure that each voter only has one vote and can only vote once, and all that in real time?

That would really shake up the structures, wouldn't it?

That is precisely what a genuinely decentralized system can guarantee. Since the truth is stored in such systems, the system knows the voter concerned. That voter's data is encrypted in the system, and only the voter has access to his or her data.

In an election, the system could grant a vote to the voter on the basis of an access code, the voter's private crypto-key. He can thus register a vote once, and once only. That the voter can only vote once is an important consequence of the solved double-spending problem. Just as it is impossible to spend a Bitcoin twice, a vote can only be registered once.

That means that 160 million votes from 160 million voters can be collected in a very short time, typically in an hour, if you are waiting for six blocks, as was explained above on the subject of double spending.

That is one advantage. Another is the security of the individual voter, since the identity of each voter is encrypted and not accessible. If nobody knows who voted how, society can be assured that every registered voter only submitted one vote. Wow — if you think about this, you soon realize that things we used to dream of (politically speaking) can come true.

A different kind of democracy

A decentralized system such as the one described above represents a completely different type of democracy, a faster one in which more voters can participate more actively and more often in important issues.

There is an even more important democratic side effect: the large fraction of non-voters can be involved more intensively. Voting slips are no longer pieces of paper on which you mark a cross; the voting slip is your own smartphone or similar device. The blockchain is accessed through the smartphone and it's easy to register a vote. Other information can be shown in the election app, secured by the blockchain, such as what the vote is about and why. An alarm function could also be integrated to inform and more actively engage the "non-voters," maybe forcing them to vote by just blocking the phone unless they do. These are radical ideas, but driverless cars and private space travel are also radical ideas whose implementation is in full flow.

It is clear that errors and interference are ruled out in such a voting system, since no more ID documents need to be checked, voting slips are no longer counted by hand, no results passed to the returning officers who then add up all the individual results. All these processes, bound up as they are with a great logistical effort and which do not preclude human error, are all done away with and not replaced.

Within a short time, everyone knows the true result of the voting, and so the result of the election. No mistakes, no lost voting slips, no incorrectly or doubly-counted votes.

What a different type of instrument for democratic control!

That would be a different kind of government. What politician who can understand that and enjoys his status and power under the current system would not suddenly become afraid that he could lose power?

It's about fear and loss of power

In these two examples alone, you can see the threat which blockchain presents and you can understand why many people approach the subject carefully and with great skepticism.
It is also completely natural that those whose power will be affected want to reject the whole idea. They speak only to the disadvantages of the technology or they are in complete denial that such a thing can even exist. In the words of a top banker, "*it is all just fraud.*" So, they compare apples to pears and a wonderful fruit salad is created in the debate that results.
Industry itself is to blame for this. Once the potential savings that a blockchain can bring was recognized, suddenly everyone was interested. That is because, as described previously, automation lead to greater efficiency and better performance with fewer employees. Fewer employees and higher efficiency leads to higher profits, that leads to higher share prices and that in turn leads to more money for management and shareholders.
But hold on! A genuinely decentralized system cannot be controlled or directed. That could lead to a real problem for management somewhere between the medium and the long term. This, as we've already shown, gives rise to the subject of fear and loss of power.

Management loses control — that cannot happen

Bitcoin should be banned. This demand was voiced more and more often beginning in mid-2016. Some politicians rushed ahead with this battle-cry, wanting to make a name for themselves. Strong activists in the establishment screamed bloody murder about the stupidity and uselessness of the new currency. In the eyes of some, Bitcoin was and still is tarred with the same brush as illegal activities like tax evasion and the drug trade.

Bitcoin has indeed been used by criminals to sell drugs and in at least one famous case, to commission a murder. But obviously that can be done with cash as well, which will be discussed later. Although there were and will continue to be criminals who use Bitcoins, these accusations are nonsense and show only that these shouting people have no idea about how Bitcoin, a truly decentralized system, functions.

It hasn't been necessary to educate them, though, because they quickly ran into a wall. You could get a judge to issue a cease and desist order to Bitcoin, or just send the police, right? That could be the way to ban it. Good idea. But... what address could you mail the documents, or send the police to? Who could you arrest? Even if there was an international arrest warrant, what use would it be? There is no company, there is no office. There is no management and no typical employees, as there are in a normal system. It is a decentralized system which runs on thousands of computers around the world, one which regulates itself and can fix itself when parts fail.

There is no centralized power—all power to the people; only this time, it is in the truest sense of the word. Everyone who owns a computer can run a Bitcoin node and so manage their money and support the whole system. Everyone can own and operate his or her own bank, completely independently and freely.

You cannot grab hold of someone and switch off the system, nor can you force anyone to interfere with the network or the data, no matter how much you were to torture any node operator or programmer. Even if you locked the programmers that work on the program in Guantanamo Bay in complete isolation, the Bitcoin network is like one of those rabbit batteries: it goes on and on and on.

Anyone who wants to stop the Bitcoin blockchain is faced with a truly heroic task and must already be master of the world because he would need to have absolute power in all countries to have everyone switch off their computers. Good luck with that.

Just switch off the internet

You could switch off the network. Just switch off the internet. It is that simple. Of course, if that were to happen, the whole world would have totally different problems than an undesired currency. Again, in a genuine decentralized system, there is no management, no leaders, no decision makers. All decisions are made by a quota of the participants. That is generally a majority, but in a blockchain system it can be specified that for some changes more votes, that is, power, must be needed — similar to democratic constitutions, which usually specify that a change is only possible with a 2/3 majority.

The rules by which a blockchain functions can in large part be freely defined, where the basis must always be a completely decentralized distribution, in which there can be and may be no government whatsoever. Naturally, these rules can only be freely defined at the start, and even then, only with an agreed consensus. It is absolutely crucial for such a system to require a consensus of all participants before carrying out a change — otherwise, the rules defined at the birth of the blockchain must apply and no action must be taken.

These are great characteristics of a decentralized system but they necessitate that people align their way of thinking. The current mode of regulation of democracy and of community life must be reimagined and redefined.

In the beginning is the individual

To be able to participate in a democracy, whether an existing or a newly-imagined one, it is necessary for there to be an individual to begin with. That is not taken as read in every country, but this is where the blockchain can help.

If a public blockchain records the truth and nothing but the truth, then such a system is naturally outstanding proof of existence. Imagine for a moment that everyone who is born is registered in the blockchain. This gives rise to evidence that cannot be manipulated afterward; not by any person, group or institution. A person has been secured and exists.

This individual can invoke this existence at any time to not only derive their human rights, but to also conduct any business imaginable. That business could be to buy something, to obtain credit, or even get married. Passports and other identity documents become superfluous as anyone can access all supporting evidence connected to his or her existence from the blockchain, where it is stored permanently, safe from forgery and manipulation.

Driving licenses are linked to identity data points, just like school certificates, nationality, family status and much more. With the blockchain system, your age to buy alcohol is now a matter of a single trustworthy scan. Entry to a foreign country can be approved with a scan from a mobile phone — if there are still borders, which hopefully won't be for much longer.

Having access to a personal, unalterable and manipulation-proof identity would significantly improve the wellbeing of so many people who are alive today, but technically do not exist. Blockchain identity has the potential to enrich society, simplify procedures and make every individual happier.

Of course, it should be stated that the data is not openly available to everyone. It is crucial that data in a genuine, decentralized system cannot be manipulated, which is equally important in the private sphere as it is in the financial. Luckily, numerous technologies have already been developed, which protect the private sphere. They are known by amusing names like 'zkSNARCKs', 'Schnorr signatures', or Zero-Knowledge.

Only if the user independently decides that his or her data can be made available to another, or maybe only gives it to others in extract form can this data be read and relied on 100%. Today, an individual's residential address is printed on most ID documents. If young people want to get into a club, they usually have to show their ID to the doorman. This third party can then see the address and could theoretically note it and do who knows what with it. Fundamentally, there is no need to know where the person concerned lives, just whether that person is old enough to be admitted. These might sound like trivial things, but with the zero-knowledge concepts mentioned above, such blockchains can be used in just the same way as is necessary for general, direct, free, fair and secret democratic elections. Just as the law demands.

A public blockchain, which is a genuine decentralized system, can do all that. It was invented in this form by the mysterious Satoshi

Nakamoto, specifically for the internet's money. Like many things in life, the blockchain system is entwined with the idea of currency and value, or what we commonly refer to as money. The next chapter will focus in on these concepts and how they relate to the blockchain system.

Chapter 6 — Money and Value

Money — what it is and where it comes from

This chapter starts with a story that might sound a little like a Grimms' fairytale.

At first, this story might sound merely trivial and disconcerting, but later you will see how it is applicable to cryptocurrency, and why it is so important to think about these fundamental basics. In the world of cryptocurrencies, it is easy to lose a lot of money with frightening speed when you do not really understand these fundamental features. If, however, you really have taken the time to educate yourself and you take into account these concepts and their effects, then all doors are open to you for successful investments in crypto. These basics apply not just to cryptocurrencies, but for all currencies and all methods of money transfer.

Money and currencies are fundamental concepts that are far too often confused, which frequently leads to costly misconceptions and mistakes. Unfortunately, even professionals working in the financial sector are not always familiar with these fundamental concepts and easily confuse cause with effect. That is a mistake that can have catastrophic economic consequences, just as it did for the blacksmith in the following example. But before we delve into this, let's first define what money is.

"Money is any item or verifiable record that is generally accepted as payment for goods and services and repayment of debts in a particular country or socio-economic context. The main functions of money are distinguished as: a medium of exchange; a unit of account; a store of value; and, sometimes, a standard of deferred payment. Any item or verifiable record that fulfills these functions can be considered as money" – that is the English Wikipedia[6] definition.

---

[6] https://en.wikipedia.org/wiki/Money

Money is a means of payment or exchange

So, money is a means of payment or exchange. If the village baker needed a shoe for his horse, he would go to the blacksmith and ask him to forge new shoes, which would mean that he would be able to till the field again with his horse. After all, his entire livelihood depends on the corn harvest. No wheat, no bread. Harvesting wheat without a horse is not an easy task. The blacksmith is happy to supply the horseshoe, but only if he receives adequate quid pro quo. For example, he might accept three loaves of bread in exchange for the horseshoe. Both men were satisfied with this mutual exchange of value and lived happily ever after. But hold on—while the blacksmith had to eat every day, the baker did not need to shoe his horse every day, and that presents a problem.

Direct exchange from person to person has only ever worked to a certain degree, as often one party could often only supply a good or service that the other party didn't need or want. Everyone needs to eat every day, so the baker, the cook and the grocery trader were always in a comfortable situation with their consumables. However, the blacksmith, the mason, the roofer and most others have far less frequent demand for their goods and services as they offer products that can last months, years, or even decades. This gives them far less purchasing power than the others.

The mason can ask for more bread than he himself needs and then exchange the spare loaves with the fishmonger for fresh fish, but that turns him from skilled mason to a bread trader. Apart from that, the fishmonger probably doesn't need any bread because he is most likely trading with the baker himself.

If you think about these very basic processes, you quickly reach the conclusion that the exchange system for using the participants' goods would never run smoothly or fairly for those involved. It was very cumbersome and generated more friction than smooth exchange transactions. There was also the small problem that consumables like bread, fish and vegetables can go bad quite quickly, while horseshoes have no real expiry date. Well, at least not until the invention of motor vehicles. Goods for goods—that is the barter economy, but it is not a practical solution for every case.

You can't just exchange goods for other goods

What was to work better would be to assign a superordinate unit to the assets being offered and use this superordinate unit, which we will call tokens, as an exchange object from one value to the other. The advantage of these tokens is that the differing values can be exchanged for greater or smaller values. It just means that you need to pay more tokens to purchase valuable exchange goods and less for items of a lesser value.

That was a very simple and rudimentary description of money. The token, as it was described here, is generally known today as money. This is a good example because the term *token* is frequently used in the blockchain, for example, in an Initial Token Sale. There is more about that in the ICOs and Investments chapter.

It is important to really get to grips with these basic concepts and make yourself aware of how they work; they are the building blocks of the blockchain system. Just as money solved many of the problems that came with the barter system, at a fundamental level, Bitcoin and the blockchain solve many of the core problems related to money and value exchange systems we use today.

Wikipedia offers the following description of money as we know it today: *"… is distinguished from exchange goods in that it does not immediately satisfy the exchange partner's needs, but can be used for further exchange due to its general acceptance."*

Money also has a catalytic effect and accelerates the exchange of goods and assets between trade partners whose needs cannot be met through direct exchange of goods or assets. The smith must eat every day, but the baker does not need a horseshoe every day. Therefore, to enable the exchange, money is needed as a facilitator and intermediate store of value.

The difference between money and a currency

In our example above, the baker is solvent because as long as he can harvest enough wheat in the field with his horse, he can always provide his trade partner with bread. He can pay. The blacksmith can't. He can only pay if his trade partner needs a shoe for his horse or some other product that the smith manufactures.

The smith is not always solvent because his products are not always needed.

Money comes in all forms; whether it is worth anything or not is essentially decided by the trade partner. If, for example, the tailor does not have a horse at all and does not wish to trade in horseshoes, then even if the blacksmith offered the tailor five horseshoes for the trousers, the tailor would not accept the exchange. Unless...

Unless the tailor and all the inhabitants of the village believe that horseshoes are lucky and that the more of them you have, the more luck they will bring. With a luck multiplier, the blacksmith is now significantly more solvent than before. In a society that believes that horseshoes bring you luck, the smith suddenly has a high level of solvency. Does that mean that money is dependent on superstition?

You can call it superstition or trust. Trust in an exchange medium which is ascribed exchange capability. Trust that this monetary medium has a value. This type of monetary medium is called a currency. In our example, it is the horseshoes to which a value can be ascribed.

You just have to believe in it

Once upon a time, a fine tailor was visiting from another village and passed by our blacksmith on his way through. This tailor offered strong trousers which did not easily rip and look like rags after just a few wears. Unlike other tailors in that village, his clothes were always crafted to the highest quality and very durable. The smith quickly offered the traveling tailor three horseshoes for a pair of trousers.

"Sorry," the tailor replied, "my horses have just been shoed a few days ago and I have two more shoes in my pack for emergencies. I don't need any more horseshoes."

"But they will bring you luck," said the smith.

The traveling tailor burst out laughing. He had never heard anything like it and he wouldn't be told any different, despite the best efforts of the smith and other curious villagers who had gathered around. He refused to sell his sturdy trousers for purported lucky charms.

A few days later, the smith needed more firewood and went to the woodcutter. "I need another half-cubic-meter of wood, my old friend," said the smith. "I've got four horseshoes here for you."

The woodcutter hummed and hawed. "I'm not sure that they really do bring luck anymore. That tailor from the next village laughed at the idea and to be honest, I am not so sure that I have had that much luck from the horseshoes I already have. When I think about it, even though I had two with me, I still cut my calf open on a branch last week," he said.

It had happened. Trust in the "horseshoe" currency vanished. First it was the woodcutter who had his doubts, then the carpenter, the roofer and suddenly no-one at all wanted to accept horseshoes as payment unless their horse needed shoeing.

Back to Wikipedia:

"Money is any generally recognized exchange and payment method. There are various forms of money, mainly cash, (coins and notes) and the claim for payment of a non-bank on a bank (deposit money or account money). The money that is legally specified as the valid payment method is known as the currency of a country."

Legal means of payment are called currencies.

The currency in our village is the horseshoes, at least until they stopped being accepted. Worried about this development, the council of elders got together and tried to restore confidence in the "horseshoe" currency. They decided it was no longer going to be dependent on belief or luck.

What if you were to take a small metal cube or disc and ascribe it a value by decree of the village elders? An imprint of some kind could denote the value of the token and then it wouldn't matter whether anyone thought a piece of iron brought luck or not. In this new system, everyone would have to agree to recognize it as the official means of exchange, as money. That would also keep the blacksmith — who was currently sitting on a pile of horseshoes that nobody wanted — in a job. No sooner said than done. The smith was tasked with turning his excess horseshoes into these metal discs and delivering them to the council of elders, who would then them distribute them to the inhabitants of the village.

The villagers happily accepted this new, convenient system and the smith was happy because he was now solvent again. In a stroke of luck, he was more solvent than most because he was uniquely positioned to produce the new exchange medium himself. The blacksmith wasted no time in creating as many of these metal tokens as possible, making himself very rich in the process. Of course, this fortunate streak did not last long. Village inhabitants realized what was happening, complained bitterly about this smith and took countermeasures.

Some copied the smith, quickly learning how to forge so they too could create their own money. In no time at all, forge furnaces were burning all over the village, and the sound of hammering and striking on anvils could be heard from every street corner.

Worried yet again, the village elders met and discussed what was to be done. There was more and more of the currency in circulation because everyone was making their own, but the result was that each disc was worth less and less with each passing day. They decided to take action and place a ban on production. No-one was allowed to make the currency without permission from the council of elders. That seemed to solve the problem — for the next few weeks, at least.

After just a few weeks, new homemade coins were discovered in the village's circulation. They differed slightly from the ones the blacksmith made. All the villagers were immediately questioned and all workshops searched, but no-one in the village was producing the coins. So where were the unauthorized coins coming from?

Forgeries

One day, an outsider was witnessed buying bread from the baker. The council elders had not realized that the baker's bread was so good that outsiders would travel just to buy it. These outsiders would walk for hours to buy his loaves and then walk hours back to their own village. It was strange. How did these strangers have the coins to pay the baker before they arrived?

The situation was investigated. A scout was sent to follow one of the strangers who led him to a forge deep in the forest where the village's coins were being produced. The money was being produced illegally. Today, that would be called forgery. But what was to be done?

The elder council met again and decided to change the imprint, thus revealing any coins from outside the village as forgeries. This was not a really good idea because what was to be done with the hundreds of coins that were already in circulation?

The only solution was, quite simply, to exchange them. The council would take them in gradually and exchange them with the newer coins. They quickly set about taking in the current coins and replacing them with new ones. The poet was nominated to take care of this and all the village inhabitants were instructed to take their coins to the poet and exchange each old one for a new one.

The new coins had a much more complex imprint, which should prove difficult to recreate on forged coins. The plan was put in motion very quickly. The new coins were produced by the smith, given to the poet, and then gradually exchanged for the older coins. The old coins were given back to the smith who melted them down and made them into horseshoes or even into new coins. The smith was inundated with work and the poet was turned from an artist into a banker without even realizing. Everyone was happy and content until ...

Forgeries again

Forged coins turned up again! Furious that the new coins had been forged, the village elders gathered again to discuss what could be done. The smith had an idea. The problem, he said, was that too many people had access to iron. Making a copy of the imprint stamp might take time, but it was not witchcraft.

Working iron was not that hard either and it was a craft that had been around for a long time. The smith suggested that a different metal would have to be used. One that not everyone had access to. He proposed that the new coins be made of silver. Silver was much harder to mine and much rarer than iron. Someone else suggested gold, which was even rarer again and would surely protect the village from fraudsters and forgeries.

It was agreed that the new coins would be made of gold. The smith was tasked with the production and the poet-turned-banker was left in charge of the exchange process again. In a short time, the forgers stood empty-handed. They kept trying to use the old iron coins at the market but were laughed at and chased out of the village. The plan had worked, and the system was finally working well for the villagers.

The rise of gold

If things were good, they were about to get even better. The inhabitants of the neighboring village saw their success and started to make their own coins. They didn't bother to make coins out of iron first; they went straight into pressing them out of gold. They implemented their own designs for the imprints and so created different currencies in the region.

The whole region benefited because the coins became exchanged with each other in neighborhood visits, and each village agreed to accept the currency of the other. The coins were made of pure gold, so even if the coins from the neighboring village should no longer be accepted to buy bread, they could always be melted down again and given the imprint of their own village and used there. The currencies did not just have an ascribed value based on confidence, but they also had an intrinsic value based on the value of the material itself.

Gold was used as the carrier of the currency and was consequently always in demand. It was rare and quickly gained a value of its own.

Gold then became worth so much that it started to attract fraudsters who realized that it was worth the effort to forge. A few clever heads started filing off the edges of the coins and selling these filings as gold. In this way, they kept the value of the coin to buy trousers or bread, but they also now had a little gold which they could sell to the smithy of the neighboring village to make more coins.

When gold coins are manipulated.

This carried on for quite some time, and the coins got smaller and smaller as people kept filing the edges away for their own gain. The elder council met yet again to discuss how to tackle this new problem. The poet had an idea. Suppose we issue a paper that is already printed and has a seal on it. We will also write a code on it in secret ink that can't be seen and only the village elders know how to find.

Then the gold coins could be replaced for these papers that had no intrinsic material value. The exchange would be made against the actual weight of the gold so that filing the edges off would become pointless because you will only get paper money based on the actual weight.

That was the solution. The poet was tasked with producing the papers and exchanging the coins, while the blacksmith would melt them down again. The gold was then given to the banker to hold in trust so that he always held as much gold as he had given out notes for.

Paper forgeries

After some time, even forged papers began to turn up in the village. However, because of the poet's clever idea, they were quickly recognized as fakes because of the secret code. The forgers had finally been disarmed and a stable exchange medium which worked for the smith, the baker and all village inhabitants had finally been ensured.

The villages elsewhere also started printing their own papers and storing the gold which would be given out against the value of the papers. The respective village elders visited each other and vouched for the gold reserves. Using the nominal value of the currencies, that is, the papers printed by a village and the amount of gold in store, they were able to define the exchange rate that the papers should have against each other. That was simple because all papers were exchangeable for gold according to the exchange rate. This system meant that everyone could be confident that the papers had a defined value and could trade them easily in and among the villages. Everyone was happy until...

Until one village began to produce more papers than it held in gold. When the villagers noticed this, they also began to produce more paper notes than they had stored in gold. Suddenly, there were arguments about the exchange rates. One side argued that their papers were worth more because they had bigger fields, more horses and better blacksmiths, so they could produce more and better bread. The others claimed that they had perfected the art of tailoring so that trousers now lasted longer and so on. There was a cut and thrust and push and shove, but eventually it was settled by supply and demand in the currencies concerned. And so, they were forced to wrangle their currencies like that to this day.

Money is decoupled from gold

This is the end of the story of the village and its neighbors. The tale of money and currency, forgeries and gold, trust and loss of confidence. But this is also where the real-world story starts. In this story, you, the reader, are the smith or the tailor or even potentially the poet-turned-banker.

In the real world, there are strong currencies at play, like the US dollar, Euro, Sterling and the Yen. There are also weak currencies like the Venezuelan bolivar or the Nigerian pound. The historical development of the first exchange objects, like shells or stones, up to today's currencies has basically followed the track of our little tale, even since the abandonment of the gold standard in 1972 under US President Richard Nixon.

The cut and thrust and push and shove of the exchange rates is also part of daily reality for all of us today. One currency area has a larger steel industry and the other more chemicals, one has more raw materials, the other has better-trained workers. The exchange rate then is set from this impenetrable set of circumstances.

All of that is no longer based on real values, like gold or other raw materials. It is all based on confidence and trust in the individual actors amongst each other. Every political report influences the exchange rate. High unemployment, low unemployment, export balance, gross domestic production, every election, even the death of an important politician. Currencies are the football of the markets and governments use them to lead a country with more or less success, but there is generally a very problematic side effect: inflation.

Static inflation and what the bread rolls really cost

This is not the statistical inflation as measured by the Federal Office, which is like measuring exhaust gas from diesel vehicles. This is the inflation in citizens' money exchanges — this is about those who have to pay $4.50 for a coffee and $4.00 for a Pain au Chocolat in large American cities. Every reader can relate to this inflation because it affects each and every one of us. We feel it personally in even our smallest day-to-day transactions.

Currencies are the football of the markets and have a fragile stability. They induce speculation. If you can exchange one currency against another at a constantly changing rate, then there are opportunities for profit — an idea that is very attractive to the gamblers.

Markets are created to enable nothing other than speculation on currencies and exchange rates. Financial instruments are created to formalize betting and to create leverage. One dollar or Euro becomes 1,000 or one million. The citizens who have to pay with the currency become nothing more the plaything of the financial instruments. City treasurers begin to invest the community's money, and company administrators invest their pension funds in such financial instruments according to the profit prospects. Derivatives are created, sold and traded on currencies and raw materials — all bets on the future that are not backed by any real value and become ever more exaggerated.

The currency protectors

Along with these bets on the future are the so-called "currency protectors." In general, it is the central banks who control the quantity of money that is put into circulation. They are responsible for ensuring that sufficient amounts — but not too much — is available so that the citizens can cover their daily needs at any time. But they too are just the plaything of the gamblers — in fact, they are quite often nothing more than a political instrument to keep the economy running. If the state needs money, additional currency is printed. If more is needed, then more is printed.

The hope with this approach is that the confidence of the citizens does not vanish, while gamblers are also kept happy. It behaves like a giant bubble that is gradually blown up further and further, always stretching the limits beyond what is safe or sustainable. The whole process is very simple because the current leading currency, the US dollar, is issued by a central bank that belongs to the banks themselves, and so this central bank is not subject to control by the government or other state-controlled organizations or even the people.

The bubble burst

The bubble finally burst in 2008 because the gamblers lost. At this time, Satoshi Nakamoto saw the bubble burst and published an alternative to these fiat currencies: Bitcoin. At the end of 2008, after the statistically improbable and shocking demise of the Lehmann Brothers Bank, he published his Bitcoin white paper which stated the following:

"A pure peer-to-peer version of an electronic payment process would make it possible for online payments to be sent from one party to another without going through a financial institution. Digital signatures form a partial the solution, but the main advantages are lost if a trusted third party is still necessary to prevent double spending."

It was an alternative concept to the money that was created by centralized organizations, governments and central banks — one that was not supported by any real value anymore. Bitcoin is a currency impervious to manipulation. It is based purely on mathematics and its transfer of value is completely independent of all economic and political factors. It is stored for all time on thousands of computers, open to scrutiny by anyone, all over the world. It is a counterfeit-proof currency with a limited supply, and which everybody in the world can trust because the currency is designed to withstand manipulation.

All of the problems of the villagers in our story, and all the problems that modern fiat currencies bring with them, are solved by Bitcoin. Bitcoin cannot be copied, as the villagers' iron coins could. Bitcoin can't have the edges filed and be used twice — once as a coin and once as raw material. Bitcoin cannot be issued by a government or a central bank, nor can they be stopped or restricted at a border. Bitcoin is available at any time of day or night, anywhere in the world, and everyone can trust them. The currency has a truly limited availability, cannot be forged, and is absolutely incorruptible. No-one can stop them, no-one can manipulate them, no-one can control them.

These properties make Bitcoin valuable, and if these properties are missing, then the door is open again to manipulation and control. Unfortunately, that is repeatedly found with other crypto-currencies and blockchains. Not every tin that says blockchain on the outside has a public blockchain within. That is why it is so important to know these fundamental connections and understand the underlying functions that money and currencies have. If you understand these connections and understand that a public blockchain makes it possible to have an ideal currency available, then you can use this knowledge to your benefit and prepare for the future.

Bitcoin is counterfeit-proof.

In the tale of our village, counterfeit money kept turning up. Everyone learned how to work iron and in a flash, everyone was making their own money. Therefore, new methods kept being devised and constructed for ensuring the authenticity of the money. Today's Euro notes, and those of other currencies, have a whole range of security features to make them more difficult to forge. However, as with every craft, there are always enough specialists to beat the systems of others. This is what Frank Stocker wrote in www.welt.de on 21.07.2017 (source):

"More counterfeit money despite new, safer Euro notes
BY Frank Stocker | AS OF: 21.07.2017 |

"With the issue of new Euro notes, the ECB was actually trying to reduce the number of counterfeits. But this number has gone up. For the coming months, though, the central bankers are promising a change in the trend. There has been the new 50-Euro note since April. Eighteen months earlier a new twenty went into circulation and there are also new tens and fives. The most important reason for the introduction of the new bank notes: they are supposed to be harder to forge. The probability of getting a counterfeit in your hand should reduce significantly.
A first glance at the current statistics brings that into doubt. In the first half of this year, 8.7 per cent more forged notes turned up in Germany than in the previous six months. The figure has fallen slightly across Europe but has also risen with the fifties. So have the new notes achieved nothing?"
"39,700 fake notes have turned up at banks, trade and police from January to June in Germany and across Europe it was 331,000. The calculated losses from the fake notes was around 2.2 million Euro, ten per cent more than in the second half of 2016. Across Europe, by contrast, losses fell from 23 to 17 million."

"The European Central Bank points out that the number of counterfeits is extremely small in relation to the number of banknotes in circulation. There are 20 billion Euro notes, and the 331,000 fakes that have now turned up are about 0.00165 per cent of them. Or put another way: In theory, you would have to have over 60,000 notes in your hand before you came across a fake."

"By the way: If you are unfortunate enough to have a fake banknote in your wallet, you must under no circumstances pass this on or try to pay for something with it. Doing so would be introducing counterfeit money into circulation and would make you liable. Fakes should be reported to the police and handed in. There are no replacements and you are saddled with the loss."

The person affected must bear the loss

Admittedly, who has ever had 60,000 €50 or €20 banknotes pass through their hands? It's highly unlikely unless your profession requires you to handle large quantities of cash on a daily basis, like a bank teller or retail worker, but even then, card transactions are becoming more and more the norm. The chances of losing out are minimal. If it happens, it is very annoying, but generally speaking, it can be said that the danger of counterfeit money is very low today. It was not always so. There was a time when governments printed the banknotes of other countries—yes, you read that right; countries forged money to destabilize another, especially in times of war.

The safety features of a bank note today are complex and fairly secure. But it is also difficult and expensive to develop and manufacture these notes. Additionally, the notes have to be exchanged to allow the old ones to be taken out of circulation. That is a lot of effort and it's expensive to do. Finally, the old notes have to be destroyed. Who knows how many of these old notes were technically destroyed twice because someone rescued them and reintroduced them into circulation. If you believe Hollywood and other filmmakers, that would almost be the perfect crime.

Bitcoin doesn't have these problems

Bitcoins cannot be forged. They do not have to be exchanged. Nakamoto's algorithm ensures that every Bitcoin ever created in the Bitcoin blockchain is unambiguously allocated to the corresponding address, and whoever has the private key to this address can send the Bitcoin to another address. Bitcoin are 100 percent counterfeit-proof because the Bitcoin blockchain prevents the double issuing of the same Bitcoin (double spending). This makes it impossible for a Bitcoin to be issued more than once and impossible for someone to smuggle a Bitcoin into the system which the system itself did not create. This is all carried out using complex mathematical formulae. No forgeries, no reprinting, no inflation. In their place, Bitcoin offers security, stability and trust.

Bitcoin is insusceptible to forgery, and the Bitcoin blockchain itself has plenty of integrated security features. Thus, all the expense of development and application of the security features of the notes do not apply to Bitcoin. As a consequence of that, neither do all the cost and effort for any exchange of old notes for new. New ones simply have to be found or created, so there is no unnecessary destruction costs like those we currently have for paper notes, and the associated risk of fraud is also eliminated.

Bitcoin cannot be filed down, as frequently happened in earlier times with gold and silver coins. In comparison with currencies of the past and present, all the problems cited in the history of money are solved with Bitcoin. That makes the score at least 3-0 to Bitcoin.

Chapter 7 — Criminals, Fraudsters and the Authorities

Only criminals use Bitcoin

Bitcoin is used for drugs and gun trading. That is true. Cash is used for drugs and gun trading. That is also true. Diamonds are used for the drugs and gun trading. That is also true.

You have to accept one thing: There have always been and always will be a drugs trade, gun-running and even human trafficking. These terrible industries exist just the same as all other illegal enterprises like black-market cigarettes, which keeps tobacco tax from the state, sales tax fraud, criminal activities within the category of so-called "white-collar crime," and other forms of commercial criminality.

Even serious crimes, like capital crime, will not disappear. People will continue to be defrauded, mugged, robbed, blackmailed, kidnapped and murdered. Nothing can be done about that, other than to forbid it by law and get the police to detect these crimes, catch the criminals and bring them before the courts.

All of these crimes have something in common; in all cases, the transfer of assets plays a significant role. In most cases, it comes down to one thing: the criminal wants money. States and the police want to prevent crime, or at least detect it. Following the trail of money was always a good approach to solving most crimes. The exceptions to this are mostly crimes of passion, which are typically not motivated by greed, but spurned love or jealousy. These crimes, however, are usually easier to solve because the circle of suspects is generally very small and socially close to the victim. For most criminal enterprises, the money trail is key to solving the crime.

The Money Trail

Criminals and fraudsters are always thinking up new methods for transferring money to hide the money trail. Because of the assumed anonymity, a cryptocurrency is of interest to the criminals of this world as a transit route for money. They believe — or, at least, they once believed — that they could be paid in Bitcoin without there being any trace of the money that the crime detection agencies could follow. They were way off-mark.

The openly accessible blockchain, the Bitcoin public ledger, in which every transaction — every single one from the very beginning — is recorded, is actually the best way to track money. Kathryn Haun, an ex-state attorney and lecturer in cybercrime and cryptocurrency at Stanford University, is a big fan of the Bitcoin blockchain, because "in the end it turned out that the blockchain can support the good guys more than the bad guys."

It was Haun who led the investigations against the dark-web website "Silk Road", after the initiator and operator of this site, a man named Roos Ulbricht, met his doom. In the summer of 2017, the "life" sentence in his case was finally confirmed by a US court[7]. Life! The court justified the verdict with statements reflecting that even though the hired hitman had betrayed him, his intention had been clear to see. In the next section, we'll learn more about this historic case.

An Exciting Story: Darknet, Bitcoin, Murder and Homicide

It was possible to buy nearly anything on the Silk Road website. While it was mostly drugs for sale, nefarious types could also purchase child pornography, forged documents, stolen credit card numbers and weapons. It was even possible to hire contract killers, which the aforementioned Roos Ulbricht also tried for himself. This made for one of the wildest criminal stories of recent years.

---

[7] *https://www.wired.com/2017/05/silk-road-creator-ross-ulbricht-loses-life-sentence-appeal/*

The story that follows is one that was only possible because of the blockchain.

In the beginning, those involved in criminal enterprise mistakenly believed that using Bitcoin was completely anonymous. What they failed realize is that this is not entirely the case; the use of Bitcoin is not what could be termed truly anonymous because it does in fact use pseudonyms.

This means that those involved can be identified under some circumstances, and every transaction is recorded for all time without any gaps. This creates an advantage for law enforcement agents who can see the entirety of the chain, which is an unalterable history of every single transaction in the Bitcoin blockchain. On the one hand, Bitcoin had provided the payment traffic for illegal products but on the other, it had made it possible to identify and catch these criminals. Does this mean the blockchain is good or evil? In any case, this new technology has provided the perfect setting for a whole lot of exciting stories.

The State Attorney's Tale

Kathryn Haun is the state attorney who led the Silk Road investigations. "Any technology worth using is used by criminals first. Criminals are the ideal beta testers for new technologies," she said at the TED conference in San Francisco in the autumn of 2016.

"The digital currency, Bitcoin, and the blockchain technology connected with it makes no difference there. It helped drugs dealers to sell their drugs on the dark net. [...] In the end, it turned out that the blockchain can support the good guys more than the bad guys."

Haun is a big fan of the blockchain because, in this case, it made her job easier. She has been working for more than ten years in crime detection and has put murderers, members of organized criminality, cartel gangsters, commercial criminals and cybercriminals behind bars.

At first, Silk Road was a difficult problem for the US authorities to solve. That is why a cross-agency special unit was established in which agents and specialists worked closely with various relevant authorities. Together, they hunted the mysterious operator of the website who hid behind the pseudonym "DPR" (Dread Pirate Roberts).

An Undercover Agent is Infiltrated

Because the Silk Road website was being operated on the dark web, and the known technologies for finding the base of operation failed, the agents drew up a plan for getting to the operator with an infiltrated agent. One of their men was to infiltrate and win the confidence of this operator and administrator, the anonymous DPR. In 2013, this role was taken on by an agent who became active in the marketplace under the pseudonym "NOB."

That year was no bed of roses for the DPR because he found himself in the situation of being blackmailed, something that is not uncommon when you deal with criminals. He received threats via his own website from somebody hiding under the pseudonym "Death from Above." Death from Above wanted hundreds of thousands of dollars for DPR's silence, and if he didn't pay, his true identity and location would be revealed to the police. This was not a good situation for DPR.

But that was far from all the trouble stirring. Another user with the name "French Maid" offered DPR insider information from the investigation team, so that he would at least know where the authorities were and what they knew. This information came with a hefty price tag—hundreds of thousands of dollars—all payable in Bitcoin, of course.

Suddenly, in the summer of 2013, the Silk Road website was hacked. It was discovered that another bad guy had managed to break into the website and had stolen 21,000 Bitcoins from the Silk Road servers. The Bitcoin rate was undergoing strong fluctuations at the time, but the damage was estimated at around $25 million.

DPR found himself under enormous pressure. To start with, the lost Bitcoins did not actually belong to DPR but to his traders, who now discovered that their trading accounts on Silk Road had been completely emptied. He acted very quickly, using all the means at his disposal to find out exactly what had happened and even managed to identify the hacker.

However, it turned out that is was not in fact a hacker who was responsible for the stolen Bitcoins. It was one of DPR's own employees, a man named Curtis Green, who had administrator rights — unrestricted access — to the servers. Green had withdrawn the 21,000 Bitcoins, sending DPR into a spiral of rage. He was so angry about the betrayal that he decided to have the traitor murdered.

The Contracted Killer

DPR turned to a user he trusted and asked if someone could take Green out. It was his bad luck that person he asked was NOB, the undercover agent from the task force.

But there was another thing that DPR didn't know, and that was that Curtis Green was in fact now working with the task force. Green had handed over his access to the system, including his passwords and login details, giving the authorities his access to the Silk Road servers. But even Green only knew DPR under his nom de guerre and he could not identify the servers or DPR himself in the dark net, nor could he identify their location. He could only administrate.

NOB knew that Green had stolen the Bitcoins and agents had been immediately dispatched to grab Green and place him in protective custody. But it could not have been Green who had stolen the Bitcoins. After all, he had a cast-iron alibi because he had already handed over his computer and access data to the task force and he was being closely monitored. At the time of the theft, he had no opportunity to do anything on the internet without the task force following his every move, so it could not have been him at all.

However, NOB's murder contract from DPR had to be accepted and fulfilled to give the task force agents a stronger lead to follow on DPR's trail. The authorities forged a series of pictures showing how Curtis Green was tortured and then a few showing his seemingly dead body. The state prosecutor did not show these pictures and did not say how DPR came by these pictures, and he was later arrested in New York. Exactly how that was done is probably still classified. It transpired that DPR was a man have named Ross Ulbricht. He was arrested, tried, and sentenced to life without parole.

This story is one that could never have happened without cryptography, upon which the dark net was constructed, or without peer-to-peer networks, which are also a significant foundation of the dark net, or without cryptocurrencies, in this case, Bitcoin. It was the perfect storm of factors that came together to not only take down a powerful and destructive website, but also reveal the identity of a supposedly unidentifiable person.

So, all's well that ends well? The bad guy was stopped and put behind bars. But, hold on! What exactly happened to the stolen $25 million?

Opportunity Makes Thieves

Along with the approximately $25 million in Bitcoins that had disappeared and the other criminals who had used Silk Road for their businesses, the investigators were particularly interested in the two other major actors in the scene: Death from Above and French Maid.

In spring of 2014, the state prosecutor got a tip-off out of the blue, one that prompted a new chapter in this strange and exciting story. The tip-off itself had nothing to do with Silk Road, and the source of the tip is not publicly known.

She was informed that NOB, the undercover agent contracted for the murder, was suddenly transferring lots of Bitcoins. Much more than his salary as an official would ever allow. In fact, he was moving Bitcoins to the tune of several hundred thousand dollars each month. The source also said that NOB was using his status as a criminal official to force the cryptocurrency exchanges he was using to delete the records of his transactions in their regular ledgers. He blackmailed them and threatened them with sanctions by the police and other authorities if they did not follow his instructions.

He had, however, failed to fully understand the power of the blockchain and its basic function. In a public Bitcoin blockchain, all transactions ever made, from the inception, are recorded without gaps and unalterably. That is the reason for the success of the Bitcoin blockchain. If the public ledger was not on the peer-to-peer network of many thousands of nodes, the blockchain would not be secure and he would probably have got away with his deception. But all the entries in the public Bitcoin blockchain are copied and confirmed on many thousands of nodes. All his activities could be seen and his pattern uncovered.

The Public Ledger Reveals the Truth

The investigators took this tip and got busy investigating where NOB had got the many Bitcoins from and what he was doing with them. Although Kathryn Haun didn't say so explicitly, it is safe to assume that it was other criminal officials in a different department, the famed and hated Internal Investigations, who were tasked with investigating their colleague.

Through an analysis of the Bitcoin blockchain, in which the transfers to individual wallets were placed in relation to each other and one or some wallet addresses were known to be used by NOB, all the connected transactions could be discovered. To their astonishment, they uncovered that NOB was not just the NOB in the Silk Road scene, but he was also the person blackmailing Ulbricht, or DPR as was then known. Up to this point, the blackmailer was known by the name of Death from Above. So, the good guy turned out to be a bad guy — and a very bad one at that.

With the help of the public ledger of the Bitcoin blockchain, it was also proven that NOB — or Death from Above — was also the user behind the name French Maid. Investigators were shocked and amazed that this undercover-agent-turned-criminal had been able to pull off so much deception right under their noses. Their agent had been playing three roles simultaneously: he was the federal agent trying to catch DPR, he blackmailed DPR with the threat that he would identify him, and finally, he had also sold him inside information from the investigation — all the same agent. However, only in the first of these endeavours, as NOB, was he working for the state. As Death from Above and French Maid, he was simply lining his own pocket. It is very likely that none of this deception would have ever come to light if the Bitcoin blockchain had not been publicly accessible to everyone, and had every single transaction not been permanently and unalterably recorded.

The Story Continues

Once the internal investigators were able to link this agent with other identities and the Bitcoin sales, it didn't take long for him to be arrested. The state prosecutors had discovered a new form of evidence: The Bitcoin blockchain public ledger.

So, why not try to use the same technology to find the stolen Bitcoins that were transferred to NOB? Although it was possible to prove that NOB was French Maid and Death from Above, there was actually no trace in the ledger that connected the 12,000 stolen Bitcoins to him directly. Ulbricht hadn't stolen from himself and it couldn't have been his colleague Green either, that much had been proven beyond doubt by the investigators. Maybe the public ledger could be the key to solving this mystery too.

Through further analysis, the investigators were able to trace the missing Bitcoins to the Mt.-Gox exchange. While it had since ceased operations, the records and the wallets associated with the stolen Bitcoins could be used to identify a bank account located in the USA that belonged to an offshore company. That sounded like surprisingly conventional criminal methods, which is bread and butter for the authorities.

The final surprise was unveiled — to everyone's great astonishment — when it was revealed that this offshore company belonged to another investigator on the Silk Road task force. This investigator was a Secret Service crypto expert. He had been present when Curtis Green handed his computer and passwords over to the task force, giving him everything he needed to pull off this crime.

The Secret Service agent used Green's access data that very evening and transferred the Bitcoins to himself. So, Ulbricht had been right when he concluded that Green was the thief. It might not have been Green himself at the keyboard, but that cannot be proved electronically. It is possible to see whose account was used, but not exactly who was used the account if no webcam was running. It is, as you will by now realize, just a question of the private key. Whoever has that can send the Bitcoins.

What a story! A mysterious cybercriminal and two corrupt officials also playing their own game and committing crimes independently of each other — if that doesn't show Bitcoin in a poor light, I don't know what does.

The Police Should Also Use a Public Blockchain

Just consider how the world could change if the police could use a public blockchain as a record system, if chains of evidence could not be changed, if the hash of a witness statement was managed on a blockchain, if the movement of seized drugs and access to evidence was recorded in a public blockchain. Opportunity makes thieves, and unfortunately that also applies to officials, as can be seen in this real case. Even law enforcement officials are human, and humans become weak. Some become weak at $10,000, others only at $1 million or $20 million. But no one becomes weak when they can be certain that they be caught using the blockchain and will land in jail.

It can be assumed that a public blockchain will not just put a stop to such temptations but could actually be a bulwark against all types of corruption. A better world could be created with a public blockchain — and Silk Road is a fine example of the opportunities that this new technology brings with it.

Crypto is Insecure

The kind of Hollywood film plots that are written by life are not rare at all in crypto world, and they do little to reassure or encourage those interested in trusting their savings to the blockchain. Fear of the blockchain and Bitcoin is always cranked up with new announcements of all sorts of catastrophes.

This is often the work of people who do not fully know or understand the system and by opponents who do not want their business model to be threatened. In fact, the very existence of many of these companies is under threat by this new technology, and managers who realize this are fearful of it. This means there is no shortage of such people who want to talk it down and make people afraid of it.

Alongside the article mentioned earlier in the book by www.welt.de (a German newspaper), in which it was reported that the fight against counterfeit money is getting increasingly difficult, there was also, coincidently, an article warning about cryptocurrencies that very same day.

Article from *Welt* of 22nd July 17:
"Doubts Grow About the Security of Bitcoin & Co."
"More and more shock news is bursting into all the hype about digital money. Investors with the Bitcoin-competitor Ether lost 27 million Euro in a "Hack". This was for account types considered secure."

"It is only a few weeks ago that the value of the digital currency Bitcoin was at the 3,000 dollar mark. Since the start of the year alone, the payment method achieved a growth in value of more than 200 per cent. But the euphoria of investors is always muted by terrible reports."

"Only last week it became known that India might want to ban Bitcoin. Its anonymity makes the currency attractive to criminals. They can move money around unnoticed over the internet money. Then there comes the next blow: the competitor currencies Ether, number two in the market after Bitcoin, was the victim of a hacking attack. In a total of three transactions, 153,037 shares at a value of nearly 27 million Euro were stolen."

"In the case of the Israeli start-up though, unknown persons hijacked the system of the company and changed the address for the Ether account to which investors paid in – it only took a few minutes for ether to a value of around 6 million dollars were diverted to other accounts. Employees noticed the losses after another three minutes but by that time, 2,000 investors had already transferred their money to the wrong etherwallet."

Based on the hysterical reactions of the bankers, it's clear that Bitcoin has now become a real threat to the banking world. The board member of the federal German Bank Carl-Ludwig Thiele warned in May 2017: *"From our point of view, the Bitcoin is not a suitable medium for keeping assets. A simple look at the rate development, subject to massive fluctuations, shows that."*

"Bitcoin is an exchange medium which is not issued by a central bank, but by unknown persons. I do not consider it a currency," stressed Thiele.

He is, of course, quite right. Well, not exactly right, but certainly about it not being issued by a central bank and thus being safe from manipulation. Whether it is a currency or not is ultimately decided by the people themselves. If John and Sally close a deal and Sally is paid in Bitcoin at her own request, then Bitcoin is a currency. True, it's not a state currency, but John and Sally probably don't care.

The boss of JP Morgan took the biscuit, however, in September 2017. He stated that Bitcoin was a "fraud" and that it would all collapse. His own daughter had acquired Bitcoin and thought she was a genius. He said he would fire any of his employees who traded in Bitcoin, and that is was not just against the rules of the bank, but would also show that those doing so were just a bit stupid. In his option, his bank didn't need that kind of person. Only a rogue would say that his own daughter is stupid.

Bitcoin fans are now watching the beads of sweat on his brow, because cryptocurrencies threaten the existence of every conventional bank and those in positions of power within them or because of them. These are reasons enough for attacking cryptocurrencies and its strongest proponents, at least verbally. It has even acquired its own expression: "FUD" which stands for "Fear, Uncertainty, Doubt." FUD is nothing more than negative propaganda, just like so-called Fake News or post-factual statements intended to shake peoples' certainty.

These or similar reports can be read, heard or seen on TV across the media landscape almost every day, and they can be very unsettling.

Just because these dangers are incorrect and unwarranted, make no mistake, there are very real dangers when it comes to dealing with cryptocurrencies today. Up to now, the Bitcoin system has been described with an emphasis on how and why it is so safe. So where do these horror stories keep coming from? In the next section, we'll look at the real dangers and where these media horror stories originate.

How Bitcoins Can Be Stolen

Horror stories are nearly always caused by someone losing some money in the crypto environment. Typically, it is not just one person, and it's often not a small amount. When we hear horror stories there are usually many investors and always many millions of dollars involved. The reasons for this are complex, and are often not really caused by the Bitcoin blockchain itself. That is important to differentiate.

Until now, the Bitcoin blockchain has run smoothly without the slightest loss due to penetration, collapse or any kind of miscalculation or malfunction.

If someone has lost money or if there have been malfunctions, it was always outside connections to the Bitcoin blockchain that were responsible, or how it affected other blockchains.

In some cases, it simply comes down to the stupid behavior of those involved — or at least their failure to take sufficient care when making transactions.

"In the case of the Israeli start-up though, unknown persons hijacked the system of the company and changed the address for the Ether account to which investors paid in — it only took a few minutes for Ether to a value of around 6 million dollars were diverted to other accounts."

What had happened?

Quite simple, really. The Israeli startup set up a website on which the Ether-wallet address was shown, and into which the investors were supposed to pay.

Someone just went in and changed this address on the website. This meant that the Ether being paid was diverted to the wallet of this person. What a simple theft. This has nothing at all to do with weaknesses in the blockchain or cryptocurrencies. If the wrong account number was shown on a charity TV show and people pay in to this account, the system has worked perfectly, hasn't it?

How Could the Wrong Address be Shown?

How can that happen? There are two basic versions, and at the time of going to print, it was not yet known how it had actually come about.

Version 1: A hacker had broken into the website and simply changed the address. Before the company noticed it, around six million dollars in Ether had been transferred to the hacker. In this scenario, a large degree of blame falls squarely on the shoulders of the company itself. The money was lost because they had neglected to take sufficient security measures for the website. It is certainly not a straightforward task, not even for professional hackers, to break into secured websites and change data without anyone noticing, but if basic security measures are neglected then, voilà, the hacker breaks in and switches it to his or her account number. If a picture editor in the charity TV show deliberately showed their own account number, then the donations would be transferred to them, and if they weren't caught the money is as good as gone.

Version 2: This scenario reflects even worse on the company. If the security was what it should be, then it could only have been an inside job. Realistically, if the website was inpenetrable from the outside, it could only have been done by someone who logged into the server with the appropriate rights and legitimately altered the address. This would be very bad because everything would point to the management or IT management. Not good!

There are still a few other mixed versions, as we've seen in the scenario that unfolded with the agent in the Silk Road case. This would require the hacker to know the password of someone with the appropriate rights for the website and then log-in in that person's name. This is actually not an improbable scenario; in fact, it's what secret services around the world have been doing for a long time. For as long as there have been famous, important or wealthy people, like celebrities, entrepreneurs and politicians, the famous honey trap has been used against them. The target will be seduced by a pretty blonde or brunette, depending on inclination, and their secrets unlocked in bed. Why not steal a password with this or similar methods?

It Doesn't Take James Bond

You don't have to switch to James Bond mode to do this. In most cases, it really is much simpler than you would think. This procedure is known in specialist circles as "Social Hacking." An example of social hacking is when someone gets involved in a conversation, mostly by telephone, to get access to another person's data. Often, the caller pretends to be a colleague from the same company or an employee of a service provider who needs to do a repair remotely. They therefore need to log in for a few minutes. To make the scam even more convincing, the real employee is even asked to change their password first and then change it back so that the caller can't get into the system any more. Neat trick, don't you think?

Finally, there is the version where computers with so-called trojan programs are conned into logging keystrokes and sending them to the hackers. These hackers then have all the information they need to log in as administrators with all rights, even from outside. That is the keylogger malware already discussed in a previous section.

Many roads lead to Rome, or in this case, to the website. However, you have to raise questions of the company itself.

It is important to completely understand that problems arise around the blockchain, but not because of it. In every major case of a theft, the blockchain itself has worked perfectly and sent the money to the addresses displayed, exactly as instructed. It's just that the hacker has found a way to put themselves between the human and the system. The blockchain does not know that it should not transfer money to the hacker. Computers know nothing at all, they are incredibly complex, but ultimately stupid. Computers can only do what they have been programmed to do – and they do that with astonishing precision, billions of times a second, if required.

This Type of Manipulation Is Completely Normal And Has Nothing To Do With The Blockchain

Unfortunately, this kind of theft – or break in – is described by the media or self-appointed experts as an insecurity of the blockchain or Bitcoin. That is fundamentally wrong – it is precisely that which prevents a decentralized application. A genuinely public blockchain cannot be corrupted easily, because it is decentralized and not just a distributed or centralized system.

Unfortunately, central services connected to the blockchain are still needed today as a way to administer transactions in the blockchain. This is especially the case for the cryptocurrency exchanges. These exchanges are generally operated by a company and, just like all other websites, are also central systems, and thus have all the associated weaknesses.

The bad guys attack these central points and steal information, data, passwords and even private keys. That is not surprising. If you give your car key to the valet to park your car, you know there's a very slight chance that the porter could take it on a little trip. Remember the famous opening scene form the Hollywood blockbuster Triple X with Vin Diesel. Or, he could pass the key on to his cousin who takes a little trip. The key could also be stolen from the valet and the thief could simply drive your car off into the sunset forever.

Whenever a central point is connected to a public blockchain, there is a potential weak point of the whole system which represents a risk for the participants.

Central Data Collections are Constantly Under Attack

In 2013, personal data was stolen from over a billion Yahoo accounts. Names and addresses were taken, along with telephone numbers and e-mail addresses. Passwords and payment data could only be stolen in their encrypted form.

That massive data haul went well. So well, in fact, that the hackers tested it again just a year later to see if Yahoo had improved the security mechanisms of its website and IT infrastructure. The web-portal had not. Once again, the hackers helped themselves to more than 500 million sets of data. Maybe they were the same ones as before, but no one could say for sure.

At least until the beginning of October 2017. After Yahoo was bought in the summer of that year Verizon Communication for $4.83 billion, the value of Yahoo quickly fell by $350 million. Why? Because the purchaser discovered in its analysis that all users of the service had been affected by the 2013 hack, and it wasn't just billion accounts that were compromised. User data for all three billion of the company's accounts were taken: names, e-mail addresses, encrypted passwords, dates of birth, telephone numbers and, in some cases, "encoded and non-encoded" security questions. Everyone who had a Yahoo e-mail was affected.

Yahoo was not the only victim, though. Not by a long stretch. The since-defunct platform FriendFinder was relieved of 412 million pieces of data, and MySpace, a predecessor of Facebook which has in the meantime succumbed to the market power of Facebook, also lost 360 million pieces of data—all with private details. The company claimed that this wasn't too bad because it only affected users who had created their passwords before June 11th of 2013. That is quite an interesting way of looking at it!

Even the platforms of large companies have been affected in the past—like the 167 million pieces of data that were taken from LinkedIn in 2012. Well, not taken, but copied. More than 160 million of these had private e-mail addresses attached to them. So many of those who got an offer at the time to purchase genuine e-mail addresses, guaranteed genuine by thousands of executives and directors, might have been purchasing stolen information. If, on the other hand, you are frequently getting unwanted Viagra advertising, you can be almost certain that your e-mail was stolen in one of these hacks. If not in these hacks, then the data might have been stolen in the cyber break-in at Adobe (2013, 30 million data sets) or at eBay (2014, 145 million data sets).

Probably the most dangerous break-in to a central system took place in September 2017. Equifax, the US financial services provider, was hacked across a few months in the summer. By the time it was noticed, extremely sensitive data of over 140 million US citizens had already been stolen. Those who know how important the social security numbers of Americans are can very well imagine peoples' shock. The social security number is, for most people, their single most important piece of identity documentation. It is even often kept secret between siblings. The social security number is supposed to be a defense against identity theft, because if it is known to someone, then they can pretend to be the actual person and vouch for themselves. Identity theft is a huge and growing problem in the USA, as the passport and ID system is not a prevalent as it is in European countries. During this Equifax hack, the hackers bagged not only names and addresses, but also all the associated social security numbers and masses of credit card details.

The question that you really have to ask is whether such systems are generally vulnerable and are you are endangering yourself when you entrust your data to such websites? The answer is clearly: Yes!

But so what? Millions of people do it every day and you live with the danger. But if it happens to a service that is acting as an interface to a blockchain, then the blockchain itself is not safe. Well, at least for those who do not know what they are doing.

Only Decentralized Data Systems are Really Safe

The cases of manipulation in the previous sections can consistently be ascribed the condition that all conventional systems and websites are centralized systems. Some company operates a website and offers a service. Generally, there are large servers or even entire computer centers associated with them, and this technical infrastructure is mostly in central hands. Therefore, by definition, it cannot be secure. Because of this, these services are repeatedly attacked, and malicious hackers try with all their resources to capture the websites or steal user data. In many cases, the feat is surprisingly easy. The data are then sold by the hackers for mere pennies.

Another popular method of attack is to capture a website or database and encrypt it. It is then unlocked against a ransom or the data decrypted. In most cases, the data are not actually stolen, just encrypted. Well, alright. That's no real loss to the customer, just to the company who has to pay the ransom money — which is often demanded in Bitcoins. Bitcoin, then, is dangerous — or so the media narrative goes.

What is certainly clear to see, is that central systems are vulnerable and constitute a significant security risk. Properly decentralized systems — not pseudo-decentralized systems — are immune to virtually everything and cannot be hacked. Data is only secure in these systems.

However, as already stated, most access to blockchains is still actually centrally organized. Typically, users open an account with an exchange, that is, with a company that operates these exchanges. This makes the exchange a central service attached to the blockchain. Therefore, these services are as vulnerable as every Facebook, LinkedIn or Yahoo website. The exchange is not a decentralized application, just like the Bitcoin blockchain itself.

This is why massive efforts are being made in the world of the crypto developers to develop decentralized exchanges which will also protect the private sphere.

Basically, all Bitcoin thefts were made at these exchanges. While only addresses and one or two credit card numbers can be taken from Yahoo and other big companies, you can find Bitcoins to the value of many millions, if not hundreds of millions of dollars on the exchanges. That is a much more lucrative target than customer data, which has to be sold on after the theft. A few thousand Bitcoins can be liquidated much more quickly in batches, and they are often worth more than 100 million credit card details. The stolen credit card data can quickly be blocked — Bitcoin cannot.

This is why the drama around stolen Bitcoin and the misinterpretations by the media began with the hacking of the first big exchange: the infamous Mt. Gox.

Mt. Gox

There was once a gamer called Jed McCaleb. He founded an exchange for electronic collector's cards for the fantasy game "Magic: The Gathering Online." Many people who are today active in the crypto world are active gamers and love online games. McCaleb was no exception to this. By and large, his platform was already an exchange — it was a platform in the same way as they are used for the exchange of fiat currencies to Bitcoin. He already had the technical infrastructure in place, so it was simply a case of whether his website could be used for buying and selling collector's cards for money, or Bitcoin for money, which was the same thing in principle.

When he found out about Bitcoin, McCaleb extended the functionality of his software and soon the first Bitcoin Exchange was born. The official start was 18th July 2010, which is very early in the life of the crypto universe, which had only been started in autumn 2008 by Satoshi Nakamoto.

Unfortunately, McCaleb soon lost interest in Bitcoin. Some say he had bitten off more than he could chew because a Bitcoin exchange was something completely different to an exchange for trading cards. As early as April 2011, he sold Mt. Gox to the 25-year-old French programmer Mark Karpelès, who lived in Tokyo.

However, McCaleb was — independently of this sale — infected by the crypto virus and has been repeatedly on and off the scene in recent years. He founded the company Ripple and the start-up Stellar was also co-initiated by him. But back to Japan...

Japan was the right place for Bitcoin, as the Japanese people love their technology, and so, Mt. Gox quickly became a vital, virtual trading post, which was made bigger and bigger by enthusiastic Asian fans. What made it even better was that the authorities in Japan were watching and waiting for now. They left Mt. Gox alone and so it quickly became a land of milk and honey in the early crypto sector. But Mt. Gox also became a kind of Wild West, where Hans and Franz, Jim and Joe and, of course, Sora and Hayato could easily exchange their money into Bitcoin and back again without any kind of regulation.

Gradually, Mt. Gox became the biggest, or possibly the only trading point for Bitcoin, and people from all over the world began to exclusively use this exchange. Exchanging money for Bitcoin was laborious and expensive if you lived in the USA or Europe. Even today it is not straightforward to transfer money to Japan, and it was much more difficult back then. It would take a few days because the banks involved wanted their cut, and apart from that, the money had to flow via various transfer banks, who also wanted their cut. One of the reasons that Bitcoin was invented — worldwide, border-free money transfer — could ironically only happen by using the old banking system to get into the new one. Despite all these inconveniences, Mt. Gox still quickly became the center of the Bitcoin trade.

The Center of the Bitcoin-World

Unfortunately, Mt. Gox became the center of the Bitcoin trade. A center is, by definition, something central and centralized systems are just not secure, as everyone knows by now. However, it was to take a while for this centrality to become a fatal problem. To begin with, Mt. Gox was the institution that exchanged fiat currencies from all over the world into Bitcoin.

However, the Euro-crisis then gave Mt. Gox wings in 2012/2013 and quickly drove up the number of users. Many believe that the Russians — who were worried about their money in Cyprus — fled en masse to Bitcoin. At that time, only Mt. Gox was well-established enough to receive these volumes and keep trade going. More than that, 90 percent of trade was going through Mt. Gox anyway.

Mt. Gox was opening 10,000 new accounts every month in the autumn of 2012, though it is thought to have reached 20,000 a day by April 2013. Bitcoins to a value of $60 million were moved in the second half of 2012, and more than a billion after this enormous growth in customer numbers. The exchange only continued to grow.

Perhaps it was this transfer volume that astonished the world, or perhaps it was a different reason. In any case, the Mt. Gox servers went down for several hours. This is a long time when such a large number of payments and receipts need to be made.

"We just hadn't counted on the sudden rush and our equipment, the servers and software just couldn't cope," said Karpelès at the time in the media. He also stated that he was not worried and reassured customers, some of whom had millions in assets on his servers. Then, as unfortunately still today, most of the account holders had also stored their private keys on these servers, so they were at the mercy of the trading capability of the servers.

Karpelès managed to get the servers working again, but only for a short time until the next failure. Ultimately, they were not contactable at all, and Karpelès had to file for bankruptcy in 2014. He was later arrested by Japanese police.

850,000 Bitcoins Disappeared

In the end, Mt. Gox remained closed and 850,000 Bitcoins had disappeared. Bitcoins to a value (at the time) of $500 million. In December 2017, these Bitcoins would have a value of $7-10 billion, depending on which rate you use. Of course, these Bitcoins are not just gone, as they are still recorded in the blockchain, but they cannot be transferred by their owners as they hadn't stored their private keys themselves. Incidentally, $28 million also disappeared from the bank accounts of Mr. Karpelès. Mt. Gox later announced that 200,000 Bitcoins had been found again.

This example just serves to further demonstrate that there is absolutely no alternative for keeping private keys with you — whether that be on paper or in a wallet which makes the private keys available. If you leave your keys in a hot wallet, you must reckon with the exchange suddenly vanishing, and with it your Bitcoins. If they haven't been stolen, there are still some circumstances under which you may not be able to transfer them anymore, which is a total loss in effect.

In the summer of 2017, proceedings against Karpelès took place in Japan. He claimed, steadfastly, that he was innocent and had been the victim of hacking. At the time of going to press, the outcome of the proceedings was not yet known.

The Mt. Gox disaster was a setback for Bitcoin because it was evidence of how dangerous Bitcoin could be, and seemed to demonstrate that the blockchain was not secure. The media did not discuss the fact that the decentralized blockchain was not hacked, only the central exchange. Only those who understand how the public blockchain functions can know the difference and understand that the Bitcoin blockchain was and is always secure.

The First Crypto Laws

One good thing did come out of the Mt. Gox affair, though. The Japanese authorities had to get to grips with Bitcoin and the crypto world. Regulations were drafted and laws brought in to regulate the crypto market, especially the exchanges in Japan. Therefore, Japan, like Asian countries in general, got their noses in front in crypto matters. They had to tackle it and used the opportunity to contribute to shaping the future. They did not make the biggest mistake of most states today, which is trying to apply existing laws and regulations to the blockchain. Japan did not try to adapt the technology to the rules, but instead created new rules for the technology, which were simply accepted.

Since the 1st April 2017, which appears not to be the date for pulling peoples' legs in Japan, Bitcoin has been recognized as a legal method of payment in Japan. Since then, it has become part of everyday life there. Many department stores and chains accept Bitcoin and, in the summer of 2017, it was estimated that more than 250,000 shops were happily accepting Bitcoins as a payment method.

But where are the 650,000 missing Bitcoins? This question was still unclear until the summer of 2017 when, at the request of the US authorities, a man named Alexander Vinnik was arrested in Greece.

Vinnik was the operator of another exchange called BTC-e. This exchange was not as well-known as Mt. Gox or other newer ones like Coinbase or Poloniex, although a greater proportion of the trade was carried out through BTC-e. Initial estimates were that coins to the value of over $4 billion were turned over through this exchange. This appeared to include very many illegal payment streams, including a lot of the Bitcoins that had previously disappeared from Mt. Gox. There were enough reasons then to keep a low profile and not put on any great marketing fanfare.

Unfortunately, at the time of going to press, there were no final outcomes in this case either. There were reports that Alexander Vinnik had nothing to do with BTC-e and that the operators, who are not known, got the Bitcoins stored on BTC-e back after the site first went offline. The domain was later seized by the US authorities.

Those Who Do Not Have Their Private Keys Are Endangered

In this case, as with the others, the investors themselves did not appear to be in possession of their own private keys, and many people — regular investors and criminal investors alike — will have had wait for many hours, sweating about whether they would ever see their Bitcoins again. The result was, as stated, not known at the time of going to press.

Those were the biggest scandals around Bitcoin. There were, of course, many others with other cryptocurrencies. A few of these will be quickly mentioned here. One of the most spectacular was the "theft" of more than $50 million in the virtual currency Ether, created as the payment method in the Ethereum blockchain.

The Ethereum blockchain system differs in one important point from Bitcoin. It can carry out so-called smart contracts. That is, payments in Ether are automatically carried out if the conditions stipulated in the smart contract are met. The advantage is that these smart contracts cannot be changed afterward, and the disadvantage is that these contracts cannot be changed afterward. For the sake of completeness, it should be said that Bitcoin can also do that to a certain extent, and many new systems are being developed to equip Bitcoin with other functions, but Ethereum is quasi-specialized on smart contracts.

Smart Contracts

The disadvantage becomes a real problem, in this case, a $53-million problem, if there is an error in the smart contract. This error — that was actually a basic design error by Ethereum — led to someone walking off with Ether to a value of about $53 million. That was even legal, because the person was only using the specified and permitted rules in the system. They used legal means to get at the Ether.

There was great outrage because, even if it had been a legal smart contract, and thus permitted, in the eyes of those affected, it was dishonest and brazen. It seems that that made no difference to the recipient of the $53 million who had a different concept of fairness and respect to the rest of the community. But there was one thing that he or she had not reckoned with: the community decided to split up the blockchain and let the "outlaw" miss out. This was anathema in the eyes of many, because if the truth can be changed, then it cannot be the truth.

This is actually a fundamental problem of the Ethereum chain. One that is running as a niche presence today as a broken-up version under the name "Ethereum Classic." But the strong main chain too, continued by the majority at that time and which also experienced a significant increase in value, is considered by some experts as insecure, at least in relation to ultimate truth. That could be problematic in the long term, especially because Ethereum turned out to be an ideal method for carrying out ICOs (Initial Coin Offerings), but more about that later.

Private Keys — The Pattern Repeats

Cryptocurrency theft reports are rampant in the media. Typically, a central website gets hacked, and the private keys stored there are taken — continuing the pattern of purloined private keys.

Cases in which even the possession of private keys could not prevent the loss are particularly galling. Making things worse, it is exactly this private key infrastructure which makes the loss possible in the first place.

In the summer of 2017, Ether to a value of about €30 million were removed through a security breach in a "secure" Ethereum wallet.

That was a "small" sum, only because a group of White-Hat hackers (the good guys) took counter-measures in the middle of the hack by black-hat hackers (the bad guys). Good hackers versus bad hackers—more exciting than a Stephen King novel!

The special thing about this case was that the hack was made possible due to a security gap in the Parity wallet. This is a wallet that should have been particularly safe, being a multi-sig wallet. In any case, several private keys were needed to sign transactions. But it was this insufficiently tested function which ultimately doomed the wallet. In fact, it doomed the wallet's users who were relying on its security, all the while having 30 million Euro stolen from them.

Isn't the Crypto World Much Too Dangerous?

If the crypto world is so dangerous, why does it have such a bright, gleaming future? Why will the crypto world change our future and our society so substantially? How can you expect to rely on the truth, when what you read here is that the truth—as happened in the case of the Ethereum blockchain—can be changed?

These are completely justified considerations and must be taken into account. This book should help to answer these questions. The basic rules are clearly laid out on the first page of this publication.

Again and again, it must be stressed that the private keys have to be guarded at all costs. If you keep your house key under the mat, you shouldn't be surprised if you come home to find your house stripped.

The same applied to the dangers in the new, not yet "grown" blockchain systems. Ethereum is not yet out of its childhood, potentially soon to reach puberty. Both life stages are dangerous. In puberty, it just gets wilder.

Blockchains in Puberty

The countless other cryptocurrencies are younger still. They are not even crawling, but always trying new things. Like attempting to iron out the disadvantages of "Grandpa" Bitcoin, to enable new ideas with faster transactions or simply more transactions per second. Bitcoin has many features in need of improvement.

All changes come with inevitable side effects. Therefore, changes in Bitcoin are undertaken very slowly and carefully. Other new blockchain variations on the other hand, can experiment a little. But experiments can many times go wrong. Everyone has to decide for themselves whether it's feasible or desirable to invest money in them. One must always be aware of the risk of losing everything when investing in new technologies.

Those who wish to invest in the grandfather of cryptocurrencies and the original public blockchain are playing it safe. Investing in Bitcoin takes strong nerves because the price is volatile. It goes up and down, sometimes at a really head-spinning rate. It could go way up in the long term, but there are no guarantees.

It must be understood that it was not the Bitcoin blockchain which was successfully hacked in the past, but the centralized points on the edge of the system. It was nearly always the exchanges that were interfered with. Invariably, the private keys of inexperienced or perhaps lazy users were stored on the exchange's servers. This backfired and allowed the thieves access to the money. While it's a given that the Bitcoin blockchain has been attacked thousands of times, no one has yet been able to break in—to either manipulate transactions, or snatch Bitcoins from the blockchain itself. It's safe to assume it's been tried many thousands of times by the best of the best. For the successful hacker, it is potentially about many hundreds of millions, if not billions of dollars. The attempt to succeed is tantalizing.

Does a Bank Robbery Mean the Entire System is Under Threat?

It was "only" the exchanges that were successfully attacked. No reason for panic then, because if a bank is robbed and 250,000 Dollar are taken from the branch, this doesn't mean the Dollar isn't safe. At least, the bank robbery would not be the cause.
We can conclude that the system itself is not under threat.
The Bitcoins will remain safe if you always abide by the following crypto rules:

*1.   Ensure that **you — and only you — have the "Private Keys"** to your cryptocurrencies (that is, Bitcoin and Co.). Always. No one else!*

*2.   You can only unconditionally trust a **genuine public blockchain** with many completely independent nodes.*

*3.   The **Computer Source Code** of a trustable blockchain system is always **openly accessible** and can be examined and used by everyone.*

If you follow these rules, you are very well secured against technical failure or theft through service provider personnel as well as hackers.
Of course, you have to be a bit clever too, and not keep the private keys near the computer. Somebody did this and lost Bitcoins valued at $50,000. The computer of the person affected actually caught fire, and the hard drive—in this case an SDD drive—was destroyed. No disaster though, because he had a backup on a stick and his private keys noted on a piece of paper. The stupidity of the situation was that the paper and the stick lay together near the computer, and both went up in smoke.

That is probably one of those exceptions which was picked up by the media. Generally, you would avoid such a grim outcome by keeping your backups far from your computer.

So, don't do anything stupid, and remain the sole possessor of your private keys. This much is clear. But what does "anything stupid" mean?

It is also stupid, unfortunately, to get taken in by fraudsters. If you become the victim of a scam, you get led up the garden path by fraudsters who make lots of big promises and you lose money that you'll never see again.

Scams: Frauds in all Guises

Scams are not unknown in the crypto sector. New markets, new opportunities to make money, have always attracted all sorts of criminals and gangsters. Often, it's a fraud scheme which has already worked in different contexts which is adapted to the new situation. Then a few specialist words from the new sector are sprinkled into the new scheme; a few quotes are taken out of context and the get-rich-quick scheme is ready to go.

"Don't miss the opportunity of the century", "Bill Gates saw it and you can be involved too."

Stupid promises of massive gains dazzle people. Some believe in modern salvation and send their money. You can earn the most money from these schemes when the lambs going to the slaughter have no idea and are impressed by historical charts. There are, of course, many of these impressive rate charts in the crypto world, and someone who is not intimately involved with them can be easily impressed by those steep, upward-shooting curves. The fraudsters know this and cook up a heady brew of real data and sharp promises, which unfortunately continue to tempt more and more people.

The most important methods of fraud are listed below. Take note and follow the advice, so you don't fall for any of them!

Up to now three different, self-propagating methods have turned up in the crypto world. Some of these have outlived themselves and gotten such a bad reputation that they don't really exist anymore. But beware, because the "XY-coin," which crashed and burned, can quickly return as the "Hurray-coin." The accompanying noise and hoopla will help herald it as the next big thing, with even faster blockchains and better payout cycles. So, you can earn more money faster with the Hurray-coin. Though the initiators and the scheme stay the same, the business opportunity is a little different, but your money is still gone in the end.

The process of fraud in the so-called multi-level-marketing systems, or "MLMs", is described below.

Recommendation Marketing — Almost Always a Scam

The principle is simple and nearly everyone has met a system like this at least once. It's all about recommending a business model to somebody else. If this person gets involved, there is a commission. So far, so simple.

It is precisely this first action which renders these systems illegal, and causes them to be denounced across the world. A commission just for getting someone else involved (this person already having paid the entry fee from which funds that commission) is a classic snowball or pyramid system. The expert — in this case, the state prosecutor — speaks of a bounty, and that is an immediate no-go. If you recognize this, you should immediately cease communication, otherwise you'll soon have to deal with the fraud squad–the police and state prosecutors.

Most fraudsters today are in fact not so stupid. They hide the bounty skilfully behind random products that are supposed to have apparent and virtual value—and at the very least—massive potential. Shares in a crypto product are ideally suited to this. Who can predict the rate in advance? If you look at the Bitcoin, or Ethereum rate, profits of several-thousand percent can be proved. Therefore, say the fraudsters, you should definitely get aboard and invest in this XY-Coin! This gets everyone convinced.

The people who operate these systems though are thoroughly trained salespeople and know exactly which buttons to push to get people enthused. The rate gains for most cryptocurrencies are just too impressive, though. How about our own coin, the system partner asks the new recruits. It would be great to be in on it from the start. That would be like if you had bought Bitcoins in 2012, at a rate of 1 dollar. Only 1,000 for 1,000 dollars. Anyone can do that, even if you have to save up for a few months. Then one or two years later, the 1,000 Bitcoins are worth $3,000,000,000! Who's in?

This kind of motivation is standard in these network marketing systems, partner sales, and partner marketing. They are almost all scams and frauds— known to law enforcement agencies as snowball systems or "Ponzis." Charles Ponzi was one of the first to divest investors in the USA of many millions of dollars with this kind of scheme. His full name was Carlo Pietro Giovanni Guglielmo Tebaldo Ponzi, but that's much too long for the name of a fraud system! So, the concept of the "Ponzi scheme" soon became established. His story is fascinating and if you want to know more, check out Wikipedia. After arriving in the USA with just $2.60 to his name, he managed a fraud worth $150 million at today's value. Respect. Only Bernie Madoff is has beaten that, and if Mr. Ponzi had not involuntarily lent his name to a fraud system—who knows— today, it might be called the Madoff scheme.

However, snowball systems roll through all sectors and are found in cosmetics, in food supplements, and have always existed in the financial sector. Naturally these systems run through the crypto sector with high criminal energy, initialized by the same people who were previously active in other sectors. Now they're clothed in another guise, loudly proclaiming "we have our own faster and better coins, mining and money-making opportunities" . . . and so on and so forth.

Fraud Easily Uncovered

Those who've been involved with blockchain and crypto, understand that it's not so simple to initialize a cryptocurrency which they can identify by careful consideration alone when an unrealistic offer is being made. If the offer is not so easy to identify, though—and if it really could be within the bounds of possibility that a great new business is being formed—then the following simple test can be carried out:

1. *Is it a public blockchain?*
2. *Is the source code public?*

All known fraud systems break down at these two questions. In most cases, the salesperson comes up with good arguments for why it wouldn't be a good idea for the source code to be public.
These can be persuasive arguments. Unfortunately, these arguments do not answer why open source would be bad for cryptocurrencies. They only supply reasons it would be bad for the pyramid scheme — a small but crucial difference that most people would not notice it all. The true reason is mostly very simple: there is no source code, there is no blockchain, and the makers of the system do not have enough qualified software experts available to engineer, construct, and support such a system. It's all lies and deceit from the outset, so leave it alone.

Mine Crypto Yourself and Get Rich

What about the many mining systems? Can't you earn a load of money with that? Those active on the internet will have seen many offers for all kinds of mining: Cloud-Mining, Solo-Mining, Group-Mining and more.
If you decide to go the mining route, you can make lots of money with the new currency. Anyone can do that, so long as it is a public blockchain and source code. If these two basic conditions are not met, then beware!

How can you see what is being mined if the software can't be analyzed? Even if a certain number of XY-coins show up in the mining results, how will you know whether you have really mined any—and if so—whether they are really available to you?

This takes us back to private keys.

If you were to buy a Black box and plug it in—within a closed XY-coin system—and then the screen showed "Congratulations, you have 0.081276 XY-Coins," that still doesn't mean anything. Any programmer can arrange for a nice message on the screen but that doesn't make anyone a jot richer, because XY-coins don't even exist.

If you attach your own Bitcoin miner to the net and connect it to its own node, the opposite is true. After a while, this node shows that you have solved a block and there are at least 12.5 Bitcoins. Plus, the transaction fees are in the wallet, hence a few more Bitcoin on top. This is not only worth it, but fun too!

Later in this book, we'll delve into just how expensive the mining process can be.

Briefly, Bitcoin mining is very expensive and specialized. If you attached one of today's top miners to the grid in most places in western countries, you can probably reckon on fees of around $3,600. You will pay around $1,200 to $2,200for the miner and possibly another few hundred for an expert to connect and support it. For simplicity's sake, let's say that is $5,000 in the first year and $4,000 each subsequent year. This is just a guesstimate. The crucial question is: how many Bitcoins can you generate with your own miner?

Unusual Offers

There are some interesting offers on the internet. For example, people on eBay are operating such miners, and offer rental of these machines for an hour or a few days. This is an offer which immediately raises doubts. If really worth it, why is the owner not mining the coins himself? Why would someone who can mine Bitcoins themselves, and earn enough money doing so, rent their miner on eBay at great expense?

It probably isn't that simple. The best answer is: it takes about a year to break even, that is, to have mined enough coins to cover the electricity and procurement costs for the first year. Naturally, this assumes that the miner has been working 24 hours a day without any problems. And these figures were established at a time when the rate for Bitcoin was the $2,700, and— most people forget this — the Difficulty of the Bitcoin network was set accordingly.

Those are details that are easy to overlook. If the rate climbs beyond the $2,700 taken we're basing it on here, more professional mining farms will go online. Then the total hash power in the network increases, and with it, difficulty. Soon your own profits drop because your own miner takes relatively longer to solve a block. It still sounds okay, because if your own miner takes longer because the price has risen, you get more for the Bitcoin you mine. If the rate rises to $5,000 per BTC, then it becomes even more intriguing.

Unfortunately, the numbers in practice are much worse. The mathematical chances of a solo miner winning the race for the right hash of the next block, as in this example, are so slim that you would need over 3,000 days to solve a single block in a worldwide competition. Over 3,000 days! Of course, you could get really lucky and get it within an hour, a day or a month. But that's what it would be–extreme luck.

So where is the profitability calculation for 360 days for the same miner?

That is easy to explain. If you got about 15 Bitcoins after 3,000 days, that's 12.5 BTC for the block and 2.5 BTC as fees. Then divide this backwards and work out the variables for about a year. This calculation example will not stand up to rigorous scrutiny because too many assumptions have been made, and many probabilities must be considered. On average, the results will be accurate, but here's what it means: solo-mining for Bitcoin is only worth it in exceptional cases or catching lucky breaks. It doesn't really make sense then to rent your miners for a fee on eBay.

To Mine or not to Mine — that is the Question

So . . . don't mine at all? Well, this chapter is about lies and fraud in the crypto world. Fraudsters always go where there is a crowd of ill-informed people and where complicated connections reign, making it hard for the layman to see through. If they lead folks to believe that mining is not worth it (anymore), then they're ready to replace it with another seemingly worthwhile concept.

So, you take a Bitcoin rate chart and show an interested person how fantastically the rate has developed. Secondly, you explain how these coins can be created out of thin air by mining. Thirdly, point out they can't do that alone. And fourthly, hit them with the good news that they can do it together with others. This is called a mining pool, and they really do exist.

Many miners actually join together to form a pool, and so combine their hashing power. That makes sense and is not unusual—in fact, more the rule. If 1,000 miners are calculating, the probability is 1,000 times greater than with a solo miner (plus or minus coincidence) that one of the 1,000 will find a block. The rewards and transaction fees are then split 1,000 times and each participant gets 1/1000 of the total.

There are such pools, but you only get the corresponding proportion of the outcome, less the operator's fees which can be high. In the end, there can in some cases be an interesting return left over, mainly if the Bitcoin rate has risen. You must look carefully at every offer.

The dangers in this pool mining are also the same as those when you use an exchange. If the pool operator also offers online wallets and the private keys are on the pool operator's server, then they and all the money can be lost or stolen. A loss through technical problems or theft is not necessarily fraud in the eyes of the law.

Mining Pools as a Fraud Ploy

Now let's look at another system of fraud, one in which the miners play a part. In fact, they are miners who don't exist, yet whose services are sold. The setup is simple: you buy or rent a miner or a part of a miner whom you have never seen, because they're based in a country where electricity is cheap. Everything is offered as a service of the operation—the service of the miner, processing, software, and the wallets too. You can get involved by taking on part of the cost, then you receive a corresponding proportion of any Bitcoins mined, along with the transfer fees.

This sounds just like the offers of the legitimate mining pools. It even sounds good.

But here is the fraud. The miners do not exist. It could be that there are miners, but not as many as are being sold. You are buying a small part of nothing. You receive nice reports about the number of Bitcoins that have been credited to the account, and how many Bitcoins you own. "Hold" is the advice, because the rate is climbing, and you should only sell your valuable Bitcoins if you really, really need money.

The operators also provide a few Bitcoins because if they do not pay out any from the very start, then the fraud will collapse around them. So, they pay a few participants. This brings good comments. That brings new customers, which is good. They send the customer the Bitcoins, but don't give him the private key so that he can get to them! This is a clear warning sign. They only allow the customer to transfer a few Bitcoins somewhere from his mining wallet. That generates a good feeling in the community. The operators do this for him too, because otherwise, they point out, it would be too much effort and he would have to bother with things like private keys. "Full-Service" is much better.

That is not only a hypothetical scenario. It happened exactly this in the USA, and in October 2017, Josh Garza was fined over $9 million there. This charge was raised by the US stock exchange authorities. A judgment against him and others in the criminal case running parallel to this has not been reached, but another civil proceeding has, in which he was also pronounced guilty and must pay back $11 million. Garza and his associates sold mining services which employed too few miners—the classic setup. Then in the second stage, they sold cloud-mining, again more than was in their possession. The indictment read: "… wrapped it in sophisticated technical jargon where the deception was actually very simple: They were selling something they did not own, and concealed what they claimed to be selling,…"

How Can You Avoid These Fraudsters?

Basically, use your common sense. If it seems too good to be true, then it probably is. The mining advocates will protest that it really is possible to make a few thousand percent profit with crypto. Yes, that is true. So, it sounds good and is true. What you've got to do is think a little more.

It is really simple. Check the company. This sounds complicated but really isn't. If you check out the website and you can't find an address in the masthead, that is not a good sign. If it states that the address of the mining machines must be kept secret to deter thieves, that's also not good. There are other reasons given for not revealing the site: "so that the police can't track down the installation," "so as not to draw the electricity supplier's attention to the installation," "to protect the investors (the owners of the machines) from the authorities." These are all arguments that can sound very rational. Especially when greed overcomes common sense. So, consider, research and judge objectively whether you'll invest your hard-earned money in such installations.

Ponzi-Mining

In essence, these mining fraudsters are doing just the same as Mr. Ponzi, Mr. Madoff, and many others. They take in money for promises of great profits and pay out a little to a few people who urgently need money — $1 million in, $80,000 out.

These Ponzi systems always turn critical when too many people want to take their money out. This also affects the normal banking system and is known as a "run" on a bank.

The President of the German Federal Bank, Jens Weidmann, warned of this in relation to cryptocurrency in the summer of 2017. He said that when using cryptocurrencies, customers could withdraw their money at the click of a mouse and the banks would not then be able to prevent a bank run. In other words, if the customer wanted to withdraw their own money, then the bank could only defend itself against that if it is fiat money? Well, thanks! Are the banks just a Ponzi scheme?

Readers can draw their own conclusions. In any case, it makes a lot of sense if you know about cryptocurrencies and develop your own strategies against all the Ponzis. In essence, it is the same with the banks as it is with the cryptos: Only the person with the key (private key) can transfer money. This is compounded for a bank or building society, in that these have lent money on a ratio of 1:10 and do not have as much money as they have lent out. So, if more than 10 percent of all investors want to withdraw their money at the same time, then there is a run, and it all goes pear-shaped. But that is not what this book is about.

In the crypto world, three things are always important:

*1. Ensure that **you—and only you—** have the "Private Keys" to your cryptocurrencies (that is, Bitcoin and Co.). Always. No one else!*

*2. You can only unconditionally trust a **genuine public blockchain** with many completely independent nodes.*

*3. The **Computer Source Code** of a trustable blockchain system is always **openly accessible** and can be examined and used by everyone.*

These basic rules have already been stated several times, so if it seems like repetition, that's because it is. However, if there is somewhere in this book where learning and deeply embedding these rules is of particular importance, then it is here, in this chapter on fraudsters, network marketing and Ponzi systems. And to end this chapter, explained for you below is another automated, high-speed fraud system.

Automatic Fraud

Fraudsters are indeed not stupid. As the state prosecutor who worked on the Silk Road case noted, new technologies are used by criminals first. Criminals and the porn industry are the first to test new technologies. If the technology works there, then it will work later in the mass market.

The criminals naturally learn a lot about technology and its application through this experience with the new technologies. This keeps them slightly ahead of the rest of the world. Why not set up a Ponzi system right on the blockchain?

There are a few systems which use the keywords "blockchain" and "Bitcoin" as marketing instruments. They do not have their own blockchain nor the appropriate experts to handle one. The modern way of setting up such a system has therefore been developed further.

It is fraudsters who have technical experts available, or the experts themselves who set up these systems. The systems that live in the blockchain and spread through it like a disease, working like a chain letter. The Ethereum blockchain, which can be programmed through the Smart contracts so that payments can be sent securely to the participant chain—and of course to the initiator—is especially popular. The perfidious thing about these systems is that they are trustworthy, and via the blockchain, they do exactly as they have been programmed to do. They are thus fraud systems that can be trusted. Isn't that great?

A team of researchers at the Italian University of Cagliari undertook a corresponding analysis of the smart contracts present on the Ethereum blockchain and found in the summer of 2017 what amounted to 191 Ponzi-structures. These same smart contracts, which run automatically and lead participants to believe they are trustworthy and secure. They run correctly too—the blockchain ensures that—but the purpose is simply to reward the initiator. It might be in Ether, but who would not want to automatically earn Ether every day?

These Smart Ponzi Systems are in a Class of their Own

The initiator or programmer can remain anonymous because anyone can set up a smart contract in the Ethereum blockchain with no checks and no questions asked. They would just have to be careful when transferring the Ether in it, but that could be solved barring any blatant stupidity.

Smart contracts are completely unalterable as part of the Ethereum blockchain and thus, totally secure against manipulation. Because governments and authorities cannot change the contract, it would be easy to get the impression that you're taking part in a secure and trustworthy international system—which indeed you are.

You also have the guarantee that the payment received cannot be demanded back by the person who sent it, nor can the payment cannot be reversed, even if the sender demands it. That is a feature of a public blockchain.

A further feature of a public blockchain is the open-source code which anyone can access and control. The smart contract is thus transparent, public and unalterable. Why should you fear losing your money then?

There is a strikingly obvious answer.

Here is an example. The fraud system unfolds as follows:

"Hello! My name is Rubixi! I am a new and verified pyramid smart contract on the Ethereum blockchain. If you send me 1 ETH, I will multiply your payment and send it back to your address when I have collected enough payments. My pay-out quota is dynamic and therefore I guarantee to pay out quickly and over many months."

So much for Rubixi. How can you fall for that? If you think about it, it is a nice system. Firstly, Rubixi can only do exactly what is in the smart contract, because that is unalterable, and no one can manipulate it. Payment will come. You can be sure of that if you believe that a public blockchain represents the truth. So why shouldn't you try it? You send a bit of Ether valued at $5, What have you got to lose? If lots of people do this, Rubixi can pay out a part to the first participants. So, if you suddenly get back 0.1 ETH and a few days later, after further payments in, another 0.2 ETH, you can quickly start to believe in Rubixi and immediately plow in more money. This time 10 ETH, because then you will get even more ETH.

Fundamentally, it's a completely standard, classical Ponzi scheme. The first investors get money from the next, and those from the next. It may seem only incremental, but it all adds up. The initiator always gets his cut and his work was really just making the smart contract. A nice little earner for Rubixi.

The whole system will run until the mass of people paying in is no longer enough to service the existing participants. But, so what?

Up until then, Rubixi and the first participants have gotten their sheep (or their ETH) safely in the barn!

In fact, it appears that Rubixi didn't actually get very far because the smart contract contained an error that suddenly brought the system to a halt. Rubixi began on 14th March 2016. The last payment was made in the smart contract on 9th April 2016, so it was short-lived. The system still managed to collect money from 98 users and, as in every Ponzi system, many fewer participants were paid—only 23 of the 98 who paid in.

In total, 191 Ponzi systems were found in the Ethereum blockchain and even if Rubixi suffered an early death, plenty are still out there, with more surely to come.

The Quintessence

To sum up, this chapter has been all about the possible criminal offers and systems and even about a contract murder, to be paid in cryptocurrency. We told of police who fell prey to the temptations of Bitcoin. We revealed that there are network marketing systems with or without their own crypto coins or blockchain. You've been warned about mining systems out there that don't have any miners, and why profitable mining is difficult in the western world.

Mainly, it has been about automatic Ponzi systems which generate income for the initiators and payments and losses for the followers—but always on a "trustworthy" system. The Devil take the hindmost, trusting or not.

Those who have now read about these various ways of falling into traps set by the fraudsters, crooks and bandits and losing their hard-earned cash, know what they are doing in crypto world and can protect themselves.

They also know the basic rules, which bear repetition: keep private keys safely to yourself, and only trust a public blockchain—and even then—only if it is an open source.

Of course, there are other rules which must not be forgotten.

If it sounds too good to be true, then it probably is. That means even if it is on a public blockchain whose code is open, as in the case of the Ethereum blockchain. Even that measure does not help against "trustworthy" Smart contracts, which faithfully execute Ponzi schemes.

It is simply too good to be true.

Chapter 8 — Other Cryptocurrencies and Blockchains

Blockchains are special database

One definition of the blockchain is: "Blockchains are special databases which can manage transaction data without the necessity of mutual trust or a central point of control and with complete transparency." That was how it was described in an article in the summer of 2017.

Even experts differ on the use of the term "database." This term falls under a very broad interpretation. "Manage" is another term which does not seem to be entirely correct if taken at its strict meaning, because the blockchain itself does not actually manage anything. It registers transactions, which is a kind of management procedure.

But wait—if smart contracts are running in a blockchain, then data is being managed, meaning, moved from A to B under circumstance X, then it is more like management in the sense of processing. Without smart contracts it is more like "filing." Punch the holes and put it in a ring binder. But really, that's just splitting hairs.

The crucial terms are: "without a central point of control," "without the necessity of mutual trust," and "with complete transparency."

Why Other Blockchains Even Exist

This chapter will introduce you to some other blockchain systems and why they even exist alongside Bitcoin. How do these systems differ and why were they created?

In some ways, it's like asking why there are different kinds of cars.

If everyone wanted a Ford Model T and in any color—as long as it's black—then there would be no other cars, neither makes nor models. No BMW, Mercedes, Ford, nor GM. And definitely no trucks, two-seaters, four-seaters, convertibles, SUVs, nor off-road vehicles.

The necessity of different models arises automatically if you want to load your shelves from Ikea into the car to get them home. You might be able to do that in a Model T, but you won't manage it if you buy a corner-sofa. A van is needed.

The same applies to the use of a blockchain. Bitcoin is the first implementation of a blockchain and it took a few years before the concept and the special truth potential was recognized by more than the pure Bitcoin enthusiasts. To start with, it was people from the financial system who realized that a blockchain could solve many of their problems. It should not be surprising that it was bankers because, ultimately, Bitcoin has garnered more and more attention as a currency and more and more people have involved themselves with Bitcoin and the concept behind it. The concept of the blockchain was analyzed and more ideas of how it could be used for other tasks were born.

The Crucial Difference

After the banks had recognized the advantages of a blockchain, they, of course, asked themselves how they could use these advantages in their own organizations. Using Bitcoin naturally ruled itself out. If you see how some banks juggle money about, an unalterable record which even laymen could completely understand would not be exactly ideal for these specialists.

On the other hand, a blockchain that transports the truth, so it naturally has an enormous potential for reducing the number of employees and cost reductions. If balances no longer need to be checked and data is moved from one system to another, then that is extremely useful and can lead to lucrative savings. But it has to be corrigible, just in case. These are the preconditions for use in the finance industry.

This was how the "private blockchain" came to be invented, although there are actually three types of blockchain and at least two other fabricated words that cause additional confusion.

In this chapter, it will become clear why we always espouse "public blockchain" and not just a run-of-the-mill blockchain because only a public one embraces the truth—and one blockchain is not necessarily the same as another. In other words, wherever "blockchain" surfaces, it is not necessarily a public blockchain internally.

It is About the Truth—All or Nothing

A private blockchain can only contain the truth until the operator changes it. It is as simple as that. A private blockchain is not necessarily promoting the truth. It is in fact just a specialized database, which can be managed inside a company "without a central point of control," "without the necessity of mutual trust," and in which "complete transparency" is often not desirable.

An organization that obviously wants to ensure that data are communicated securely and reliably without processors in controlling, must check whether the parts that have arrived in the warehouse were also installed. A blockchain can do this. A blockchain can also manage employees' holidays and all certificates that need to be produced together with a timestamp, without these data needing to be checked by a human being again. There are many more areas in which a blockchain which functions only as an IT solution within a company can save that company a lot of manpower, and thus a lot of money.

This blockchain system then lies in the organization's own servers, and the miners that verify the blocks each time are also installed on its own servers. As these servers are attended by the organization's own employees, it is also easy to change the algorithms and so manipulate the data. Basically, the data 5, 50 or 500 blocks back can be changed, and the miners instructed to recalculate them. It is possible to take a miner and attach to it a new block with different data while the others are temporarily switched off. Then, when the data have been changed and recalculated, and the manipulated miner, working in-house, has calculated a few blocks on after the manipulation, the other miners are simply started again. After a while, they again become synchronized. Someone who finds that too complicated or too much effort can just change the whole chain itself. Who can stop the organization from doing that?

That is the disadvantage of every blockchain whose nodes are not operated decentrally. The more decentralized, the safer.

The Banks and the Blockchain

It is easy to understand that bank directors are sweating a little each year. A few years ago, it reached the point where they had to actively deal with blockchains. The trigger for this was a blockchain-like system created especially for the banks. The system, named "Ripple," was created to take over the function of a central clearing house in international payment traffic. That works because Ripple is not a public blockchain in this sense; it just uses some functions of a blockchain in the framework of the whole concept.

Apart from Ripple, the banks also want to keep an eye on all the other technologies and, of course, keep up with them. This was the motive for a few banks to form a consortium under the name "R3," which has been romping around in the crypto market since September 2015. Initially founded by nine financial institutions, the consortium had expanded to over 80 participants by the summer of 2017. The technology flagship is its own (blockchain) software called "Corda."

Corda was formed because of the general frustration of many financial institutions which had various generations of IT infrastructure that could not always communicate with each other—and were thus the cause of inefficiency, risks and ever-increasing costs. At least that's what it said on the consortium's website. To what extent a real blockchain was developed and the software used, is not completely clear because the history of R3 is somewhat murky.

Goldman Sachs—the In-Out Game

One of the biggest banks in the world, perhaps even the biggest and most influential of them all, Goldman-Sachs, left the R3 consortium. That can happen. It is, however, rare for a founder-member to leave, isn't it? Maybe they were not seeing eye-to-eye with the other peers in this peer-to-peer network? Did the typical disputes—and there are always disputes when it comes to money or power—arise? Nobody knows.

Goldman Sachs did not renew its membership, which costs $100,000 a year. Together with Goldman, the Bank of Santander left. The reasons for its departure were, according to a Forbes Report, "even less comprehensible." Whatever the case, it could be that they just ran out of money to pay the membership fee, or reached the conclusion that too many cooks were spoiling the broth. The consortium is still active and still making headlines.

So, the management of the consortium acted against previous programmers and online magazines. They acted aggressively, using injunctions, for example, instruction from attorneys to cease and desist claiming something as fact, or risk prosecution. What had the recipients of those injunctions done? There were probably several reasons why the R3 lawyers had acted so hard and swiftly. The most important: it was not blockchain technology that was being developed, but distributed ledger technology—something completely different. Therefore, anyone who claimed that R3 was developing blockchains, was a potential target for the lawyers.

Distributed Ledger Technology

Well, that's clear then. Distributed ledger technology is not a blockchain, and anyone who says it is, needs to be put straight—by a lawyer.

So, what is distributed ledger technology? Basically, nothing more than a shared general ledger of accounts. A ledger is the record itself, so for the Bitcoin blockchain—the blockchain itself. It's the data inventory, in which all transactions are recorded. The word "distributed" explains it. So, it is a shared record of transactions? Or is it?

Nobody really knows, but the spokesman for the consortium has not used the word blockchain since this legal action, nor can you find it on the website or in any recent documents. In fact, this author himself has seen representatives at conferences stumble in the middle of their presentations, confusing themselves with "Blockchain ... excuse me, distributed ledger," while looking down anxiously and keeping a lookout for lawyers, before carrying on. It is disconcerting.

Wicked tongues even claim that the R3 developers failed in developing a blockchain system and they are, therefore, now concentrating on development of distributed ledger technology.

Whatever the truth of it, it is definitely not a public blockchain and the system does not transport the truth. It should not be forgotten that R3 does not claim to do this at all.

Private, Permissioned, and Public Blockchains

Distributed ledger technology or DLT, an often-used abbreviation, and blockchain are terms used by many interchangeably. The uninformed listener or reader can be confused more quickly than he or she can listen or read. For this reason, clarification is needed, which is the aim of this section.

First, you must know that there are no effective definitions because there are no corresponding reference points to come up with them. They are concepts that either grow and become viable—or not. You can explain them best if you also consider the technical background.

A blockchain—a chain of blocks of data—is a sensible name for a chain of blocks. That is what a blockchain is. A distributed ledger is also a blockchain from a technical point of view. The difference is that the blockchain can be stored on a computer and is still a chain of data blocks. It is only when it is distributed through different computers and nodes that a blockchain becomes secure and can transport the truth. Then it would be a blockchain, which is a ledger; and if distributed, would be a distributed ledger. Confusing, no?

So, it's if you follow the majority and see blockchain as an umbrella term for a distributed ledger with an appropriate consensus mechanism. The consensus mechanism means the mining, which provides security for the construction and distribution of the blocks to different nodes, assuring the unalterability of the data.

There are three types of blockchain working on this conceptual premise. Only one of these, however, contains the truth that you can trust blindly.

Public Blockchain

This is the only true blockchain—the one that carries the truth. It's the one in which the truth is stored with no possibility of manipulation. This kind of blockchain is used by Bitcoin, Ethereum, Zcash, Monero and others. A public blockchain must provide certain important features.

The software, or technically speaking, the source code, must be publicly accessible, controllable, and usable by everyone. People speak of open-source software. Well-known open-source systems include the Linux operating system and Apache web-server software. If that doesn't mean anything to you, you don't need to worry about it. You do not need to know one open-source software from another. You only need to know that the software is always free, publicly accessible, and that anyone can and may use them and change them.

There are several different license models, but all of these simply confirm that the software can be used at no charge. One condition, however, is that even when welcome changes are made, the software must be passed on freely. A further condition is that changes must also be published as open source.

The Source Code Must be Publicly Accessible

This is a very important aspect because if the software code is publicly accessible, then many experts can see it. True to the proverb that two heads are better than one, errors in the code can be found much faster by many experts than by the developer alone. Open-source software, like Bitcoin, are therefore monitored. When it's being used by so many people, it benefits from being discussed and improved by many, often hundreds of experts.

This is a very efficient quality model and has already given rise to many great software packages.

Together with monitoring and improvement by experts, who usually publicize their opinions mercilessly (as it is all for a good cause), there is another important aspect which provides greater security to the individual. Open-source software can be checked for any malware. So, by using open-source software, you can protect yourself against possible components in a program that aren't open source, and lurking to attack the private sphere.

If you have installed windows, you must trust Microsoft. You must trust that Microsoft is not sending any data off your hard drive anywhere, even if it is for quality control. Only Microsoft itself has the source code and no one knows what goes on from their side. Everyone has to trust the central point of Microsoft.

If you have understood the blockchain and you want to rely on true data which can only be delivered by a public blockchain, then your hackles will rise when you hear the words "central" or "central point". That's because a public blockchain is never allowed to contain non-visible program code which no one can check. It's self-contradictory.

Why do organizations develop their own software? It's only logical. If Microsoft published its software as open source, that anyone could copy, install, change, and use, then the software manufacturer would no longer earn any money.

So, there are good commercial reasons for developing proprietary software and protecting it. Every profit-orientated organization must do this; otherwise, they couldn't survive. Open-source software is more for the community, so more and more large companies are following a mixed strategy.

IBM produces huge amounts of software that it publishes as open source, and even a large bank, JP Morgan, has developed an open-source module and basically given it to the blockchain community. The company model has thus changed from purely selling software to consultancy. This is a pleasing development and a still-young model, which will inevitably lead to better software and a more peaceful world.

A public blockchain must-have open-source software — nothing else is acceptable.

Inclusive Participation — with Equal Rights for Everyone

This open-source software must be of the type that anyone, anywhere in the world, can and may download and install on their computer. As soon as the software is running, the computer is connected to the network as a node, enabling exactly the same rights as any other. In this way, the network can expand while also becoming larger and more stable. The freer the nodes in the network, the harder it is for fraudsters to manipulate the ledger—the content in the blocks.

Since the open-source software of the Bitcoin real public blockchain is being used without access limitations all over the world, about 12,000 Bitcoin nodes[8] are in computing centers, industrial complexes, office buildings and peoples' homes. Those are the ones that are publicly accessible. Then there is an unknown quantity hidden behind a firewall. This means they are protected from involuntary access from outside via the internet, so they cannot be manipulated. Viruses and Trojans usually have no chance. The positive side effect is that these nodes cannot be found, either by pinging them from outside or over the internet. Therefore, no one, no matter how much money or power they have, can get to all of them or maliciously manipulate or threaten them.

If someone—a government, international group, or individual in the Bitcoin blockchain—wants to attack and manipulate, they will fail, if only because they will not even be able to talk to many of the nodes carrying the truth, since they can't be found!

In this way, public blockchains with many nodes form an autonomous and secure system on whose data you can blindly rely. Therefore, you must look very closely if someone is lauding a "blockchain that is secure" or a distributed ledger aka DLT. If it says "blockchain" on the tin, there is not always a blockchain in it. This takes us to a non-secure subcategory of blockchain.

---

[8] *You can find a good overview here: https://bitnodes.earn.com/*

Permissioned Blockchain

If a group of companies wants to exchange data, the transaction is always associated with some insecurities and incompatibilities. Their IT's infrastructure may not be compatible with each other, and the data must be converted or sent in some other way. "Some other way" might be a horseback messenger — only joking — but something similar, like a fax. Now comes the surprise, and this is not a joke: in the USA alone, an estimated 17 billion faxes were sent in 2015 by over 45 million still-active fax machines!

That's only because the companies had all developed their own IT software technology, and these systems now do not understand each other. Sometimes the systems do not even understand each other within the same company!

Thousands of people do nothing else but transfer data, check the transfer, and then afterward deal with the found and notified conversion and transfer errors—all of what a blockchain can do from its inception.

Therefore, it makes great sense for such companies or groups of companies to use a blockchain to make the data available in a more liquid way and with the greatest integrity. What is crucial is that the data integrity for the participants in the blockchain. In this context, it means that the transfer goes through without problems. Faxed data no longer needs to be typed in or transferred by manual or automatic conversion. Through this, the data can be transferred and used without checking. That means trust in this kind of blockchain is limited to the data integrity, since the data was placed in the system. If a participant enters false information, for whatever reason, then this is passed on incorrectly. That's also the case with a public blockchain.

The important difference is, however, that data are not placed into a cryptocurrency; they are generated in it. This argument becomes void, though, if you use public blockchain to monitor sensors, for example. In this scenario, you cannot completely rule out incorrect data being entered and faithfully passed on. The data is wrong, but it is transported securely.

The Public Ledger

Another feature of a public blockchain is the public ledger, which means the data in the blockchain can be seen by anyone at any time. In this way, everyone can check the transaction history, a very important property of a public blockchain that engenders trust. Along with advantages, this does bring some disadvantages, depending on what it is being used for. It depends on what an individual perceives as being a disadvantage.

In the case of the Silk Road investigation, it was a great advantage to the state prosecutors that all transactions in the Bitcoin blockchain were publicly accessible. Everyone could see all the information, using a so-called Block Explorer, at any time. For Ross Ulbricht and the two law enforcement agents who were arrested with the help of the public ledger—and are now serving long stretches—it was a serious disadvantage. As always . . . it just depends.

At this point, however, a limitation must be made. In order to trust a public blockchain, the data in the ledger do not need to be visible to everyone. Indeed, they could all be completely encrypted. What is important is that everyone can see the software and can operate a node in the network. If enough nodes are present, then it makes no difference whether data are public. It is ensured that after a certain number of blocks, the data corresponds to the truth. It's completely okay if there are no public transactions.

Public records of transactions are not ideal for organizations anyway. That is because if companies used a public blockchain with public data, then the whole world could see who was interacting with whom. Who owed whom, how much money, whom was being bought by whom, and at what price. Also, which credits and rebates were in play, when what services are to be provided by whom, and so on and so on. People around the globe could see the margins that industry was aiming for. Everyone could see purchase prices and profits, salaries and special payments. No company wants that, firstly because there would now be transparent companies which would have to be managed within social norms, and secondly, for reasons of competitive disadvantage. Companies do not want either. If you want to use the advantages of a trustworthy system and at the same time keep the world in the dark about your internal affairs, then a blockchain that is not public is recommended. This is a so-called "permissioned blockchain."

The nodes within a permissioned blockchain are only operated by approved partners and also in effect provide the mining functionality of the network. The mining algorithm is also adjusted to the needs, and mostly a so-called "proof-of-stake algorithm" is used. The partners get a corresponding number of votes and the majority or a certain quorum of approved transactions. More about this later.

The transactions in a permissioned blockchain are typically only stored truthfully in blocks if the majority of the partners or the agreed quorum play fair. Where a literal majority exists, there is the possibility of an illegal agreement to change the data, involving only 51 percent of the partners if necessary. Trust is also needed among the circle of partners, more so than the technology itself.

Who Trusts Whom?

This is an important difference, because how can you trust a system that is—yet again—ruled and contolled by just a handful of people? That is neither secure nor unalterable. It is just a system to simplify internal working procedures.

It is close to the banks' aim of "t0". The "t" means the time required to process a transaction. If, for example, you buy shares—say, in Apple or Tesla from the bank—then these shares must be sold by somebody else, or the company itself. But who knows whom they belong to now?

If in doubt, another bank or a broker can be tried. This means the purchaser's bank must contact the seller's bank and transfer the shares. This needs people to process the transaction, on the one hand to remove the shares from the portfolio of the seller and record them against the money the other bank has sent. Then this record is notified to the purchaser's bank, which carries out the counter-entry. If the shares are registered ones—in which the name of the owner must be entered in the company's share register—then the process must be notified to the company and they must update the register accordingly. This process can easily take several days.

The whole process is not the same as "t0," where "0" is the time in days, hours or minutes. "T0" represents an immediate clearing, as the bankers call it. In a transfer of shares, it can take 2-3 (days) until the last i is dotted and t crossed.

And that is for a simple procedure. When the gamblers really let loose, as they did in the late 2000s, good property credits were wildly mixed with bad property credits. To secure pseudo-secure investment products for the investors, the paperwork increases dramatically.

Closing "Consolidated Loans," according to insider reports, can last many weeks. This is also because many faxes and many workers are needed to go through the forms. How simple would it be with a blockchain, in which the starting data would be reliable and one hundred percent robust, and the whole check and data exchange would just be done away with. Couldn't the banks use it to speed up the derivatives roulette and earn even more?

You would assume that, because everyone knows that the banks have the customers' interests . . . er . . . their money at heart. It can only be hoped that blockchain is quickly understood by lots of people so that the financial acrobats do not succeed in speeding up the roulette for the benefit of the banks. And conversely, to the detriment of the consumer and customer with the argument "You can trust our blockchain, because the blockchain is the truth."

A Permissioned Blockchain is at Best, Internally Secure

A permissioned blockchain is never safe for outsiders and you cannot—and should not—rely on the data of such a system. A permissioned blockchain is an interesting technology which enables a company that interacts with other companies, to process interactions more reliably. That can lead to great savings because the whole checking and data administration expense is spared.

Bad news for the binders and folders manufactories—their folders are no longer needed because no one needs to file anything anymore. No one needs to look anything up anymore because the data—within the group—are reliable. Provided, mind you, that there are no majority agreements behind the backs of the others, to manipulate the data and thereby give only the appearance of security.

That is terrible news for the employees! Why does the company need staff for now? Staff who check documents, administrate and file? They would no longer be needed, as the data are in a permissioned blockchain and thus are true. If you want to, you can inspect the permissioned ledger, but even that would be unnecessary because of the unerring truth of the data. So, neither the staff nor controlling is needed any longer.

Accounts? These are not needed either, because if an internal accounting unit is used, like Bitcoin or Ether, accounting is immediately dealt with through the blockchain. Ripple, for example, integrated such a token as a precaution. This token can be traded under the abbreviation "XRP." You can kill other birds with the same stone, no matter whether you use a permissioned blockchain or a distributed ledger. The employees are left by the wayside or sent on their way.

More Unemployed

This scenario will be a massive challenge for modern society and politicians. It is shocking that so few politicians are dealing with it while industry is gearing up in matters of blockchain—especially permissioned blockchain—and want to use the systems as soon as possible.

At the executive level, the thoughts of commerce, and especially the banks, are easy to read. If wage expenses can be saved, then costs are lowered. Lower costs lead to higher profits, higher profits to rising share prices, and higher share prices to bonuses. The thinking of business leaders is understandable.

The thinking of politicians (those with no idea), is not. That is not entirely true, because if you don't know what's coming, you can't really plan for it. But as a comedian who is well-known on German TV would say, it's enough to ban local Bitcoin. That will ensure social peace in Germany for years. At least, until the next election.

Those who think that permissioned blockchain is the peak of corruption of the data encryption standard ideals of blockchain have not reckoned with the private blockchain.

Private Blockchain

This is a real centralized system and with this assumption, it can never transport the truth because if all the miners and all the nodes are under the control of one organization, where is the protection against manipulation? The organization can change the data or swap it for new data anytime. Who is to stop them?

In a permissioned blockchain, there is at least a defined number of partners, say, ten. If they all have equal voting and miner rights, then six of them would have to oppose the other four. This is difficult but possible, and in any case more difficult than if all the voting rights were gathered in one organization.

A private blockchain is a blockchain in the technical sense as long as mining computers and nodes are present, but it is not a public blockchain as the inventor intended.

A private blockchain could be a very interesting data processing system for a company, especially if parts of the concern works with other parts of the same corporate chain. Processing, accounting and processes like production control can all be undertaken by a private blockchain, with many advantages compared to existing systems. Again, we find more efficient processing, lower staff costs, more profits, higher share prices, and higher bonuses.

No wonder the ecosystem around blockchains is growing and growing. Nakamoto gave the world the blockchain concept, and with it, Bitcoin—perhaps altruistically, perhaps not. If he or she, or the group behind the pseudonym was thinking long-term, and foresaw that Bitcoin would become a currency to be taken seriously, accruing a value of a few thousand Euro, then hats off! Anyway, to begin with, Satoshi Nakamoto mined many thousands, if not millions of Bitcoins, which today could be worth billions. Again—congrats! If he, she, or they did it for pure delight in the technology, or completely altruistically—it's all good.

Today there are many enthusiasts and those who want to change the world for the better in the blockchain industry, as in any other industry, but most of the players are following commercial interests. If the world wants to employ systems which improve efficiency, then companies quickly spring up to help with that. And further interactions of the blockchain arise which are tailored to individual uses.

To illuminate this phenomenon, some other blockchain systems are presented below.

Ethereum

What Satoshi Nakamoto is to Bitcoin, Vitalik Buterin is to the world's second-biggest public blockchain, known as Ethereum. Of course, there is a certain technical difference between the two systems, but the noticeable difference is that Vitalik is a living person who is regularly heard from. He is a regular guest at conferences, advises companies, and has been the guest of one or two heads of government. It's the exact opposite of Satoshi Nakamoto. The cult around Vitalik Buterin extends so far, that a false report of his death in an accident led to an immediate crash in the rate for the cryptocurrency Ether. Vitalik represents the Ethereum blockchain personally, and published a concept in late 2013 of how an even better blockchain than the Bitcoin one could be constructed. Gavin Wood built on this concept, and together with other experts, brought the Ethereum project to life in the summer of 2015.

The Ethereum blockchain is exactly like the Bitcoin blockchain in that it's public and the entire program code is publicly accessible. It runs on many thousands of computers and the mining process is a typical proof-of-work mining algorithm. So far, so good. However, the two systems differ significantly in some areas.

While Bitcoin has only limited programming possibilities — which can affect a transaction — Ethereum is not limited in this respect. This is perhaps the most important difference that you need to know and understand.

Alan Turing

Bitcoin has a so-called "Scripting Language", meaning a programming language which can carry out a series of instructions in a forward sequence and thus only has a limited functionality compared with a normal computer. The most important limitation is that jumps backward are not possible within a script. This is a security measure that Nakamoto built into Bitcoin. The built-in programming language of Bitcoin is by definition, not "Turing complete".

This specialist term is named after Alan Turing. He lived in England as a mathematician, logician, and crypto analyst. He was born in 1912 in London and was crucially involved in decoding the German Enigma. This cipher machine was perhaps the most important communication method for the Nazis, which ensured a great strategic advantage during the second world war.

Turing was the brains behind the decoding of the Enigma code. This was a master achievement which contributed significantly to defeating the-mass murderer Hitler and his henchmen. But although Alan Turing probably saved England by doing so, he received no thanks. He was hounded to death and was only rehabilitated by a royal pardon a few years ago by the Queen herself. His crime: he was homosexual. In the post-war years, he was tried for his "criminal" homosexuality and in 1952 subjected to chemical castration. Two years later, he committed suicide, apparently due to the hormone treatment and the depression that resulted from it. All in all, events that the English nation should still be ashamed of today.

Through the deciphering of the German enigma code, the U-boat orders could be read and consequently track down or avoid the U-boats which operated in the notorious 'wolf packs'. With that, the cargo vessels bringing products vital to survival, to England from the USA, were protected from the attacks of the very efficient U-boat weapon.

Along with saving England by deciphering the German Enigma code, Alan Turing created many of the basics of today's computer world and ingeniously characterized developments. The Turing machine was his invention.

He had already designed this machine in 1936, even before there were computers as we know them today. For this reason, a Turing machine is basically just a calculating device and not a real computer. The Turing machine models a computer and tries to find out whether a problem can be solved by a computer or not; put simply, the Turing test will prove whether a task is solvable or not. Even if that sounds very theoretical, it is still of enormous importance in today's world. The machine fulfills a very important function in the age of artificial intelligence: can computers calculate our thoughts? If our thoughts pass the Turing test, then computers will be able to predict our thoughts.

In the world of blockchain, the Turing test is used to establish how extensive of a programming language is needed in a blockchain solution for the necessary definition. This again sounds more complicated than it really is. If such a language passes the Turing test, then it is Turing complete — otherwise, it's not.

Bitcoin does not have a Turing-complete language, while Ethereum does.

Turing complete Language

That means that Ethereum should be able to—as is the case so far—actually solve all programs and tasks that a computer typically should be able to solve. These include in particular the so-called Loops, that is, jumps backward in the program to then come back again. By contrast to the script language of Bitcoin, which can carry out commands in sequence, the Ethereum language, called "Solidity," can do nearly everything that a "normal" computer can — provided someone writes such a program and runs it on the Ethereum nodes.

With the Bitcoin script language, 1+1+1+2 is calculated and the result stored. Then comes the next script 1+1+1+2 and this result is also saved. If that is needed ten times, then ten scripts need to be run one after the other. This can be done differently with Solidity: "Calculate 1+1+1+2 and return to the start. Count how often you have returned to the start and stop returning to the start when the counter is on '10'." When simplified, like it has been here, it sounds trivial. In practice, however, the two methods are worlds apart.

These Solidity programs are called smart contracts. The multitude of possibilities for these smart contracts makes Ethereum different and desirable. But to avoid confusion, there are also smart contracts within Bitcoin, and there too, further modules are being created to extend the range of functions of smart contracts. Because of the limitations of the Bitcoin script language, which is not Turing complete, there are certain programs that just cannot be run with Bitcoin, as they can be with Ethereum. That is a security issue for Bitcoin, yet the most important feature of Ethereum. As always, it's both a blessing and a curse at once.

If you can do everything, then that is an invitation to the bad people to try to do "everything" and exploit it. That is what happened in the summer of 2016, when Ethereum was robbed and hackers pocketed over $50 million. That only happened because Ethereum, in Solidity, made a Turing-complete programming language available.

Ethereum Smart contracts

Smart contracts are at the center of Ethereum. Therefore, Ethereum is not described necessarily as a cryptocurrency, but rather (by fans) as a computer spanning the world. As Ethereum, like Bitcoin, is a decentralized blockchain with a proof-of-work consensus, there are also Ethereum nodes around the world which are storing the Ethereum ledger. Ethereum is thus a genuine public blockchain.

Along with the public ledger, the smart contracts themselves run in a so-called virtual machine, that is an appropriate Ethereum program, on the nodes. As soon as a transaction is placed in the transaction pool, the recipient address can be a smart contract and only needs to be a pure recipient address.

If the recipient address is a smart contract, then this is carried out in the EVM (Ethereum Virtual Machine) according to the rules set in it, and the result is stored. This result is then mined in one of the next blocks and can itself, in turn, be checked by every node, if a block contains this smart contract transaction. This is because the EVM (Ethereum Virtual Machine) runs on every node.

After a smart contract has been placed in the Ethereum net, it is shared over the peer-to-peer network and then run on every EVM—on every node. In other words, the smart contract can no longer be stopped and does exactly what it was created to do. It checks and calculates results and calculates them maybe a few times or possibly repeatedly. Smart contracts can do that on Ethereum because the programming language is Turing complete.

Calculating over and over and then starting and calculating again, is the most dangerous moment. You are in a never-ending loop and going around in circles — the nightmare of software developers. If that happens, in general, we speak of computers having "frozen." Previously, that would have meant closing the program by pressing a few buttons simultaneously. In bad cases, it would mean switching off the computer. In the worst of all cases, it meant pulling out the power cord.

Today though, there is a worse case: a never-ending loop on a decentralized system, where switching off one computer does not achieve anything. An almost endless loop can then lead to a large theft.

The "Decentralized Autonomous Organization" (DAO)

Smart contracts work completely independently and do only their programmed job. If they are used in a decentralized system, thousands of them are doing so, always in the same way. If one or a few of these computers are switched off, that does not disrupt the system. The system is completely independent and cannot be manipulated, due to the decentralized arrangement. By using a blockchain, the past cannot be manipulated either. These are ideal conditions for an independent, autonomous organization. Precisely that was created in the summer of 2016. The "DAO,"—the "Decentralized Autonomous Organization".

Enthusiasm in the crypto community was unbounded because you could follow the basic principle of "Code is Law." People were no longer closing agreements which later had to be disputed in court with the usual unclear starting points. Rather, computers were doing it by following Smart contracts in an incorruptible system in which the results did not need to be questioned. In a system where judges were no longer needed because the correctness of the result left zero room for doubt, "Code is Law" meant the software itself was the law!

The approach is still fascinating, and Code is Law is certainly a subject which needs to be tackled. This is certainly true for lawyers because Code is Law means that ultimately a judge does not have to decide whether the contract has been kept, only whether the contract itself is within applicable laws. It would certainly be adhered to in a decentralized system, but the question to be answered is whether it was legally permissible at all.

This is the important question that quickly arose for the DAO. To answer a question like this, the judges and lawyers first must understand what defines a smart contract. In other words, lawyers have to understand programming. At least, solicitors will have to stock up on software experts who understand smart contracts. This gives rise to a new legal discipline because, just like patent lawyers have extensive legal training and are also technical experts, the lawyers of the future will have to be lawyers and software experts all in one! Very few would have foreseen that.

It was the idea of the DAO that investors pay money in and the DAO would manage the money via smart contracts. Payments were made in Ether, the cryptocurrency integrated into the Ethereum blockchain. Ether is, so to speak, the Bitcoin of the Ethereum blockchain. Everyone could pay Ether into the DAO and receive voting rights, via smart contracts. Thereafter, the DAO would, based on the votes of those with voting rights, independently invest in other companies—again via Smart contracts. This allayed the fears of someone making their own investment against the will of the shareholders. Nor could anyone—no banker, director, authorized signatory nor anybody else—run off with the money. Everything would run in a decentralized blockchain system via smart contracts. It was a new and great idea which many were ecstatic about.

The Great Ethereum Robbery

It started on April 30th, 2016: Investors could acquire their share rights in the DAO by paying in Ether. The sale was intended to last 28 days, and on May 10th, more than $34 million had flowed into the DAO. But that was far from the end of it. On May 15th, it was more than $100 million, and finally, on May 21st, 2016, over $150 million paid in by over 11,000 investors.

The grand total: over $150 million!

But as always, when it seems too good to be true, when the enthusiasm is greatest, the spoilsports turn up. This was no different. As early as May, the first analyses by software experts appeared, which listed potential attack points for a hacker in the smart contracts. These experts were not nobodies, but people with solid reputations—university professors and notable crypto experts. Investors were warned and asked not to invest anymore until these potential attack points had been secured.

At the beginning of June, another expert then pointed out the possibility that a never-ending loop could be programmed and used to divert Ether. The bad news compounded quickly, and a hacker struck on June 17th, 2016. He exploited the Turing complete language, used a form of infinite loop and stole a third of the assets collected in the DAO— over $50 million!

The enthusiasm evaporated immediately. There was a deep shock and the whole Ethereum community wondered what to do about it.

Because firstly, the stolen Ether were locked in a smart contract for another twenty-eight days before they could be moved. That was good. The experts animatedly discussed how to proceed. Various people put forward different points of view. The proponents of Code is Law said it was okay, because if the code is law and the hacker was just following this law, then it was his right to keep the money. You could see it like that. But more than 50 million?

The majority of the community found what he had done despicable. "Code is Law" or not, surely those actions can't be right? In the end, the community decided that they did not want to let the hacker get away with it, and programmed a "Hard Fork." It seems that a decentralized system can be changed that simply. A hard fork is not backward compatible, meaning the Ether that the hacker had could not be used in the new branch of the chain and he would be left just sitting on them.

To what extent this was the right way to go, and to what extent we can still speak of a manipulation-proof system is now a vital question. Where and when exactly does the manipulation stop—or start? This is the reason that the Ethereum blockchain is not considered secure. The argument does not really apply, because a hard fork is nothing unusual, it is just new rules for the future.

The real insecurity affects the reliability of the Ethereum community. In future, if someone wants to send, say, $100 million or more via the Ethereum blockchain, and the community, miners and nodes decide to quickly initialize a hard fork, then you should indeed be worried.

In any case, the Ethereum blockchain was split and that is why today there is Ethereum with the exchange symbol ETH and the continuation of the old chain, the one with the DAO hack, under the abbreviation ETC, which stands for Ethereum classic. Both chains continue to be mined and both are still in operation. Ethereum Classic is only traded at $40, while ETH—the "new" Ethereum, was at nearly $1,200 at the time of going to press. However, this is still a sign that you cannot just switch off a public blockchain. Not even with a hard fork.

The hard fork generated for Bitcoin on August 1st, 2017 is another example that such systems cannot just be switched off. By contrast, a permissioned blockchain or even a private blockchain can be forked or switched off by the operators at any time. At that point, it's just gone or functions under different rules, depending on what the operator wants.

Dangers for Ethereum and the Future

What makes the Ethereum blockchain so special, are the almost unlimited opportunities to present nearly every kind of software function via smart contracts. Along with the legitimate programs, there can also be malware, where the definition of malware can only be relative to the applicable legal framework, because a smart contract knows no legal framework, morals or ethics. In the previous chapter about automatic pyramid systems, we saw it's the smart contracts that make it possible. Smart contracts don't care what they are calculating, they just do their job.

Regardless of morals and rights, there is a constant uncertainty that somewhere in the Ethereum network, a smart contract could be lurking that has not yet been active. The concern is that at some point it will do something nasty to the network, simply because it can, and because it does its job. This residual risk is latent with Ethereum; it cannot happen with Bitcoin because the script language is not Turing complete. You always have to keep that in mind.

The number of fans and market participants in Ethereum is growing day by day, despite all these gloomy predictions. With this support, there is an increase in confidence and the number of computers mining or reinforcing, and securing and stabilizing the network as nodes. This is a very positive development, which is further supported by another mechanism which makes it easy to collect money for other projects within the Ethereum chain. Called the "ERC 20" mechanism, it's the basis for many ICOs (Initial Coin Offerings). More about this later.

The growth of the Ethereum blockchain comes with a price tag of course. As more users generate more transactions, more smart contracts generate more calculating effort at the nodes, so it's necessary (just as with Bitcoin) for the network to adjust and be extended. It must also become quicker and more efficient. The inventors had already foreseen that, and therefore a solution is being worked on that is intended to improve the Ethereum blockchain's efficiency. One of these planned measures is the resetting of the consensus algorithm from proof-of-work to proof-of-stake. We'll learn more about that in the next chapter.

These actions are unfortunately seen by many as also being security risks. It is thus yet to be seen whether Ethereum can sustain itself as the second-biggest blockchain of the future.

Chapter 9 — Nodes, Consensus and Mining

Why some work is needed

On the one hand, a blockchain consists of cryptographically connected data blocks in which the individual transactions of system participants are recorded. That is where the name "blockchain" comes from. A blockchain itself is relatively worthless because it is not safe in and of itself. The security is achieved by various measures. The single most important thing about this is that the chain is distributed over as many computers (nodes) as possible at the same time. Only this can make a blockchain secure, because if data is changed on only one part of the nodes, this change will sooner or later get overwritten and the data on the majority of the nodes becomes the truth. The truth then gets synchronized. The rules for maintaining this truth are also called the "Consensus Algorithm."

This consensus algorithm must of course also be known to the nodes, just as with any other specifications they must adhere to. Software must basically run on every node to get that node to work at all. For all intents and purposes, that's the node application. And this raises the interesting question . . . *what* software?

It was very easy to answer this question in 2009 because there was only one version—Nakamoto's. Of course, the software was far from error-free. Actually, all software is. Working with other programmers, these errors were gradually eliminated. After every significant change in the code, the nodes were bought up to date with the latest version, so that all nodes ran on the same software. It was, and still is, called "Bitcoin Core."

Bitcoin Core

Bitcoin Core is the software program which makes the nodes work—it is quasi-Word or Excel. At the same time, it's the software which transfers the scope of functionality to the node, which would be by comparison the bold font or mathematical function symbols in Word and Excel formulae. The consensus algorithm, which defines which blocks the node can and may accept and in what form, is also in the scope of function of Bitcoin Core. Bitcoin Core defines the checks that a node must make to confirm the correctness of a block. For example, the node must measure the size of a block and it must be smaller than 1 megabyte. If the block delivered by the miner is larger than 1 MB, then it is ignored by the node and not added to the copy of the ledger which is stored locally—its blockchain.

The protocol is also defined for the miners in Bitcoin Core. The miners too must also know the format in which a block is generated for them to be accepted by the nodes. The miners only get the reward of 12.5 Bitcoins (from 2016 to 2020, from 2020 only 6.25 BTC) if the majority of the nodes accept the block and attach it to the existing chain. The size of the payment is also defined in Bitcoin Core.

To be sure that the blockchain cannot make an unpermitted split and that the transactions are secure and cannot be reversed on short notice, you should, as previously stated, wait at least six blocks before passing on the Bitcoins you have received. That is not defined in the protocol, but if a value that can be calculated. It is a result of the mathematics of the whole system. However, it's also defined in the protocol that the miners only get their reward after 100 blocks—and it's an important incentive—so that the miners cannot do anything silly or try to defraud.

All that and much more is defined in Bitcoin Core. Bitcoin Core is maintained by the so-called "Core developers" (Core devs) and alterations are only approved gradually, conservatively and with great care.

First Dissatisfactions

To begin with, there were only a few programmers operating a few nodes and miners. Miners and nodes ran on the same computers and these programmers invested time in their hobby, Bitcoin. Gradually, this hobby spread, till at some point no one knew all the operators personally anymore, and even then, only via electronic communications channels.

Some people just downloaded and installed the Bitcoin open-source software. All over the world, more and more nodes were running, all of which had a copy of the blockchain or were calculating blocks in the mining procedure.

As the Bitcoin software was becoming more and more popular, many experts began analyzing it. Some caught on and decided to work on the project to point out errors to others. Naturally, it wasn't just moaning, people helped each other on the principle that two heads are better than one, and fifty heads are better than two!

Because the software was on the GitHub platform as open source, close collaboration between these top experts was easily realizable, even internationally and across all time zones. GitHub enabled that and it's still used today—not just for Bitcoin Core, but for thousands of software projects in all countries.

On GitHub, you can see not just who did what and when, but experts can make decisions on parts of the software code lines that have been built in so that changes are always checked and tested by many people. This is a crucial quality criterion for software projects and should definitely be a basis of such projects, as will be explained in the later chapter on investing in crypto projects.

On the https://bitcoin.team/ website, it can be seen how many programmers deliver new software code, who they are, and when they delivered it. If you compare that to other crypto projects, you can see an inordinately higher number of so-called "Commits," as changes and deliveries are known. In this too, Bitcoin sets the gold standard for these projects. It's also interesting that it can be viewed on this site how a developer with the pseudonym Satoshi Nakamoto at some point just stopped working on the project.

As the entire software is publicly accessible, many programmers have developed new ideas and communicated them in GitHub and other fora. Many of these ideas were taken up enthusiastically by the community and discussed intensively. All ideas live by intensive discussion in the online fora and they are being constantly improved, and people help each other by finding errors that others have overlooked.

The good ideas have always been taken up by the community—which is constantly growing—and accepted into the "BIP." BIP stands for "Bitcoin Improvement Proposals".

Bitcoin Improvement Proposals

These BIPs are sorted and numbered according to importance and usefulness and if the community thinks that a BIP has been discussed enough and is free of errors, Bitcoin Core (the software for the nodes), is updated accordingly. The discussion of such BIPs from the first proposal to implementation can sometimes last for years. It is not a process in which one person has an idea and then updates the software overnight. There must be a broad consensus of programmers before the code is implemented. This implementation can only be undertaken by a few programmers in the Core team who have the cryptographic keys for this. This works like it does in films where it is shown that nuclear weapons can only be launched when two people turn keys simultaneously. It's just not as dramatic.

This situation only applies to Bitcoin though. Open-source software can be used, changed, and offered by anyone. Anyone can build modifications into Bitcoin Core if it is done in a copy of the software. That is exactly what continually happens if an individual or group does not wish to wait for the consensus of the Core team, or if they are against the opinion of the community. If the Bitcoin Core code is copied and then published with changes, then a new version of the software for the nodes or the miners—or both—is created. This is then called a fork. Anyone in the world can carry out a fork at any time. It's far from unusual occurrence!

The Fork — the "AltCoin"

The word "fork" was frequently heard in the summer of 2017. Bitcoin was splitting itself, according to the media. You could read about a civil war within the Bitcoin community and even of the end of Bitcoin. Basically, it was a fork, and this gave rise to a new chain with the name "Bitcoin Cash."

There have been forks for a long time and there always will be. That is just in the nature of the system itself, the liberal type of the software, and the community. Everyone can do what they want. Anyone can construct their own Bitcoin anytime, anywhere in the world.

To distinguish these forked, or split off, versions of Bitcoin, they were named "AltCoins". This is nothing special and there are more than 1000 of them. Some are forks from Bitcoin Core and others are cryptocurrencies with newly designed blockchains, offering different functions and features. In the Altcoin Top Ten are Ethereum, Dash, Monero, Zcash, LiteCoin and others. These are also traded on the crypto exchanges, sometimes with a market value of more than a billion dollars. Most of them have a niche presence though, and are often just experiments. Some have a market value of a few million but are not really solvent, and are in fact only suitable for gamblers and speculators.

The first AltCoin known to have been created was called "IXCoin" and was a fork of Bitcoin Core. The developers changed a few parameters in the basic software and soon a new blockchain and cryptocurrency came into being. That was in August 2011.

The developers decided to take this step because they wanted to create the coins more quickly, or did not want to wait as long as the Bitcoin-Core protocol intended. They set the reward for their IXCoin at 96 coins per block.

LiteCoin

It is no problem to create a new AltCoin, such as the IXCoin. You only have to find new people to mine the coin and set up the appropriate nodes. The future importance of this AltCoin can be decided immediately.

Mining costs a lot of energy, and energy costs money. There are always people who will set up a miner and invest if there is enough money to be made. The more earning potential there is, the more people there will be willing to mine the new coin. It is that simple.

Of course, it was not so simple when Bitcoin first began. At the time, there were only a few enthusiasts who wanted to drive the technology forward for technology's sake. The crypto industry was born in 2009, and whether computers were mining Bitcoin or IXCoin was a commercially relevant question. IXCoin is still being traded and investors were paying from 0.05 to 0.8 US dollars for it in 2017. IXCoin was the first well-known AltCoin and as such, it deserves a mention.

A month after IXCoin's inception, the next cryptocurrency, Tenebrix, appeared. As with many forks, or copies, Tenebrix was ultimately unsuccessful. However, Tenebrix did change the consensus mechanism of block calculation. The blocks no longer needed to be calculated using the Bitcoin method, but could now be calculated using a method known as *Scrypt*, which uses the main memory of the computer more than the Bitcoin method does. Scrypt mining functions differently than Bitcoin mining does. The algorithm allows shorter separations between blocks because the braking effect previously described is achieved differently. That led to another new currency under the name *LiteCoin*, which used the Scrypt-mining mechanism. LiteCoin came from the experiments with Tenebrix. In contrast with Bitcoin, with LiteCoin, a block is produced every 2.5 minutes, and the maximum number of coins generated is defined as 84 million, compared to Bitcoin's 21 million. LiteCoin described itself as the crypto silver currency in relation to Bitcoin, which enjoys the reputation of being crypto gold.

LiteCoin was a very successful fork, and enjoys great popularity today. As of December 2017, LiteCoin had a market value of over US 12 billion and reached a price of over US $220 per coin. It can easily be found under the ticker symbol "LTC."

The significance of LiteCoin is not only from a monetary point of view, but also from a technical perspective. It is a simpler and more attractive means of mining cryptocurrency as the change in the algorithm requires less specialized computing power than necessary for mining Bitcoin, but more storage space is required. Storage units are fairly expensive, and if you cannot gain any significant benefit from pure computing power, then the specialized miners, such as the ASIC miners, are not practical.

That is why Scrypt, which LiteCoin was the first to use, is a very interesting way to keep mining costs under control and thereby allow more people to install and operate miners. This leads to greater equality of opportunity than the Bitcoin algorithm allows. Therefore, it is not surprising that more branches were created from the LiteCoin code, and that new cryptocurrencies—forks of LiteCoin—arose.

Today, hundreds of the thousands of cryptocurrencies are derived from LiteCoin.

How Is the Price of a Cryptocurrency Determined?

For an AltCoin, it is not only crucial that the software itself functions, but also that there are enough people operating nodes and miners. The risk of operation is initially with those who participate in and invest in mining. The lower the investment and the higher the expected income, the greater the number of participants. That is a simple economic consideration.

If LiteCoin were to be traded tomorrow at a higher rate than other Scrypt-Coins, and the final reckoning were to the advantage of LiteCoin, then the miners would convert their software to LiteCoin and calculate LiteCoin blocks until the rate dropped again and it is more lucrative to mine a different currency. This constant ebb and flow is not always applicable, however, because not all cryptocurrencies can be mined reasonably with all hardware. This switching between different currencies is illustrated in the August 2017 arrival of Bitcoin Cash, Bcash, an AltCoin derived from Bitcoin (Bcash is a combination of the words "Bitcoin" and "cash"). Bcash raised the upper limit of 1MB per block hat in the hope that more transactions could be placed in one block, and as a result, the throughput of the blockchain could be increased.

An inconvenient side effect was that the difficulty algorithm had to be modified because Bcash was only being mined by a few miners, who were already challenged by the existing Bitcoin difficulty. That is why the so-called "EDA-Algorithm" (Emergency Difficulty Adjustment Algorithm) was built. The EDA-Algorithm allows the difficulty to be changed very quickly, thereby making mining easier. That makes mining Bcash lucrative again, and the Bitcoin mining farms are switched over to mine Bcash.

As a result, Bcash-Blocks were calculated much too quickly. In October 2017, the rate sometimes reached 50 blocks per hour, or nearly a block a minute. The braking effect was gone, and this was not healthy for the system. The EDA-Algorithm braked it strongly again and massively increased the difficulty. But this made it once again too difficult for the miners, and so they switched back to Bitcoin mining, which was much more commercially attractive. The switching back and forth continued for days. It remains to be seen how it will play out in the future, and whether Bcash can survive. It is probably not long until the next hard-fork of Bcash.

The Profitability of Mining

The switching back and forth between different cryptocurrencies is not unusual. GPU miners — that is, those who use graphics cards to calculate the blocks — generally switch between Ethereum, Zcash and Monero according to which is most lucrative at the time. However, there are not the same fluctuations and upheavals as there are with Bcash. Mostly, the switch to another coin is influenced less by the difficulty and more by the exchange rate of the currency. If the price of Monero rises disproportionately, then it makes sense to mine Monero and not Zcash. Modern mining software switches back and forth automatically.

So, it always depends on the profitability of mining, which itself depends on the value of the cryptocurrency. The price of every individual crypto coin depends exclusively on supply and demand. If somebody offers $5,000 for a Bitcoin , then the price is $5,000 per Bitcoin. It is as easy as that. Of course, someone would only offer $5,000 if they really believed in the system, or if they saw that lots of people really believe in the system. It is all about belief, isn't it?

Yes and no. You have to separate science from faith. As a rule, belief in a system on a scientific basis lasts longer than unfounded belief in some AltCoin quickly brought onto the chain. If the fundamental scientific facts are not right, it will perish or sink out of sight.

It is all about trust in the stability of the system, the intrinsic value, the independence, the defense against attacks from hackers and from authorities and politicians. The more independent and the more stable a cryptocurrency is, the more people will trust it, and the higher it is traded. It is of no use to construct a miner that mines a currency that is unstable or easily manipulated. Or worse, a currency that can be influenced or even controlled centrally.

So where does the stability and robustness against attacks from outside come from? It's very simple: if a system can be changed easily, then it can also be manipulated easily. Bitcoin, and the great effort needed to keep the system running has been explained in this book. Thousands of people invest time and money in hardware and infrastructure for the operation of Bitcoin. That represents a lot of trust in Bitcoin. The hardware and the enormous energy costs (the Bitcoin network uses more electricity than the whole of Iceland) are caused by the consensus mechanism, which the miners are subject to in the calculation of a new block. Bitcoin uses a mechanism called *proof of work.*

Proof of Work

As the name suggests, this is proof that the work has been done. If enough electricity flows for millions of miners to be working and one of them correctly calculates the result using a complex formula, then electrical expenses have been incurred in creating this new block. The electricity costs incurred in calculating a block can be gauged precisely, and so can the computing power with which you can, on average, calculate a block before anyone else to get the payment. That is what mining is all about.

If the algorithm is very complicated and hard to calculate, then a lot of energy will be needed. In fall of 2017, rough estimates of 1.2-gigawatt hours per day were used by the Bitcoin network. At normal domestic electricity prices, that is an investment of US $156,000 a day!

However, each day, 144 blocks were mined, which equates to 1,800 new Bitcoins generated. These have a value, at a rate of "only" US $10,000 per Bitcoin, or US $18.8 million. Added to that are the transaction fees of, on average, 160 Bitcoins. That is another US $1,600,000. So, in total, Bitcoins at a value of around US $20 million a day are credited with energy costs of about US $156,000. This calculation is, however, only an approximation, because investment and operating costs of the mining installations are not considered, and neither the higher rate — in December 2017 it was US $10,000 per Bitcoin — nor the cheaper locations where mining farms are typically found are considered either. Instead of US $0.13 per kWh, only US $0.06-0.08 per kWh are charged.

The nonetheless enormous energy costs result mainly from the complexity of the calculations as they become more challenging with the increasing difficulty. The more miners that connect to the system, the higher the difficulty and the more energy is needed.

If the formula were simpler, then there would be correspondingly less energy required. If the formula were much too simple, then anyone could calculate a block with an abacus or in their heads. With a simple formula and the same hash power in the whole network, there would naturally be chaos. Everyone would find a block every second, the network would be inundated with new blocks and new chains would constantly be formed, which would then have to be deleted a few seconds later.

That is nothing bad in itself because at some point the longest chain would come through and win, but the system could be dominated by someone with a lot of money and would thus not be safe. Theoretically, an entity with a lot of resources, say a state, could simply acquire enough computing power to calculate the simple formula, and then generate the most blocks, thus replacing the blockchain on the nodes as they wished. That would be possible with only 51 percent of the total hash power in the net, because the blocks would then come from one place and form the main chain. All other nodes would overwhelmingly have to follow this chain.

The more difficult and expensive it is to consolidate this mining power, the more secure the whole network is. For Bitcoin, the expense for the miners is enormous and bound up with high electricity costs. This is why the net is secure and very stable.

The costs and effort with, for example, LiteCoin are not as high, and this is reflected directly in the price. It is basically the same with silver and gold. Mining for gold is more expensive and takes more effort than mining for silver, and that is why the gold price is correspondingly higher.

Bitcoin Mining is a Question of National Security

Bitcoin mining has become so important that it is even important for states to be involved. State involvement came about as more and more politicians and policy-makers began to understand Bitcoin and blockchains. This is a good thing because it leads to higher security of the Bitcoin blockchain.

The temporary dominance of China in mining could have lead to larger issues. China's dominance was due to the fact that the miners in China had access to cheaper electricity, and therefore the returns on the mining farms were accordingly high. Also, the Chinese operators simply installed the hardware in halls near little-used or de-commissioned hydro-electric power stations in the mountains. In addition to resulting in a cheaper electrical source, the cool air at high altitudes leads to easier cooling of the miner hardware, which can get very hot.

All in all, these are very good conditions that the Chinese operators exploited. That led to a large proportion of the hash power being located in China. Theoretically, this meant that the Chinese government could have indirect control of over 50 percent of the hash power, giving it the potential to manipulate the Bitcoin blockchain to a certain extent. This made many uneasy.

The subject of crypto has come to the attention of high-level authorities in many countries, and is being taken very seriously as a result of the potential national security risks. Many countries have begun to take direct and indirect steps to counter this risk. A close acquaintance of Russia's President Putin announced in late summer of 2017 that over $100 million was to be invested in a mining farm in Russia. Americans are also building large mining farms, especially in the state of Washington. In Washington State, on the west coast of the United States, there is also cheap hydroelectric power. It is also not as hot as it is in the South, so the combination of a cool climate and cheap electricity makes mining very lucrative.

Other countries are building up as well—there are more and more mining installations in Northern Europe, including Scandinavia and Iceland, Japan is undertaking intensive research and testing new technologies that will make mining faster, and the first ASCI chips with a slimmer design, better performance and less energy consumption have already been announced.

One way to create trust is by using complex calculations that require expensive, specialized computers. It has proved itself so far for Bitcoin and the other cryptocurrencies that mine with Scrypt—that is, LiteCoin and its clones. Of course, many developers have also thought about alternatives that allow consensus on the blocks and allow numerous transactions without sacrificing that trust.

For this reason, there are a few other consensus procedures to achieve this aim. The most prominent is the *proof of stake*.

Proof of Stake

This is, in principle, evidence of stakeholding. This is comparable to a share of a company. If you own shares, you have a vote. If you have ten shares, you have ten votes. That does not appear particularly secure, but it can be implemented without the great expense of energy.

To guarantee security, a further mechanism has been conceptualized. If you want to vote, you have to deposit some of your coins into the affected blockchain. That means the miner does not have to pay for any electricity but does have to deposit coins, which are not liquidated, as long as it is active as a miner. Only when it has been established that its block validation complies with the rules, and that the security of the blockchain has been maintained, does the mining node get back its deposit, which had been blocked. As a reward, the miner also gets a part of the transaction fees.

The blockade lasts many blocks — anywhere from 30 to 100 blocks, for an example — depending on the blockchain to ensure fair play. If the node "cheats" and, for example, passes on a block in a prohibited format, then it loses the deposited coins. That is the fine and should lead to everyone acting honestly.

Proof of stake is disputed though, mainly for the following two reasons: First, the deposit of coins requires that those who want to mine — that is, those who can either adhere to or change the rules — already own coins. Those who own more coins can mine more, and those who mine more receive more rewards. In other words, the rich become richer. That is certainly a point of criticism within the community, which at its core represents liberal and humane views. This criticism, however, is only of a philosophical or political nature and not really dangerous to the function or security of a proof-of-stake blockchain itself.

The second point of criticism is much trickier from a security standpoint. As the deposited coins are of the same currency that is being mined, a rise in the rate could lead to the reward for mining being higher in total than the coins deposited for voting. So, if you had to deposit ten tokens with a value of US $3, and after 100 blocks at ten minutes a block you receive seven coins in total as a transaction fee, you would take a loss at that rate. But if the rate rose from US $3 to $7 over the 100 blocks at ten minutes, or 16.6 hours, then a profit has been made even though the 10 coins deposited are lost. That comes to US $30 invested and, despite the fine, US $49 received. It makes sense to cheat.

This financial mechanism cannot be simply applied with proof-of-work mining, because deployment and profit are not done with the same monetary instrument. If you buy electricity to mine, you do not get electricity back but just newly mined coins, which are traded at a certain rate. Both assets are completely independent of each other because the electricity must be paid for anyway.

Against this background, it is very important to investigate closely how the proof-of-stake process is implemented in detail. The Ethereum blockchain, which at the moment works with a proof of work, is to be converted to proof of stake. It remains to be seen how it will be converted and whether the trust in this blockchain and with it, the cryptocurrency Ether will remain.

Delegated Proof of Stake

In another type of the proof-of-stake procedure, the consensus about the right block can be transferred to authorized nodes. Participants can thus transfer their votes to a delegate, or a representative. These nodes are called validator nodes or supernodes, depending on the system.

Nodes that do not wish to be active themselves send coins to the supernodes, and these supernodes deposit the coins, check the blockchain, and validate blocks and transactions. If the supernodes then receive the transaction fees as payment, they share this with their voters, according to a certain key.

Proof-of-stake algorithms make sense in some circumstances in a permissioned blockchain. In this type of blockchain, which generally cannot guarantee the truth of the data, the consortium partners involved can determine the decision, or the stake, in accordance with their share, and vote accordingly.

Depending on how it is applied, then, proof of stake is the better version of a consensus algorithm but is far from being as trustworthy as a proof-of-work system. It is advantageous that a proof-of-stake system can be very fast because it does not require any complex calculations. As always, advantages and disadvantages must always be weighed against each other, and you must choose one process or another.

Alongside these two proof-of procedures there are a few others, and more are constantly being added. There are no limits to creativity.

Other Proof-of Procedures

With a proof-of procedure, it must be demonstrated that the data in a block corresponds to the truth. The more broadly these procedures are applied, and the more times they are used to demonstrate the truth, the better. If the proof-of procedure is complicated, complex and expensive, then it might be ideal, but not necessary in every case. Proof of stake within a permissioned blockchain is a good example of a simplified procedure that still serves its purpose adequately and can be used considerably more easily, more efficiently and primarily, more cost-effectively.

You can, of course, combine proof of stake and proof of work and create, for example, a proof-of-activity algorithm. In a proof-of-activity algorithm, the data blocks are mined with low difficulty by proof-of-work miners but then transferred to the validator nodes, which for their part select a block as legitimate by proof of stake. Through the simplified proof-of-work algorithm, the calculation does not cost as much, which lowers the security. To increase the security again, an additional proof-of-stake algorithm is added in afterward.

The purpose of mining is generally not just the generation of new coins, but also the securing of the network against attacks. The more expensive it is, the less an attack is worth it. Some thought, what if the whole of mining was just turned on its head? With the proof-of-burn algorithm, bought coins that were generated previously, are sold, and the miner must prove that it has destroyed these to be able to vote. That also costs money and quickly becomes too expensive for an attacker.

For other blockchains, the proof of space is used. The proof-of-space method determines whether the participant makes enough storage space available for writing and reading procedures, and then provides the corresponding confirmation rights accordingly.

Other methods include proof-of-authority, proof-of-elapsed-time, proof-of-luck, proof-of-minimum-aged stake, proof-of-Hodl, proof-of-ownership, proof-of-retrievability, proof-of-secure erasure, proof-of-storage, proof-of-stake-time, proof-of-time, proof-of-use and others.

Up to now the original model, proof of work, has clearly prevailed and proved itself.

Together with the confirmation of the blocks and the receipt of the reward for this confirmation, the consensus methods are also responsible for another very important function within the network—they determine, in some cases, the new functions that a network gets.

The Network is Forked

It has already been described how AltCoins arise from copying the code. A net's existence and functionality depend on whether the miners and the nodes all have the same understanding regarding the functionality and use the right consensus mechanisms. If a miner generates a proof-of-work block according to the rules of Bitcoin Core and another proof of stake according to other rules, then that is not compatible.

People are different, and everyone has their own ideas and their own economic incentives for going left and not right. Anyone can copy the open-source code and start his or her own AltCoin at any time. The problem is the miners that then support this blockchain. You always need appropriate computers, GPUs or ASICS to build the blocks together, regardless of which mining algorithm you use. So, it is not about a new coin, an AltCoin, which may have one or several new properties; it is about adding new properties to an existing blockchain and being able to continue using the existing mining power. This is where opinions divide and there are lively debates in the community involved that sometimes become very personal.

Bcash is a good example.

The Scaling Debate

In recent years, the interest in Bitcoin has risen enormously and more and more people have bought Bitcoin. Many people are trading with them, and others want to use Bitcoins to make purchases. Others, the so-called "Hodlers" just want to use Bitcoin as a long-term investment.

The term hodlers come from a typo—"hodl" instead of "hold." As it sometimes happens, the term became entrenched in the Bitcoin community. Instead of being called "holders," long-term Bitcoin investors are referred to as hodlers.

For hodlers, the Bitcoin is like gold. Buy it, let it sit, and then after a few years, sell it if needed. An enormous growth in value can be expected. Others see Bitcoin as money, and if money is in your pocket, you can buy the everyday things you need. Bitcoin should − like the dollar, the pound, the Euro and the yen − be just like money that you can use anywhere.

Along with Bitcoin users themselves, there are a few other actors in the Bitcoin network whose interests are completely different. The miners are entirely concerned with transactions. They receive a transaction fee for every transaction. For miners, the idea of using Bitcoin as money is very lucrative.

The throughput of the Bitcoin network was technically limited due to the complex mining algorithm and the long block times. Even in an ideal scenario, the Bitcoin network couldn't carry out more than seven transactions per second with the existing algorithms. That far too few, if you consider how many around the world wish to use Bitcoin as a regular currency. To compare, Visa, with its centralized network, can process 2,000 transactions per second (tps). PayPal can handle 115 tps[9]. So there had to be a change in Bitcoin's software if it were to work as a regular currency.

In response to this, developers began to develop an upgrade of the Bitcoin Core software, named *SegWit*. This upgrade was intended to remedy a few errors that could lead to serious problems, and also to make a higher throughput of transactions possible. SegWit would clean up the blocks and create the conditions for a new network that was run on and securely connected to the Bitcoin network. This made hundreds of thousands of transactions per second possible. The whole thing was published as BIP 141, or Bitcoin Improvement Proposal Number 141.

Everyone Must Participate

The basic algorithm of the blockchain requires many participate, and the new software also must be installed. To signal that they

---

[9] https://cointelegraph.com/news/how-sharding-based-blockchains-could-handle-more-transactions-than-visa

were on board, those who wanted to support BIP 141 had to set a Bit, or software code, in the new software.

It was important that the miners and all the nodes made this software upgrade because they would have to deliver the blocks in a new format, and the nodes would need to accept this new format. Installing the new software ensured that everything could run automatically and that the signals from to miners could be transmuted correctly. If 95 percent were to signal that they were participating, the new software would be automatically activated. From then on, mining would be done with the SegWit method, and the blocks would be attached to the existing blockchain according to the new standards. That was the plan.

In the beginning, there was no doubt that SegWit would be accepted, because, ultimately, security updates and the capacity for more transactions are always good. It surprised the community that a large proportion of the miners were not sending any SegWit signals. There was a dispute that went on for years until developers found a way to get SegWit up and running. This route was very turbulent, however, and will be described in more detail in the following section. It is as exciting as a whodunit, and the debate had still not been settled by the time this book went to print.

What needs to be clear first are the advantages and disadvantages of updates and upgrades, because not every change to the Bitcoin core code is welcomed by everyone. One or more interest groups can quickly form.

Dispute in the Bitcoin Community

The Bitcoin Core devs, that is, the programmers who took over the work on the code from Nakamoto, are very rational and conservative people and highly qualified experts in the field of software development and cryptography. They take a very conservative approach to changes to the basic software — that is, to the blockchain itself. Security is the most important requirement. That makes sense for a system currently worth over US $220 billion. That is as much as the International Space Station is worth. There, too, safety is the number one priority, because no one wants to risk lives and the invested assets must be protected.

No one would take up a module that had not been thoroughly tested and attach that module to the ISS, if it was unknown how that module would affect the pressure on the whole structure, or whether the other modules could withstand it. There could easily be a group of companies, however, that would take the risk if they could be relatively sure that their experiments were going to be carried out safely within weeks, before the new model made the whole structure unstable. This group would want to activate the new module.

Another scenario could be that NASA and the ESA would want to send up a module that could pass on radio signals better and faster than the current technology. Unfortunately, one of the suppliers for this module is also a manufacturer of transmitter amplifiers for use on Earth and makes a lot of money with these amplifiers. If this company were to support the new ISS module, then business with the transmitter amplifiers would decrease and a lot of money would be lost. On the other hand, the supplier would not want to risk losing business from NASA and ESA. The best strategy, then, would be to join in with the development of the new modules and slow it down, without anyone noticing. Whenever a lot of money is involved, the true interests are often divergent, and everyone plays their own game.

Only about 25 to 30 percent of the miners were sending SegWit signals. Too few. The activation threshold was set at 95 percent. The Core devs wanted to be certain that the Bitcoin net would run through it without any problems. That is why they wanted the 95 percent agreement that never came.

So, there was no new software and the community argued. Some wanted to treat Bitcoin like gold, others wanted fast transactions with low fees. The limit of the individual blocks, set at 1 MB, was repeatedly identified as the restriction, which may not have necessarily been true.

The money faction wanted larger blocks, and one of the well-known people in the crypto scene, Roger Ver, who is also known as "Bitcoin Jesus," became the spokesperson for the so-called *Big Blockers*, the faction that wanted to introduce the larger blocks of 8 to 16MB. The Bitcoin core faction wouldn't listen, because for them the technical risk was far too high. And, explained the few who intervened in the discussion from Core, the demand on the nodes from the larger blocks would be so high that the hardware would become too expensive. That, in turn, would enable fewer people to operate a node, which would lead to centralization. Centralization is exactly the opposite of what Bitcoin was created for.

Bitcoin Unlimited

Roger Ver started Bitcoin Unlimited, and a few developers then started to write software that could generate larger blocks. Some nodes and a few miners were equipped with it. However, the whole thing seemed to have been put together in a hurry and there were failures and fatal malfunctions of the Bitcoin-Unlimited nodes. The normal Bitcoin network remained unaffected and functioned like a well-oiled machine. The Bitcoin Core developers never batted an eyelid. There seemed to be no solution.

That was to change in the summer of 2017 with the *New York Agreement* (NYA). Representatives of the different groups met at a conference in New York. A paper was drafted and signed in which the representatives agreed that *SegWit2x* would be developed. SegWit2x would allow SegWit to be introduced, and block size to be increased from 1 MB to 2 MB.

SegWit2x was introduced as BIP 91. Since SegWit controlled the blocks in terms of their content along with the other upgrades, and thus could create more room for transactions, and 2x-blocks with up to 8 MB capacities would be possible. To do this, a *Hard Fork* would be necessary.

At the same time, the sword of Damocles was over the miners in the form of BIP 148, which was a *UASF*, or User Activated Soft Fork.

Soft Fork vs. Hard Fork

It is actually very simple. A soft fork is when the nodes and wallets can accept and check the new blocks without having to run new software. In a hard fork, the nodes and wallets would all have to run a new software version.

A soft fork is compatible with the past and all old data is processed just the same as the new data and block formats. It makes no difference whether an exchange or a wallet provider is running new software or not; the new data structures that are propagated across the network can be processed by every participant in the system without requiring new software.

A hard fork is different. Everyone is forced to run new software because otherwise, they can no longer participate. You can imagine the anger of users who look in their wallets and may still see their Bitcoins, but can no longer move them.

This is most easily understood using the size of the blocks as an illustration. Nakamoto set the upper limit for individual blocks at 1 MB. One of the things the nodes check is that the blocks are all no larger than 1 MB. If they are just one byte larger, then they are immediately rejected as invalid by the nodes. Thus, no block that is too big can ever be attached to its own existing chain, much less passed on to other nodes. The miner can receive no payment and has mined for nothing. The energy invested has gone to waste, the electricity costs paid for nothing. These measures keep the system stable and secured against tricks.

What about blocks that are smaller than 1 MB? No problem. Nakamoto only set the upper limit at 1 MB. Anything smaller can be processed without difficulty.

If the Bitcoin Core software is changed into a form such that, from a certain date, the block size may only be 0.5 MB, then that is no problem for the whole system, because the new rule is included within the old rule. Blocks that are 0.5 MB can be processed without difficulty in the existing system. That is a soft fork, a backwards-compatible change. If 51 percent of the nodes run this software, then in the future, only blocks with a maximum size of 0.5 MB will continue the blockchain, because these 51 percent of the nodes no longer accept the other blocks and these 51 percent generate the longest chain. It makes no difference whether the remaining nodes update their software to the latest status or not, because they function either way.

If, however, software is installed that can accept blocks larger than 1 MB and this software runs on 51 percent of all nodes, only that 51 percent can accept and process the new blocks, because the remaining 49 percent must reject the blocks as too big. The others will be forced into updating if they wish to continue their participation. This is a hard fork.

In reality the result is not so black and white. In general, a hard fork just results in a new chain that operates independently of the existing chain, mostly by fewer nodes and miners. This is what happened when Bcash branched off from the Bitcoin blockchain on August 1st, 2017.

What that means will be explained shortly. First, you need to know the sub-categories of these forks. That is, those with a "UA" before hard fork (HF) or soft fork (SF).

UASF and UAHF

The UA stands for "User Activated." But who are these users?

Users in Bitcoin, and every other cryptocurrency, are those who buy and sell the coins, as well as those who use them as currency. Contributing users are those who keep the system running and secure, i.e., the node operators and the miners. The service providers, the exchanges and wallet operators are users who have to access a node and can participate.

There are over 12,000 nodes in the Bitcoin blockchain saving the current blockchain and adding on the current blocks. That is already more than 12,000 users in this category. That means that there are many more users in this category than there are miners, who carry out no functions at all that would be important or necessary for distribution over the net. It is, in fact, the nodes that have the power because they decide whether they are going to accept a block from a miner or ignore it because it does not comply with the rules. This is the most frequently misunderstood aspect of the Bitcoin network and the concept eludes even many experts. It is only because of the power of the nodes that the pseudo-power of the miners could be broken at all in the case of Bcash. If the power really had been with the miners, then BIP 148 would have remained an empty bluff.

BIP 148 — a UASF

The agreement with the miners about a signal in the blocks was introduced a few years ago by the Bitcoin Core developers to communicate with the miners and give them an opportunity to bring their mining software up to date before an upgrade. That is, to a status that the developers, with their conservative style, regarded as secure, and used software that had previously been discussed and tested sufficiently. The idea was to allow the miners to be involved seamlessly and it was suited to the signal mechanism that was also used for SegWit. In any case, any miner who did not run the new software promptly would not be able to generate any reliable new blocks, and would therefore not be able to receive any payments or transaction fees. To prevent the loss of earning opportunities for the miners, this communication was built-in via a signalling Bit, that is, a marker in the generated block.

When the miners did not signal sufficiently and the discussion about the larger blocks began, there was a group of developers who did not want to watch this game anymore. For whatever reason, there were a few miners who had no interest in SegWit, although SegWit made more transactions possible, which was the express wish of most miners, as it led to more transaction fees. If everyone paid for their coffee in Bitcoin, the transaction fees would add up.

In response, BIP 148 was published. If sufficient nodes installed these updates, then these nodes would just refuse blocks from August 1st, 2017 in which SegWit was not signalled. It should be noted that the nodes had to run this software, not the miners. That is a very important distinction.

This was a user activated soft fork. An action that now forced the miners to act quickly because August 1st was just around the corner, and the nodes had been equipped with the new software. If the miners wanted to continue to earn money with Bitcoin mining after August 1st, 2017, then they would have to signal SegWit long enough before the 1st to get around this UASF.

Then the original SegWit would be initiated a short time later, because 95 percent of the miners would have to have signalled SegWit. That was a wicked trap into which the miners stumbled. The only way out seemed to be to signal SegWit2x as per the NYA quickly enough so that the UASF was not activated. Unlike the original SegWit BIP, where 95 percent signalling was needed, it was only 80 percent for SegWit2x, and thus it was easier to achieve.

In the weeks before August 1st, the miners began to signal SegWit2x and, two weeks before the deadline, an 80 percent agreement had been achieved. SegWit2x was activated and after a short time. Everyone was pulling together because the remaining 20 percent had to either activate 2x or no longer mine after the 1st.

A technical lock-in sequence was started. After this, an activation sequence was started, which also lasted two weeks. After that, SegWit was activated.

The 95 percent SegWit threshold had been exceeded because all miners had, in the meantime, signalled SegWit2x, and therefore, the original SegWit could be activated. It took a few years longer than anticipated but ultimately, it succeeded. SegWit has been running since then without instability, and has significantly increased the data throughput in the Bitcoin blockchain through the new structures. Fees have sunk, and the basis for *secondary layer solutions* is in place. This is considered by the crypto community to be a great breakthrough.

To SegWit or Not to SegWit; That Was the Question

What follows is mostly unproven. It is largely pure speculation, but it does appear to be the reason why a certain group of miners did not support SegWit.

Different motivations in relation to the ISS , the International Space Station were illustrated previously. One was that the manufacturer of ground radio amplifiers might have lost money if the ISS module were to improve the connection. At the same time, suppliers might want to stay on board because there was also a lot of money to be made with the ISS program. This dilemma was best solved by the manufacturer biding time without the other participants knowing.

A miner that was also a manufacturer of ASIC mining chips had a similar problem. This manufacturer produced specialized chips and built miners. It sold these miners all over the world and operated mining farms, predominantly in China, as it was also a Chinese manufacturer. Up to 30 percent of the total hash power of the Bitcoin network was assigned directly or indirectly by this pool.

So far, so good. But the manufacturer had a dirty little secret. It had designed, developed and produced the chips itself, and it had built in a little back door. The chip could be controlled so that it could calculate faster — 10-15 percent faster. That might not sound like much, but extrapolation suggests a monetary advantage of over US $100 million per year — US $100 million at a rate of US

$3,000 per Bitcoin. At the time of going to print, the rate was over US $10,000.

The manufacturer, which was using its own chips, used, or would have used, these secret codes and in doing so could mine itself a significant advantage. As said, that has not yet been proved, but there are many indicators that it must have been so.

100 Million Reasons for Preventing SegWit

The question now is what all that about SegWit has to do with activating the module. SegWit would have prevented the execution of the secret code and the advantage would have been lost. So the miners had at least 100 million reasons to prevent this and delay it as long as possible.

As far as anyone knows, the manufacturer did not send this code to its clients, but only sped up its own installations with it. Illegal? No, because in a public system, everyone can do what they want, as long as the community permits it. The UASF disrupted this. The community had a lever that leveled the playing field for everyone. This is how things regulate themselves over time in a worldwide distributed network — if enough participants work together.

After the UASF became a threat for this miner, the decision for SegWit2x was accelerated, because at least the 1 MB upper limit would be lifted, and the 2 MB block size would be introduced. If you were going to lose the mining advantage, then at least the blocks should be bigger.

That was the plan, but it didn't work out that way because the 95 percent was reached, and the original SegWit was activated. As a result, the 2x hard fork was canceled in November 2017 after a lot of back and forth. The majority of users had resisted it.

These users were right to resist it because a decentralized system cannot be changed by contract, even if it was signed in New York. The NYA was not signed by everyone, nor could it have been, and so it was nothing more than an attempt to regulate Bitcoin by decree. This was an action that could have shaken trust in Bitcoin, had it worked. The system and the participants were strong enough to successfully defend against this centralized, very well-organized and professionally orchestrated attack and maintain the decentralized and manipulation-proof properties.

But when hundreds of millions are at stake, people do not give up easily. In the summer of 2017, another company that many assumed was close to the previously mentioned miner announced an emergency plan in case the SegWit upgrade failed. The emergency plan was a hard fork with bigger blocks that could function without SegWit.

Bcash is Born by Hard Fork

At some point, the strategy changed; it is not clear whether this change was connected to the original SegWit's sudden activation instead of the 2x. The hard fork was going be made anyway because a group of people claimed that they were not convinced that SegWit would work. All sorts of PR announcements were produced and on August 1st, this hard fork was produced. Thus, as the initiators claimed, Bitcoin Cash, the "true" Bitcoin, was initiated.

In general, hard forks are used to create a new cryptocurrency. This begins with the first block, the genesis block. Miners help with building up the network because they are hoping for financial success, and a group of activists and participants use this new cryptocurrency from that point. That is what happened with LiteCoin, Monero, Zcash and many others. It was not so for Bcash, which was assigned the ticker symbol BCH instead of BTC, like the original Bitcoin.

Bcash branched off from a certain block in the main chain. The same code was used, and that led to the historic inventory of the chain being transferred as well, or every Bcash coin having its beginning in the original chain. That in turn meant that everyone who had a Bitcoin at the time of the branching off now also owned a Bcash coin. Everyone suddenly had exactly as many Bcash as they had previously had Bitcoins. This gave rise to a host of problems.

Problems upon Problems

For one thing, there was the problem of the high difficulty already described. A much bigger problem, however, was the question of how a user could get at the Bcash. To do that, you had to log into a Bcash wallet with a private key and transfer the Bcash. Anyone who has read this book this far will understand immediately that that is an absolute no-no. No one with half an understanding of how important the private keys are would ever use them in a strange wallet that is new to the market. You would still use the private key for your Bitcoins, but what if the Bcash wallet had an error and then all the Bitcoins disappeared?

The wallets of the exchanges were plagued by the same problems except, in this case, it would be customers' money that disappeared. For that reason, some exchanges announced that they would not be supporting Bcash. Period.

But that would not do either because it would mean that customers would be deprived of Bcash's value. This was a completely new situation. Some exchanges have enabled payments, while others are still working on it. Nobody is enthusiastic about it because there are additional costs for the programming that is required of the exchanges and wallet-producers.

The Bcash rate was very volatile and reached US $700 at its peak, sometimes with a low volume of trading. It then underwent a succession of losses. At the time of printing this book, the Bcash rate was hovering at about $2.000.

Although the rate is only 10−15 percent of that of Bitcoin, it is gifted money for most Bitcoin hodlers. The question is how can you change this Bcash into Bitcoin without running the risk of Bitcoins being lost. In this case, as always, it is crucial to keep your own private keys. Absolutely crucial.

Securing Forked Coins

Securing forked coins requires some effort, but it is the safest way to make a little more money − about 10−15 percent more.

The first and most important step is to secure your Bitcoins.

First, you transfer your Bitcoins to a new address, so that they are safe so long as you have the private key for this new address. Next, you take the old private key and use it in a Bcash wallet so that the Bcash coins are displayed and can be transferred from there. Nothing can happen to the Bitcoins because they are no longer under the old address generated with the old key.

The next step is to send the Bcash to an exchange and change them into Bitcoins. You then send these Bitcoins to the new Bitcoin address. Done!

You must be careful to do it exactly like this, because if you accidentally send the Bitcoins to a Bcash address due to a faulty Bcash wallet, or a faulty exchange function, they are irretrievably lost.

In public systems, different people follow different philosophies. That is a good thing and means a little freedom. But people need to be assured that nothing is lost, and it needs to be easy for everyone to manage. But the blockchain will not disappear, and more and more specialists are developing systems that can be operated easily and conveniently. Just like the internet itself. In its early days, the internet was very complicated, and then came the world wide web simplified things. Today almost everyone uses the internet and most people can manage it well.

The Future of Bitcoin

SegWit laid the basis for an enhancement that could allow Bitcoin to become a real alternative to credit cards. Using *payment channels* based on SegWit, Bitcoin can be quickly and cheaply scaled. Several hundred thousand transactions a second would be possible without difficulty and that would certainly be enough for everyday transactions. In addition to the fast throughput, the fees are nearly null and the transactions are almost always carried out immediately. This would be a dream payment network that satisfies all requirements.

A payment system for the 21st century, even. The banks are still operating a payment system that came out of the 1950s. At that time, a whole series of processing staff was necessary to carry out a whole range of checks before a payment process could be closed. It was necessary to check a ledger to see whether credit was available, and then the sum needed to be entered into a new ledger and deleted from the old one. Then the other bank had to be informed so that it could do the same thing on its side, and then they needed to check that both sides had done it correctly. This was complex and work-intensive. It was no wonder that it took days before a payment was debited and credited. If it was outside of business hours, it took even longer.

Eventually, the processing staff was replaced by computers, and banks began touting "a new branch that will never close." That was the birth of the ATM.

The computer also made an entrance into the bank offices, and the banks were able to move, debit and loan more money faster, and make money on interest.

Bitcoin changes everything. Blockchain changes everything. Using the new SegWit-based payment channels, more people will be able to free themselves from the stranglehold of banks and bid them farewell. It is just a matter of a few years.

Payment Channels

Payment channels are realized with a technology known as *Lightning*, which is the best known among these technologies. Lightning is one of the Second Layer Solutions previously mentioned, which only became realizable through SegWit.

Lightning makes a direct connection between peers. That is the basic principle. One of the two participants places a minimum sum in this Lightning channel. He sends, say, 0.001 BTC to the Lightning address and thus initially finances the channel. Generally, the customer does this. This transaction is also recorded in the Bitcoin blockchain and entered in the ledger.

The Lightning channel now has a credit that is assigned to the customer. The customer now goes to the corner cafe for breakfast and pays for it from the Lightning channel. The café receives the payment immediately because the channel shows credit. As not all the credit is used up, the customer goes several times over the next days to the baker, has breakfast, pays with Bitcoin via the Lightning channel, and the café owner is always paid immediately just as he would be with cash or a credit card. These transactions are not recorded in the blockchain; they are administered only within the channel. This is a kind of proof-of-stake process. Thus, no fees are due and the whole thing can happen in real time. No

Bitcoin miner and no Bitcoin node sees these transactions in the first place.

At some point, the channel is closed, either because one of the participants wishes it or because the credit is used up. The remaining sum and the closing balance is now entered into the Bitcoin blockchain. That means that only the first and last transactions are entered into the ledger while hundreds or even thousands of transactions may have been processed within the Lightning channel in real time, with no fees. That is a payment channel. Fast, free of fees and yet, blockchain-secure, because at the beginning and end there is a manipulation-proof entry into the ledger.

The system is easily understood, but it cannot be the final word. If you have to deposit payments everywhere, you will lose money, and the café will become like a bank, running customer accounts, even if this is automatic. This is not really practical but that is only the basis of a Lightning system. The real magic power is yet to come.

Payment Channels Become Networked

Assume Alice pays for breakfast in the corner café by payment channel and then goes to the butcher to buy meat for dinner. As in the café, she pays the butcher with her payment channel. The Lightning system can automatically connect the different participants, process the die payment bases and record them. It is not necessary for Alice to open a payment channel with the butcher and make another deposit there. The system connects the butcher to the café automatically and processes the whole thing. Lightning systems based on SegWit can automatically construct these channels, undertake payments in real time and record the crucial transactions securely in the Bitcoin blockchain. That is the real magic, and it will ring in a new payments era.

The future, then, looks rosy. Life will become simpler. But the future has not yet arrived, and so it must be constructed. Many approaches are being discussed, in all sectors and for all situations in life. But building the future, bringing new products into being and activating services costs money. Billions need to be invested. The question arises: Where to get it honestly?

The crypto sector would not be innovative if it did not have its own answer to this question. The answer is ICO, or Initial Coin Offering — that is, the first issue of a new cryptocurrency.
What that is all about, what the opportunities and risks are, is the subject of the next chapter.

Chapter 10 — The Basis of the ICO Investment Decision

The white paper

The white paper still plays an important role in investment decisions. It is the most important document to read and understand before investing in an ICO. Unfortunately, few understand the technical details and, as described, the technical papers often mutate into marketing papers that promise the moon. A real white paper is a technical description, in which the idea and its possible implementation are presented on a technical level. Everyone should read the white paper by Satoshi Nakamoto to at least understand the form, if not to be able to understand the content. Satoshi's approach and structure is a good one because he had no need to motivate anyone to make a monetary investment. You will not find any marketing-speak in his white paper — there are no profit forecasts or short charts — because he did not need to persuade or convince anyone. These sorts of promises are not found in any of the white papers at the basis of other successful ICOs. With this in mind, here is an important investment rule:

Investment Analysis Rule 1 — The White Paper

There are no marketing slogans, persuasive language or clever buzzwords in a white paper. It should never explain how much money you can potentially make by investing in a project, nor should it detail the risk of loss. You should find no profit charts from other crypto projects for comparison. That is not the purpose of a white paper. A white paper is a technical paper that the average layperson would not understand. Despite that, or perhaps because of it, it is the basis of a successful project.

Okay — if you can't understand it, why should you read it? A very fair question. Even a layperson with a minimal technical background can look at a document and recognize quite quickly whether it is a technical paper or a marketing paper. As humans, we have a natural sense of language; we don't have to understand the terms to instinctively know the difference between factual, technical language and marketing spiel. In the latter case, it is dubious! Leave it alone!

If you recognize that the white paper you have been presented with is actually is a technical paper, then there is a decision to make as to whether this technical idea is valid and sensible. That is somewhat more difficult for the layperson to determine, which is why the big investors consult with technical experts who have an in-depth knowledge and understanding of the subject and the marketplace. They will only invest in an ICO if a white paper is positively evaluated by these experts.

That makes sense for large investors, but how can the non-expert get involved? There are certain rules that have to be observed to protect the layperson in potential investments.

Investment Analysis Rule 2 — Who is Behind it?

Who has published this white paper? If there are no details about the author or authors behind a white paper, just a pay-in address for Bitcoin or Ether, this should ring alarm bells! Leave it alone!

For legitimate and credible white papers, the initiators are publicised and well-known in the sector. Due diligence can be carried out with a simple Google search.

A professional ICO investor crystallizes his approach in a very simple question he always asks at the start of his analysis, which is "How probable is it that the guys behind this are going to run off with my money ?"

To answer that, a simple Google search is not usually enough. However, it is typically quite easy to do some further research to get the answers and reassurance that you need.

One way to gather more information is to check out the relevant forums. Look at how and with whom the initiator(s) communicate. Keep in mind that it is not enough to just see here that the initiator once tweeted Vitalik Buterin, the co-founder of Ethereum. You have to evaluate how the initiator communicates with others and on what subjects. When he or she has exchanges with other technical experts, what do they write about? Are technical questions discussed? How do others respond to them? Do they seem to be held in good regard by others in the community? Even if you can't judge the questions and answers yourself, you will know whether it is technical details or whether they are getting a lot of praise or blame from colleagues. Getting heat or blame is not a red flag in itself — it can sometimes just be a sign this person has awoken interest in the community. Trust your instincts. If you do your due diligence and dig into enough research, you'll have an instinctive sense of whether the person is credible or not.

If you have identified that the person knows what they're talking about and is in relatively good standing, then that is a good basis for a small investment. However, it is still not enough to justify the risk of a larger investment. For that, you'll have to delve deeper.

To deepen your own analysis, you'll have to look at how many software codes have been published in the past by the initiator on the professional platform *GitHub*, and what happened to them. *GitHub* is an international platform that basically stores all the codes written by the programmers using the platform. The programmer can choose whether the codes are stored openly, just for the programmer themselves, or for the programmer's company. If they are stored openly, it is called *open source*, and this leads to another very important investment criterion.

Investment Analysis Rule 3 — Open Source

Only if the software is, or will be, available as open source, is an investment appropriate. The more other experts have worked on the same open-source code, the more valuable the project and the more secure the investment.

I know that sounds a bit strange because surely if there is only one white paper, there is only one code. That depends. In any case, there should be older codes by the initiator and the initiator should have worked on other crypto projects. If they have worked on other projects — or at least left helpful comments — you will be able to see these on *GitHub*. Basically, the more comments and so-called Forks and Commits, the more stable the code and the greater the chances of profit.

Another important indicator is the number of contributors to the project. Here, too, the rule stands; the more, the better. Up to a sensible upper limit, of course. If you've ever worked on a large group project, you'll know that the proverb "too many cooks spoil the broth" can all too often be true.

Ultimately, it is important to understand who is joining in and contributing. If you can see that several of the top people in the sector have been working on the project for a few years, you'll know the blockchains and the crypto project's code is going to be solid, which is a good investment signal.

However, you should not let yourself be deceived by so-called experts whose profiles on *GitHub* or other platforms claim that they have twenty years of experience as a professional developer and have worked for McDonald's and Coca-Cola, or for Boeing and for the White House. Even the evidence— usually links to purported references—are just a cheap trick and are often completely worthless. Judge people by quality work indicators. Real experts have submitted or commented on code lines, pointed out errors in codes, and generally been a helpful resource to the developer community. Anyone else is strictly for the birds and should be regarded as a hazard for investment.

Wow! All of that seems to be a lot of work—and it really is! Everyone has to decide for themselves whether they are going to invest or participate in an unregulated game of chance. If you are investing large sums, you are definitely advised to make this effort. Remember; no miracles happen in the crypto world, but you can make extraordinary amounts of money if you have done your homework properly.

The rule described here is commonly known. Anyone who wants to make an ICO—especially those following unspoken motives— often try to hide their lack of competence by linking with experts, allegedly! So please beware and put the time into doing your due diligence before you part with your hard-earned money.

Investment Analysis Rule 4 — The Advisor Ploy

With ICOs, an advisory board is often quickly founded and announced, which is intended to act in the role of advisor for the project. The existence of such a board engenders trust, because if Vitalik Buterin is advising a project, then nothing can go wrong, can it? Theoretically, the project stands a better chance, but in practice...

There have been reports of cases in which Vitalik Buterin was listed an advisor on a project board and he knew nothing about it. The initiators asked him a question about some technicality at a conference and he answered the question because he is a nice person. It must have been a great honor for him to have been instantly and unknowingly elevated to the advisory committee of the project. It was doubtless no honor for the investors who invested in a very dubious ICO.

Nowadays, you can find an advisory committee on nearly every ICO website. Many white papers will also include details of their advisory board. Many of the advisors are actually the initiators' advisors and are aware — unlike in the previous case — that they are listed there. Before you invest, you have to ask a couple of questions.

What is the advisor doing for the project, and can he really help or have influence? If he can help at all, how much time will he be able to devote to the project? Is this person a paid advisor who advises on a lot of projects because that is his or her job? Is this person truly contributing to the project? Will the project be any better because this consultant is advising?

If the answers to these question can be ticked off and you are satisfied that the advisor or advisors are contributing real value to the project, then that is another green light for investment in this ICO.

However, if this advisory board is just for show or is filled with paid positions, then you have to consider whether it really makes sense. It can be assumed that the wheat is quickly sorted from the chaff with this procedure because most ICOs are watched like hawks by the authorities around the world. Genuine advisors do not commit easily to projects because — time and energy aside — they are publicly named as associated with a project and thus could be personally liable if something goes wrong. Not to mention potentially tarnishing their professional reputation and credibility if a project goes very wrong. This would certainly cause anyone getting involved in a project to be cautious and check more closely when they are asked to publicly endorse a project and its initiators.

As already stated, a white paper has mutated from a purely technical discussion paper to a marketing paper in recent months. In fact, in many cases, these papers look a lot more like a financial prospectus than a technical document. So, it is time to dedicate some time to the regulations and check what ICOs are, or what they can be.

What are the Differences Between ICOs and IPOs?

IPOs (Initial Public Offerings) are stock floatations. IPOs are extensively regulated all over the world and are subject to strict conditions. These strict regulations are intended to protect the investor, though opinions vary as to whether they do or do not. The real debate is whether many these regulations are truly necessary or whether they simply line their pockets of advisors and bankers at the expense of the investors. Regardless of the legitimacy of these arguments, the plethora of regulations and requirements for stock floatation do exist and must be satisfied.

The same applies to any other kind of capital and investment brokerage. In nearly all cases, and in all jurisdictions across the world, a license is needed for such a business. That is typically in the form of an expensive bank license, which is likely out of the reach of a group of cryptocurrency enthusiasts—not that they would wish to conform to traditional banking regulations! In any case, crypto projects are usually started by liberal-thinking people who wish to break away from the power of the banks and state regulation. A bank license is the last thing they would want. That is where ICOs come in.

An ICO is a completely different affair because no money changes hands. The only thing exchanged is cryptocurrency, and these are not even qualified or recognized as financial instruments in most countries. For that reason, they should be unaffected by the regulations of the traditional financial markets.

This is a position taken by many. In fact, most authorities are at a loss for how to deal with the whole situation. It is not just different from country to country; even within one country, there can be differing views taken depending on which official, institution, or department you speak to.

In the USA, there are so many state centers and financial monitoring authorities that it would be a miracle if they all agreed. Is Bitcoin a currency or a commodity? Is it an exchange item, a private accounting system, or is it a financial instrument? What about the new belly-draft coin?

Are the stock exchange supervisors responsible for Bitcoin? Or is it the Securities & Exchange Commission (SEC), the Commodity Futures Trading Commission (CFTC), the Federal Reserve System ("Fed"), the Federal Deposit Insurance Corporation (FDIC), the Financial Crimes Enforcement Network (FinCEN), the Financial Industry Regulatory Authority (FINRA), the Office of the Comptroller of the Currency (OCC), the National Credit Union Administration (NCUA), the Consumer Financial Protection Bureau (CFPB), the National Association of Insurance Commissioners (NAIC), the National Futures Association (NFA)? Or is the responsibility placed on the president himself? Each institution has its own rules and regulations, along with their own opinion on cryptocurrency and ICOs.

This question becomes especially relevant to an investor if he has invested in an ICO and the ICO is then prohibited. If that happens, what happens to the money they have paid into the ICO?

Until autumn 2017, there was a whirlwind of various conferences all created to attempt to classify the newcomer. At the meetings and conferences, the employees of the state centers all said their piece, all countries, all authorities. The wilder the ICOs became, the greater the pressure placed on the officials.

In late summer, the American stock exchange supervisors (SEC) investigated the DAO ICO of 2016 and established that this constituted an issue of financial instruments. As a result, this ICO should have been subject to the same regulations as an IPO. However, since nobody had actually done that in person, no prosecution would follow.

The sector classified this as a warning. The SEC is said to have deliberately investigated DAO because the Decentralized Autonomous Organization was not actually a company with conventional structures. It was not structured like a company — it didn't have a board, officers or shareholders — and therefore could not be treated as one. The SEC could only fire a warning shot and wag a finger so they wouldn't lose face. Strictly speaking, they could have found against anyone who had supported the DAO, because even the offer to acquire an instrument is prohibited. However, many believed the SEC did not want to go that far. Instead, it is following a watching brie and watching every new ICO like a hawk.

If the DAO had been a Company

One additional factor to consider is that the SEC had probably become aware that it was not possible to just shut the system down. At the beginning of the 1990s — a time that is now known as the infamous dot-com bubble—things were much simpler. The SEC had a lot to do and was — in their view — very successful.
A crypto system on a blockchain is something very different — something they had no experience dealing with. Especially because it was a public blockchain that simply could not be switched off. If the DAO had been operated by a company, then the servers would no doubt have been deactivated and the handcuffs snapped shut.
However, in mid-September of 2017, just a few weeks after the statement by the SEC, an ICO prohibition was announced in China. This was not a surprising development. The ICO wheel was spinning faster than ever before, now reaching alarming speeds. And more and more people with no idea what they were doing were tempted into all kinds ICOs by blustering advertisers and finance providers peddling wild promises of fat profits.
May be it was the ICO of a bakery that finally broke the camel's back. They produced mooncakes, a popular snack in China, and wanted to earn a bit of money. The business of baking these little cakes was more effort than an ICO, so an ICO was propagated to expand. Maybe they wanted to hash the mooncakes and save this hash in a blockchain so that if it came to it, the customer would at least know what was making them feeling ill. However, many people raided their piggy banks for this and other similar ICOs. They blindly invested in all sorts of things without knowing what a blockchain is, what it means, or even without knowing what cryptocurrencies are. They knew nothing. They just saw the rate of Ethereum jump from $3 to $300—just like Bitcoin had jumped from $40 to $4,000—and it seemed like they had a once-in-a-lifetime chance to get in on the opportunity early. They didn't care what the project was called. Bitcoin, MoonCoin or Mooncake—it didn't matter. Their only aim was to get rich.
No wonder the authorities got involved and quickly shut them down. They immediately took a radical approach and ordered all the exchanges to close, but they might open again in a few months when they have the appropriate licenses.

Now, it appears that the sheriffs are regaining control of the Wild West and that cryptocurrencies are also going to be ordered and regulated. It remains to be seen how strongly they will try to access the markets and with what motivation. If it is up to the banks and most politicians, they will try to control or prohibit cryptocurrencies. These demands are repeatedly voiced by people who have absolutely no idea how decentralized systems operate. You can only wish them luck in switching off or controlling a genuine blockchain.

Investment Analysis Rule 5 — ICO Jurisdiction

Despite all of this, ICOs will not disappear. In fact, it will be quite the opposite. For a few months now, there has been some competition across the globe for the ICO site advantage. Come to Zug in Switzerland, say the Swiss. Come to the Isle of Man, say the British. Or there is Gibraltar, Malta, Singapore, and a few others who want their location to be chosen.

Switzerland seems to be in the lead because foundations are, and always have been, the hobby horse of the Swiss. Therefore, Switzerland seems to be the ideal site for ICOs with the foundation model. They specialized in this market long before others woke up, and in the pretty canton of Zug, they founded "Crypto Valley." "We quickly institutionalised the coincidence of the Ethereum Foundation and their ICO in Switzerland," said a spokesperson of the Crypto Valley Association.

The Ethereum Association also started its ICO from Zug in Switzerland in July 2014. Within just forty-two days, 31,591 Bitcoins, with a value at the time of $18,439,086, were sold for 60,102,216 ETH. That all happened completely legally under Swiss law. It was also more or less the birth of the Crypto Valley, where many more ICOs would be initiated in the following years.

Until the summer of 2017, the only competition was coming from Singapore, where lots of project groups and companies were situated and undertook their ICOs under the favorable regulations of the city-state.

The starting point of an ICO, the seat of the foundation, or the seat of the company are thus an important criterion for the investment. Switzerland and Singapore would probably not allow Mooncake ICOs. Nor would Gibraltar, the Isle of Man, or Malta. If the seat cannot be determined or is located in a lesser-known region, that should be a warning sign.

Exception to the Rule

A genuine technical paper, one that is verified technical experts, and a solid Foundation site are things to pay attention to when considering an investment in an ICO. These three factors will ensure you don't suddenly get a mooncake in front of you instead of a legitimate crypto project with great profit opportunities. Of course, just as with any rules, there are exceptions. For example, if the ICO maybe you haven't heard of the people behind the ICO but it is being made by an established and credible company or companies.

That was the case with the Kik ICO. Kik is a Canadian company that was founded in 2009 and produces a messenger app. Kik is in direct competition with Skype, WhatsApp and WeChat. Despite this tough competition, the Canadian's behind Kik have managed to gain popularity with over 300 million users — predominantly in North America — actively using their app. In addition, Kik has also received $120 million from traditional investors and venture capital firms. We can safely assume that these investors have carried out their own careful due diligence before investing.

After the Kik team experimented with various internal "currencies" like bonus points, loyalty points, and in-app purchasing, they discovered Bitcoin and cryptocurrencies. In late-summer 2017, they carried out an ICO with the KinCoin for the internal currency of the Kik Messenger. This rewarded users for certain activities in the future, and allowed them to earn internal Kin tokens, which they could then use to purchase things like stickers or emojis.

The ICO was very successful and brought in nearly $100 million for the company, which came from more than 10,000 backers in 117 countries. It was a complete success.

Not all Tokens are equal

Investment Analysis Rule 6 — The Type of Token

The initiators — the founders of the ICO — should have put careful thought and consideration into what kind of coin or token they want to issue. There are basically two types: the equity token and the internal currency, also known as utility token.

The equity token is generally directly or indirectly linked to the success of the company. The investors in an ICO receive a mid-term or long-term payment of interest for their investment if the project works. Token purchasers seldom get any voting rights or shares in the issuing company. In fact, in many cases, it is not a company issuing the tokens but a project or foundation that doesn't belong to anyone, therefore ruling out the possibility of acquiring shares.

There are a few completely "flat" ICOs that do nothing more than distribute a ten percent share — or however much is stated — to new investors via an ICO. Most of these shares are issued without voting rights and have nothing to do with the blockchain itself, nor do they give the investor any chance of disproportionate gain. It is precisely these types of ICOs that are catching the attention of authorities across the world. What this sort of ICO is doing is simple and is easily comparable with the public issue of shares in a company. It is sometimes even comparable with a stock offering, but it is only possible and legal in countries with appropriate requirements. For that reason, we categorize these ICOs as a *security* or *security coin*.

Anyone who invests in an ICO like this must be aware of the possibility that they have not acquired any shares, even though their money has been taken. In the worst-case scenario, those who have received the money wind up in jail and the company falls apart while the leader is behind bars. Even if only an investigation by the authorities and supervisory bodies is undertaken, investors must remember that the management can easily become distracted from their actual task, which is to develop the project. This is not ideal for the investor who has put their hard-earned money into funding the project. Along with that, it must be considered that acquisition of shares is very strictly regulated in some countries. In Germany, for example, you can only purchase shares in a limited company via a notarial contract. There is not yet a way for a notary to certify a transfer of shares by ICO.

The rule of thumb here is that there should be no investment in equity tokens.

Equity tokens are not ideal

As equity tokens are not ideal in the context of an ICO — and are also probably illegal — internal currency is the remaining option available to potential investors. This is the category that makes the most sense and that you can confidently support if you take all the other precautions outlined in this book.

An internal currency — or utility coin or token — basically means a currency within a project, where only these new tokens can be used to pay. If you want to buy stickers in the Kik Messenger app, you have to use their Kin-Tokens to pay. The system does not permit any other payment system. Users are forced to use the Kin-Tokens or else they cannot purchase any stickers. The token has utility.

Other examples are the various decentralized storage solutions like SIA and STORJ. Both of these blockchain systems allow people who have large hard drives, but who only use a part of it, to rent the unused part. Most computers now come supplied with hard drives of at least 500 MB, if not 1 or 2 TB. This solution makes sense because more and more digital merchandise is being purchased and saved by individuals, but unlike the cupboards at home where you can reorganize the shelves in spring, hard drives are constantly filling up faster than the capacity available. If you reach your limit and the 250 MB disks are full, a new computer or at least a new hard disk is bought. But this time, it is a 1 TB because you now know you will inevitably fill it in time.

This overcapacity on the hard drives of millions of users can now be utilized with the help of blockchain solutions like SIA und STORJ, where the blockchain manages the origin of the data, ensuring its properties are free from risk of manipulation. Additionally, the destination storage and other data are also written permanently into the blockchain, so all data owners are that their data demonstrably belongs to them and they can get it back at any time. If someone wants to store their data securely, like the author of this book during its creation, then decentralized storage methods are ideal. That's why there are half a dozen versions of the book draft stored decentrally on maybe thousands of hard drives and being secured via the SIA blockchain.

Why go for decentralized and not just use Dropbox or some other cloud service? This is a question that is frequently asked, and it makes sense because everyone has cloud storage these days and it is mostly free—at least, up to a certain volume. Even large volumes of cloud storage can be obtained very cheaply, and small- and medium-sized companies can very easily use the professional versions of online storage systems.

There are a few significant differences between a traditional cloud storage system—like Dropbox—and a decentralized storage system. Firstly, there is the price for the usage. Decentralized storage systems are significantly cheaper and offer larger volumes. More importantly, however, is the decentralized aspect itself. If you place data in cloud storage, then you are clearly handing the data over to a third party for safekeeping. If this third party—Dropbox, Microsoft, Google, Amazon or whoever—should fail, then the data is lost for the duration of this disruption in service.

You could argue that it is highly improbable that Microsoft or Google will fail because the data is stored in several versions in multiple redundant computing centres. And that is true—it is secure, including the various copies, barring theft by hackers. If hackers manage to break into the cloud, the data can be manipulated or stolen. And this type of security breach happens every day. To break into a decentralized system, however, is significantly harder and more complex than that—if not impossible. As a result, data stored decentrally is far more secure.

The WannaCry Virus and Others

Recently, hackers were repeatedly able to overcome the security measures of many companies and encrypt the data on their own storage systems. The virus that did this smugly notified those affected with a message stating that it would be happy to decode the data again if a certain number of Bitcoins were received in its Bitcoin address. Yes, wicked hackers also know and understand the advantages of Bitcoin, and they like the security of assets it provides. Naturally, these sorts of attacks are to be condemned, but it illustrates precisely why decentralized storage is so important.

In decentralized storage, the data are proportionally distributed and encrypted on the thousands of hard drives participating in the system. That would not be so simple without the blockchain; you would always need one central position to store the locations of all the data so that they could be accessed again. This central point would be the weakest point of the whole system because if this particular computer were attacked and cracked, all the data would be vulnerable again. Only a blockchain system can deliver the appropriate security mechanisms to secure data.

An additional advantage offered by the blockchain system is that the whole history is unalterably stored in the blockchain. The author can prove at any time when these texts were written, and if it came to it, any copyright disputes could be settled quickly and efficiently. In a cloud storage system, however, this time stamp has the potential to be changed. For a book project like this, that is a completely unfounded fear, but what if a pharmaceutical company has stored the research data for a multi-million-dollar drug patent and needs to find the conclusive evidence in a patent dispute? When it comes to potentially many millions of dollars, it's not outside the realm of reason to think that a competitor, rival or hacker would spend a substantial sum on hacking file data that is kept in cloud storage.

A Closed Value Circle

As such, systems are best implemented with a blockchain. It makes sense to have your own currency (tokens) running alongside the blockchain as accounting unit between storage provider and storage user.

If you want to store your files, say, on the SIA network, you will need SIA coins to pay for this service. Conversely, the provider, in return for the offer of his hard drive in the system, receives corresponding credits of SIA coins for storing the files of complete strangers.

If Alice wants to store her data in the SIA network, then she has to pay some SIA coins for this. Bob still has 600MB free on his hard drive and makes this available to the SIA network. The blockchain then takes the appropriate amount of SIA coins and credits them to Bob. At the same time, the data is also distributed and stored on other hard drives being offered by other participants in the SIA network, and they also receive the appropriate amount of SIA coins.

This alone constitutes a new value creation chain. Now anyone who has a PC can market it to earn some extra money in the background, so to speak. This may only be a few cents, but a few cents are better than nothing. This kind of value creation is only just beginning and will, with the continued success and spread of such systems, certainly lead to a redistribution of income and assets.

These blockchain-based, decentralized services around computers are parade applications of a blockchain. In the area of storage alone, there are three blockchain systems with outstanding ICO success.

One of the developers, David Vorick of SIA, made a remarkable statement at a conference, which made examples of these crypto companies for the sector. He said: "You cannot pay for our services by Visa because we take decentralization very seriously. Payment processing by Visa is a central service and is out of the question."

You Should Invest in People of Conviction

What types of people should ICO investors look for? For the most part, the ideal people to invest with have certain convictions and beliefs that they stand by, and which make the projects good investments. One such conviction is that it is not about money, but about changing the world. These people are generally not easily compromised by money, and people invest in them because they want to support their freedom—and because they can shape the future. Ultimately, that is something you can profit from as an investor. Of course, this only applies to those taking a long-term view, because systems have to be built up or at least introduced into and accepted by the market. That is a process that can take years, which is a factor that good investors will always consider.

Of course, there are also other motives related to why people invest in decentralized storage solutions. A participant on a discussion panel at a conference recently explained his motivation. He was revealed that he was playing with the idea of storing his brain on the internet, and as that required an enormous amount of storage, he took the precaution of buying lots of coins and secured a huge amount of storage at a good price. Perhaps he was also scared of someone stealing or hacking his thoughts from a central point. It sounds like a ludicrous idea, a fantasy from a futuristic movie, but it is anything but that when you truly think about it. One thing we know for sure is that the world will store more — not less. If sometime in the future hundreds of millions of sensors are all linked and are recording and saving data, then a guarantee of truth is needed. At the moment, that guarantee can only be provided by a blockchain storage system. Someone uploading his or her brain may seem far-fetched right now, but artificial intelligence is just around the corner.

Hard drives are not the only module that you can hire out on your computer. You can also rent out the computing power itself, which is made possible by the GOLEM system. Instead of storage space, CPU power is sold for GOLEM tokens.

Another project, named "RNDR" targets the user's graphic cards (GPU) and promises a significantly more lucrative use of the GPU than 3D animation by utilizing it for mining.

This is a remodeled sharing economy, and only the blockchain makes it possible.

The unanswered question is, naturally, how you use the SIA coins you have earned in the real world. Say, for example, if to buy something to eat. That is done indirectly by exchanging SIA coins into other currencies, such as Bitcoin or other cryptos, or even directly into a fiat currency. This will be discussed in more detail later because whether a currency is traded at an exchange or not is an important investment criterion.

However, another question arises: Why a currency of its own? There are over a thousand currencies by now, and it can be assumed that there will soon be ten or a hundred thousand. So, why is there an SIA coin, a FileCoin and a STORJ coin? The question becomes more pressing when you realize that most coins are issued on the Ethereum blockchain.

The ERC-20 Mechanism

One of the reasons why Ethereum (ETH) is currently trading at a rate of hundreds of dollars is the ERC-20 system. The ERC-20 is a standard that can be used as a basis for your own coin by using the Ethereum blockchain. The overwhelming majority of all ICOs are these kinds of ERC-20 coins.

ERC-20 tokens have become a sort of industry standard. But the question as to why a currency is based on another currency remains unanswered.

The most important reason is, of course, to decouple your own currency from the basis currency. If a new coin based on Ethereum with an ERC-20 token were to generate great demand, then only the new currency would profit and not every owner of Ether, the Ethereum's blockchain cryptocurrency. Conversely, the new coin would not be dragged down if there were a massive sale of Ether. That is the thinking behind it this system.

In an economic sense, having your own currency guarantees that the economic aspects of the project are more strongly considered than just the fluctuations of the underlying technology. You would also — theoretically, at least — miss out on the upward movements of Ethereum. However, both movements — upwards and downwards — each affect the new coin anyway.

The price of ICO coins is not dependent on the fluctuations in Ethereum itself, but rather by the lead cryptocurrency, Bitcoin.

Just like the tides of the sea, Bitcoin draws the market upwards and downwards with it. If Bitcoin rises, the others rise. If there is a correction with Bitcoin, all AltCoins are massively affected and lose value disproportionally.

If there was a total failure of Bitcoin, there is a good probability — approaching certainty — that the entire sector would collapse with it. All value would be destroyed within a very short time and it would be all over for the truth in a blockchain system. That could only happen if someone succeeded in hacking Bitcoin and interfering with it. Despite the millions of attacks on Bitcoin, we have not even come close to this kind of scenario playing out, nor can it be assumed it will ever happen. However, if you were to follow a strictly theoretical line of thinking, the inevitable consequence you will arrive at in this scenario is a total loss of all blockchain systems. The same would happen to the gold price if gold were to suddenly start growing on trees. In both cases, the chances of this happening are zero. So, back to reality, and back to the new tokens being sold in the framework of an ICO.

Regardless of the type of token or coin, there is another important aspect which plays a role in the investment decision. That is the so-called *token economy.*

Investment Analysis Rule 7 — The Token Economy

The token economy is another important factor for consideration when trying to evaluate a good investment opportunity. How are the tokens paid in used? Who gets how many tokens, and for what? When are tokens issued and under what conditions? How many tokens are there?

The economic interplay of all participants is of crucial importance for the success of an ICO investment.

The Bitcoin token economy is very well balanced and that is an important contributing factor for why Bitcoin is the most important and valuable cryptocurrency in the world. To begin with, the coins are not just distributed freely and easily. That is different for many other currencies that are available.

Coins Before the ICO

Coins that exist before the ICO is known as "pre-mining." These are coins already existed, even with the genesis block, which is the very first block. For example, let's consider a scenario where the initiators have generated, say, 10 million coins already and now generate 10 million more through an ERC-20 smart contract. If this second batch is then sold in an ICO for 1 million dollars, then the coins already present are now also worth 1 million dollars. You can become a millionaire that quickly and easily.

In an alternative scenario, it might happen that the mining algorithm has an error in it and the founders find themselves with a few million tokens because these were mined too quickly. The error is the remedied and the blockchain now runs perfectly. In fact, this very scenario has already happened and this cryptocurrency is worth a few billion despite that. However, that should remain the exception.

It is completely different for Bitcoin. From the very first block—the genesis block—mining was done with proof of work, and no one has simply been awarded millions of Bitcoins. This is certainly a huge quality feature which should be noted.

But Bitcoins are a cryptocurrency that have to be created, and a predefined quantity of new coins is generated through mining.

With ICOs, however, other stimuli are used for creating coins, and exactly how that happens could be divisive.

Quantity in Circulation and Total Quantity

Along with the number of coins that might already exist, there are other factors of great importance, including how new coins are generated, when they are generated, and how many are generated in total.

In the Bitcoin system, an average of 12.5 new Bitcoins are mined every 10 minutes. About every four years, the number of Bitcoins is halved by the system. Accordingly, in 2020, only 6.25 Bitcoins will be generated every 10 minutes. There is also a defined end of new Bitcoins. In total, there will never be more than 21 million Bitcoins. That fact is fixed and cannot be changed.

That is what gives Bitcoin its value; it has pre-defined inflation and is calculable. Ethereum also produces ETH according to defined rules and is to a large extent calculable. However, the Ethereum developers did not define an upper limit and thus ETH is subject to a completely different inflation model to Bitcoin. When making an ICO investment decision, you should certainly look at whether the number of new tokens is limited, how quickly they are created, and the method by which they are created. These are crucial criteria to take on board when considering the potential future value of a token. If the tokens can be produced indefinitely, increasing or decreasing depending on the mood and whim of the management, that should be a huge red flag that investors should not ignore.

The ideal scenario is a token that has a maximum number and is issued over the course of time depending on success. Of course, no one should be able to affect the issue of later tokens except the system itself. That is to say that there is no management, but, of course, with a decentralized blockchain, that goes without saying.

Together with the inflationary aspects, how and why these tokens are distributed is also important.

Who Receives How many and For What

The Kik ICO was probably so successful because lessons had been learned from the ICOs of the previous months, and because the token economy was well-balanced. Kik defined that there would be 10 billion tokens in total, and that 1 billion of them would be distributed during the ICO. That is a lot, but there is an upper limit that you can consider, even when figures in exponential form are constantly shown when calculating. Another three billion Kin are assigned to the foundation and serve the technical development and support for the system for the next years. These are released according to a precise plan and can only be used in accordance with the rules that are laid out in the foundation charter.

This leaves about six billion tokens, which are automatically issued to the users via the blockchain in a system that Kik calls the Kin Reward Engine. Users can get these Kin if, for example, they generate and distribute news or moderate an online group. That means that the Kin tokens are distributed within the community as a stimulus for users to actively participate on the platform. The users can make purchases within the system using the Kin, and the whole thing is a self-contained circulation.

This kind of neat token economy is not found in every ICO. In the meantime, the proportion that the founders assign to themselves has swung from about twelve to eighteen percent, which does not seem like a sensible decision. When you consider that the eighteen percent is relative, one has to wonder whether founders should really keep $18 million of a $100 million ICO just for their idea. Plus, there are new positions being invented which are also assigned a few percent here and a few percent there. Management makes six percent, marketing makes four percent, community service makes six percent, and so on. This type of structure should be closely examined before investing. The whole model is sometimes very complex in construction and not very transparent. Kik, for example, is not without complexities, but at least it is comprehensible and transparent. Better to leave it alone if there is too much complexity.

Although there is a total of 10 billion Kin tokens, only 1 billion of these will be available for distribution outside the system or to be traded via exchanges. Anyone who motivates a user with lots of friends and followers in Kik Messenger to open and moderate a group will need Kin to pay this user. An artist or fashion company has to either be heavy users of the Kin network themselves to earn corresponding amounts of Kin to open such groups themselves, or they will need to buy Kin from the exchanges and use these. Kik is assuming that after a few years, enough users can be reached that large brands will have to buy Kin to pay users. As there are only 1 billion Kin in the ICO, the price should rise, which is the purpose of investing after all.

From the investor's point of view, the aim of an ICO is that the price of the tokens rises. For that to happen, the new coin must, however, first be traded.

Investment Analysis Rule 8 — Exchanges and CoinMarketCap

Liquidity and fungibility of a new coin are the alpha and omega for investment. What is the use of 10,000 Turbo coins if they are not listed on the exchange and traded? If no one is buying these Turbo coins or exchanging them for other cryptocurrencies, then it is written into the blockchain unalterably and free from manipulation forever that the 10,000 Turbo coins are assigned to an specific address. The person with the private key to this address can move the coins. But where can they be moved to?

For this reason, it is of crucial importance to follow the media and online news carefully. It is a lot of work, but it is related to a lot of money, and that should not be forgotten.

The chatter on the various channels, predominantly Twitter, then Telegram and Slack, as well as the relevant blogs and crypto websites frequently discuss ICOs. If you keep yourself apprised of all the latest happenings as they occur, you will inevitably develop an instinctive feel for the coins that are sooner or later going to be listed on the exchanges.

Initiators are frequently interviewed in the various media, appear at conferences or maintain some kind of internet presence. You have to try to find information on exchange listings. You can, of course, go directly to the exchanges online and read their blogs to find the information you need. As previously stated, you have to make some effort if you want to invest your money sensibly and profitably.

Many ICOs in the past sold out very quickly. Sometimes, that was a matter of seconds, as in the case of BRAVE, an ICO that took in $35 million in under thirty seconds. That was a new record, but other ICOs have also sold out in a flash. Anything is possible in the crypto world.

When these things happen, many annoyed investors stand on the sidelines with long faces. Somewhere, though, there is someone who wants to sell their coins, but a lot of people then buy these coins from the ICO. Sometimes this is done directly, peer-to-peer, or via an online exchange.

While this is an opportunity, you must tread very carefully. There are small exchanges that are very flaky in their function and are not to be recommended. It might even be an exchange set up specifically for these coins. You have to examine the exchange very carefully before you make a transaction. A Twitter user commented on this situation as follows: "Any coin that can only be sold/traded/used in one place, would be a big red flag for me."

Luckily, there is a website you can go to for help:
 coinmarketcap.com, which has over 1,400 cryptocurrencies listed at the time of writing. This website provides information about market volumes of coins, the volumes of the last 24 hours, and other helpful indicators.

If the new coin makes it to this website, that is a positive indicator that you can even get on board after the ICO. However, the volume must definitely be noted because if a coin has risen by 80 percent, that is a long way from meaning that it is a winner. In a total trading volume of $300, 80 percent or even 8,000 percent doesn't mean very much in terms of value. For comparison, the Bitcoin trading volume in December 2017 was $450 billion, Ethereum was $129 billion, both of which are robust and compelling sales. Comparatively, sales of $300 or even $130,000 are not compelling by a long way. So, beware.

Investment Analysis Rule 9 — Pump and Dump

The website mentioned above (coinmarketcap.com) is, however, only an indicator. It provides only general indications which then need to be combined to give an overall picture. In many cases, these indicators are severely manipulated — but even that is a strong indicator.

If a value, an ICO, is too heavily promoted — if it is recommended by everyone on every channel and an unnatural level of hype is generated — then it can be compared to the stock floatation of any pink sheet share.

The more an ICO is hyped, the more celebrities — and by that, I mean people who are not from the crypto scene itself, but from Hollywood or superstars in other fields like musicians, artists, and athletes — the greater the caution that needs to be exercised. In some cases, that these hyped campaigns are part of a strategy commonly known as a "pump and dump."

The initiators make an agreement with so-called influencers, that they will receive, in advance, a certain number of tokens. Then the promoters of the ICO can officially advertise using these celebrity endorsements and the celebrities even advertise the coin and the ICO themselves. Because of the participation and endorsement of these celebrities, other media catch wind of the story and becomes more intensely widely spoken about, written about, and tweeted about.

The outside world gets the impression that a monster ICO is coming and everyone absolutely must be involved. This is true. It becomes a monster ICO. The initiators have ensured that the token is quickly liquid and that the token economy looks good. All the criteria are fulfilled, and it is safe to invest — at least that is what they want you to think.

However, for the sharp-eyed observer, two key things are missing. For one thing, there are no endorsements by crypto celebrities; no blockchain experts — real experts — are involved in these ICOs, and it is not discussed within the community. Secondly, either a pre-sale has taken place or there are previously generated coins that have been pre-mined.

Those who now participate in the official ICO will get coins at the issue price and as soon as trading starts, the rate drops for a short time. Why? Because the celebrities and those who are pulling the strings are selling the coins in huge numbers.

Those who think that it does not make sense to purchase at the issue price are thinking correctly from a business point of view, but they have overlooked the fact that these celebrities got their coins at a huge reduction. If you bought at a fifty percent reduction, you could easily sell at one hundred percent, can't you? Those who purchase cheaply and then push the ICO with their brand and media power ("pump"), can then sell immediately after the ICO at a higher rate than the issue price ("dump"). This is a bargain for them. It is the ordinary ICO participant who is left looking stupid because sometimes the issue price is never regained. A small consolation is that this does not just happen in the crypto world. Nothing different is done in many stock floatations than is done in the world of the big banks.

Behind every pump and dump are the types of people who are willing to do this type of thing, and there are a lot of them. As soon as the truth is no longer guaranteed by a public blockchain, it is no longer the truth. It is the truth that people have invented, and that is why you must look closely at who is behind every ICO before you make a decision to invest.

Investment Analysis Rule 9 — Technology

When conducting your pre-investment research, there is one thing you must never forget: An ICO should — according to the original concept — keep a technical team financially free to develop and support new blockchain technologies. That was always the idea, but current ICOs are, for the most part, operating far from those original standards. Mooncakes definitely was and Kik tokens too. It is therefore not surprising that the most successful ICOs were carried out by founders who had the original concept at heart and developed blockchain enhancements and protocols.

Many in the crypto world talk of a change in the epoch and a so-called "FAT Protocol." Historically speaking — at least in the history of the internet — at some point, the TCP/IP communication protocol, which is still used today, became available to the wider world. Everybody used it and everyone was happy. Well, everyone who could use computers at command line level at that time. If you don't know what that is about, you weren't on the internet in those days. It doesn't matter because all of that changed with Sir Tim Berners-Lee and his world-changing invention. From his underground laboratory at CERN, in Switzerland, Berners-Lee published the protocol that everyone knows: the www. Protocol, and thus invented the world wide web that we know and use today.

Neither Sir Tim Berners-Lee nor any other TCP/IP developers earned any money from the invention of the world wide web. Others, like Amazon, Google, Facebook, and many others, however, earned their billions on the internet. These companies use these two basic protocols to communicate with their users, clients and suppliers. While these millionaires and billionaires earned fortunes selling goods or services, or networking users to earn money with through advertising, the original developers of the protocols went empty-pocketed.

That is something that is going to change with the ICOs and the FAT protocol, because so-called "DApps", that is, apps that are based on a blockchain, can only run if the protocol that keeps the blockchain itself running, allows them to do so. Therefore, value creation is stored on a protocol-level and is financed by ICOs. In the future, large, profitable companies will inevitably develop based on these protocols, but this time, the developers and ICO investors will profit from their success too.

The Inverted Pyramid

This model functions much like a pyramid. The DApps, decentralized applications, are based on the protocol and deliver the users a cool interface, for example, with which they can use the blockchain. In contrast to the use of the free TCP/IP or www. protocols on the internet, the DApp must pay to use the underlying protocol.

In the case of Bitcoin, an example of a DApp would be a miner. Although everything is open source and the use of the software is free, the user still has to pay a transaction fee to the network which the miner then keeps. In this case, the miners represent the second level of the pyramid, which is based on the Bitcoin protocol itself. Facebook can still offer and market its services, but if they wanted to do that using the Bitcoin protocol, transaction fees would always be charged.

The difference between the TCP/IP and the www. protocols and the FAT protocol becomes clearer if a company like Google, for example, wanted to offer its users the possibility of storing their pictures decentrally. If these suppliers wanted to do that on the basis of SIA or STORJ, then the users need the corresponding SIA or STORJ coins. This guarantees that the blockchain concerned cannot be used for free. If Google wanted to construct its own decentralized storage system, which would certainly be no problem for its experts, then they would have to pay the users themselves for the use of the hard drives. Most people would not just allow Google free access to their hard drives.

Based on this principle, it is easy to see where the profit in an ICO lies, along with a possible short-term price gain. If this new DApp, based on SIA or STORJ, gains great popularity and acquires millions of users, the corresponding SIA or STOJ coins are needed. However, we must remember that, if the token economy is correctly managed, there will only be a certain number of these coins available. If that is the case, the users or providers will have to buy the coins somewhere, and that usually means either via an exchange or from a dealer. If demand increases, then so does the price and the value of each one of the coins issued by the ICO. That is the principle of an ICO.

Up to today, it has been the exact opposite of that. Up until now, the pyramid has been inverted. Everything was based on a free protocol, (TCP/IP and www.), and the profits were primarily earned at the top end by massive companies like Google, Facebook and Amazon, among others. The average investor could get involved, but they would have to buy shares of these companies when these were issued. The issue was always made too late, and the average person didn't really have the chance to get involved right at the start, other than as founders or as employees.

The average investor was always on the outside of the inverted pyramid looking in. The bankers and brokers lined their pockets and the average investor could only hope for higher exchange rates. Oftentimes, this happened so that the model — when viewed from the outside — worked very well. The the old proverb "the Devil always shits on the biggest pile" was true, and in these models, those who already owned assets could increase them, while the developers and people who delivered at the sharp end of the pyramid were fobbed off with salaries. They could generally live quite comfortably, but they very rarely came into the big money that was being earned from their work and expertise.

Bitcoin and the blockchain are now turning that on its head. Everyone can now be in at the start and everyone can invest in this opportunity, even with only a little money. Of course, you must watch like a hawk and heed the advice in this book to make sure you are only investing in the best opportunities. As repeatedly stated throughout this book, the ICO market is teeming with fraudsters, hustlers and charlatans. It sounds repetitive, but when it comes to your money, it is bears repeating.

Professional crypto investors like to invest long-term on the basis of the previously mentioned FAT protocol, and they only invest in ICOs that intend to develop technical protocols. Pros would never invest in Mooncakes, pyramid systems or cloud mining.

Look very closely at the proposals and analyze the token economy. Ask yourself the crucial questions, like are the founders are going to run off with the money? What happens to the ICO profits? Who is managing them? If all of these questions return a green light, then you can confidently get on board with the ICO.

When you know the right questions to ask, it becomes easy to see which ICOs have fulfilled these criteria, because the success of many ICOs speaks volumes and you can assume that the conditions stated were met.

The Most Successful ICOs

There are a few potential factors to consider when drawing up a list of the most successful ICOs. One of these is the sum collected and another would be the time it took to be collected. ICOs are often sorted by time span, which does not mean that the size of the sum is of no interest.

This practice started with the first ICO in 2013 by the MasterCoin group. This ICO was very successful, and 5,000 Bitcoins were collected with a value of around half a million dollars. However, MasterCoin was not as successful as Ethereum, for example, and is still listed today as OmniCoin, as MasterCoin was renamed Omni in March 2015.

Ethereum is currently listed as the second most important blockchain and is attracting more and more developers and investors. Ethereum's rate has risen from a few cents to nearly $1,300 as of January 2018.

While the rise has tailed off, there is certainly still potential there if the extensive usage continues to go well. Of course, there are also large fluctuations in both directions. The Ethereum ICO started in July 2014 and collected 31,591 Bitcoins in just 42 days. Using the rate at the time, that translates into over $18 million. In total, just over 60 million ether were issued. Using the highest value of both cryptocurrencies in the January of 2018 as a basis, around $310 million were collected, and the investors received ether at a value of a cool $70 billion — impressive!

You can see that the Hodl Principle can be a recipe for success. It is also very probable that the Ethereum foundation is hodling and not all of the Bitcoins from that time were changed into fiat currencies. Thus, the foundation has a solid basis for adequately supporting the future development of the Ethereum blockchain.

The figures from those days are impressive enough, but they are nothing compared to the madness of 2017.

It Doesn't Take Days Anymore — Hours or Minutes are Enough

Golem is building the decentralized supercomputer that everyone can use, but only if they have GolemCoins to use. These coins only existed since the ICO, which sold out very quickly. It took only twenty-nine minutes before all the tokens were purchased and a total of (at the rate of the time) $8.6 million had been collected.

Golem makes it possible to use the CPU power of many different computers if the owners do not need it themselves. This is a concept to set the pulse rates of software enthusiasts racing. That is why many crypto experts were eagerly anticipating this ICO, and quickly invested when they got the chance.

Then came the Gnosis ICO. Gnosis is a decentralized system that allows users to bet on anything and everything. It runs decentrally, meaning a bet can never be changed as it is in a smart contract, and the bet will be paid out no matter what happens.

If you were to bet against your boss that it would be sunny at midday on 1st September 2018, then the smart contract will look up whether it is sunny or not and will pay out to the winning participant. Of course, the primary purpose of these bets is for the makers to acquire insights and information that can be used for a variety of other purposes. That might be significant for, say, predicting election results. Therefore, Gnosis is not known as a betting product, but is a so-called "prediction market." Despite the initial skepticism of the community, the ICO was very successful and $12 million was collected within ten minutes.

Collecting $12 million in just ten minutes is setting the bar pretty high, but better was to come. Bancor, a project for developing smart contracts, made $152 million from its ICO in three hours. The project was very technology-orientated and thus appealed directly to the developer community. That was certainly a large part of the success, as many in the community had lots of Bitcoins from early days and investing these in new technologies was an easy decision for the techies.

It was an ICO called the Brave Browser that finally broke the record with $35 million collected in thirty seconds!

Those are just some examples of the fast and *very* fast ICOs in the past. Others needed longer but collected more. At the time of publishing, the largest ICO of all was FileCoin which collected a total of $257 million.

FileCoin is working on a protocol for decentralized storage and thus represents an alternative to SIA and STORJ. This is, yet again, another technical offer. No Mooncakes!

The next largest protocol ICO was Tezos. Tezos is developing a solution for digital identity. That is one of the greatest challenges to humanity, and a solution to this problem will significantly change and influence the way in which we live together. This idea alone collected $232 million, however, before going to press, Tezos encountered big problems. The money was collected for a Swiss foundation and the two founders, a married couple, accused the foundation board president of not managing the money properly. They claimed that he wanted to pay himself a few bonuses that were not in order. The foundation board president accused the founders of wanting to maintain control over the foundation and use the monies for purposes other than those agreed. At the time of this book being published, no end to the conflict was known.

EOS pledged itself to the scaling of decentralized apps and collected $185 million for this project. The next biggest ICO was Bancor, followed by Kik.

It can be assumed that bigger ICOs will follow and there will surely be one that collects more in less time. It is also very likely that these new ICO superstars will be more entrenched the technical world and will be more concerned with new technologies on the blockchain basis. Those who really get to grips it and do their research will certainly be able to make sensible investments.

Simply throwing money into all ICOs in a scattergun approach will never be a formula for sustainable success.

Important Warnings

It can be assumed that many readers don't want to miss out on the opportunities and chances in this new industry. FOMO — the "Fear of Missing Out" — sets in and the idea of missing out on a once-in-a-lifetime chance drives many investors to take unnecessary risks.

There are some valuable notes in this book that will guide you as you evaluate the opportunities presented to you. By asking the right questions and doing your due diligence, you can make an informed decision about whether or not to participate in an ICO. The whole landscape is very complex, and there is always news of scams rearing their heads, which is why you must always be careful. When in doubt, invest in solid Bitcoin before investing in a flimsy ICO and losing your hard-earned cash.

An investment itself is not always easy, which is why you have to take great care. There are a few technical hurdles to overcome. Those who are not careful quickly lose their coins forever.

With this chapter now under your belt, you should be in a good position to combat any potential pitfalls, but I would recommend that you also read the chapter on criminals, fraudsters and the authorities before making any investment decisions. It is not just informative, but also quite entertaining, and it highlights a few of the important dangers that arise when investing in an ICO.

We know that investors' money is sent securely and reliably through a blockchain, but where does it go? Everyone who has already participated in an ICO has lost money. Therefore, you have to stay very alert. If possible, try to test it out first with small sums. If everything goes smoothly, you can move onto investing larger sums. If an ICO is running over several days and does not sell out, you could invest crypto to a value of $50 and if it all works as expected, you can always follow it up with larger sums. The author has lost $50 a couple of times using this method, but not hundreds straight away. It was usually technical problems at the root of this loss, but other times it was sheer stupidity. If you lose your private key, it is your own fault.

So, caution is the mother of wisdom; education is the basis. In that spirit, the author wishes every success to all crypto investors!

The Famous Last Words

Over the last year and a half, I have seen many, many offers promising potential investors that they too can get rich quickly with cryptocurrencies. I've seen hundreds, if not thousands of these promises of salvation, from all corners of the earth. Printed offers and online, videos or on social media. In all languages. When I look at these offers, ninety-nine percent of them had one thing in common: they were nearly always frivolous. At the very least they were spreading false information, either intentionally or for the purpose of manipulation.

Unfortunately, the offers have not improved over the course of time. The more popular Bitcoin and the blockchain become, the more experts and people with the ultimate method for earning money, lots of money, crawl out of their holes and siphon it off. I know that I am using quite a coarse expression, but I am doing so deliberately because I find it disgusting how people try to rip off those who are not sufficiently familiar with this new crypto world. How they use every trick in the fraudster's book and all sorts of scams to take money, reader, out of your pocket.

Only education can help in this regard because the law itself can't at the moment. Bafflement reigns there too. If you don't understand what is happening yourself, you can't act or protect others adequately. Education is the best defense. Knowledge is power. Knowledge protects.

I hope that I have been able to give you some of this knowledge with this book, and I hope I have been able to raise your awareness and provide enough information for you to be able to distinguish the nonsense, rip-offs and con artists from the truth, and that you can enjoy Bitcoin and blockchain.

Of course, you will be told that the situation is not portrayed correctly in this book. Some will warn that a government will switch off Bitcoin at some point. You will be told that it is better to store your private keys with the miner or the exchange because blockchains are not secure. You will be told that everything will be cracked once quantum computers arrive. That is one (incorrect) perspective.

Those on the other side will praise this book and try to use it to lure you into some rip-off scheme, to sell you involvement in some crypto cloud so-and-so system, to lead you astray, to stimulate your natural greed. A mixture of both formulae will probably be used, depending what they have in mind.

Judge for yourself against the basics of the wise and ignore offers that do not correspond to the rules.

Those who want to tell you something else, show you something, or prove something are motivated by other reasons. For most of these people, the only focus is on your money or keeping up your diminishing power. Be strong. I have just one request to close with. If you have enjoyed this book, please pass the word on so that your friends and acquaintances can acquire this knowledge too. Everyone should have a basic knowledge of crypto so that they are not standing open-mouthed having to watch helplessly from the sidelines as the future passes them by.

With this in mind, I wish you all the best and juicy spoils.

Joe Martin
bitcoin-knowhow.com

PS: Please rate this book on Amazon and write a few lines about how you liked it. Thank you in anticipation of that.

Remarks

1944

In 1944, three years before George Orwell started to write his bestseller *1984*, which was to appear five years later, he formulated in a letter his thought that history would be written by the winners and that "2+2" could easily make "5".

"Already history has in a sense ceased to exist, i.e., there is no such thing as a history of our own times which could be universally accepted, and the exact sciences are endangered as soon as military necessity ceases to keep people up to the mark. Hitler can say that the Jews started the war, and if he survives that will become official history. He can't say that two and two are five, because for the purposes of, say, ballistics they have to make four. But if the sort of world that I am afraid of arrives, a world of two or three great superstates which are unable to conquer one another, two and two could become five if the fuhrer wished it."

History is Written By the Winners
George Orwell
Tribune, 4 February 1944
George Orwell: A Life in Letters, [10]

2014

"Bitcoin is an extremely important innovation, but not in the way most people think. Bitcoin's real innovation is a globally verifiable proof publishing at a certain time. The whole system is built on that concept and many other systems can also be built on it. The blockchain nails down history, breaking Orwell's dictum of "He who controls the present controls the past and he who controls the past controls the future." [11]

---

[10] https://www.thedailybeast.com/george-orwells-letter-on-why-he-wrote-1984
http://alexpeak.com/twr/hiwbtw/

[11] *https://www.reddit.com/r/technology/comments/2ghp54/*
i_am_julian_assange_ama_about_my_new_book_when/

www.ingramcontent.com/pod-product-compliance
Lightning Source LLC
Chambersburg PA
CBHW031923190326
41519CB00007B/394